EC-Council

E-Business Certification Series

Customer Relationship Management (CRM)

Student Courseware

Course: Certified E-business Associate - Exam 212-16

Customer Relationship Management

Developer
Thomas Mathew

Publisher
OSB Publisher

ISBN No
981-04-8162-4

Trademarks

EC-Council and EC-Council logo is a trademark of International Council of E-Commerce Consultants. All product names and services identified throughout this book are trademarks or registered trademarks of their respective companies. They are used throughout this book in editorial fashion only. No such use or the use of any trade name is, intended to convey endorsement or other affiliation with the book. Copyrights of any screen captures in this book are the property of the software's manufacturer.

Disclaimer

EC-Council makes a genuine attempt to ensure the accuracy and quality of the content described herein: however EC-Council, makes no warranty, express or implied, with respect to the quality, reliability, accuracy, or freedom from error of this document or the products it describes. EC-Council makes no representation or warranty with request to the contents hereof and specifically disclaims any implied warranties of fitness for any particular purpose. EC-Council disclaims all liability for any direct, indirect, incidental or consequential, special or exemplary damages resulting from the use of the information in this document. Mention of any product or organization does not constitute an endorsement by EC-Council of that product or corporation. Data is used in examples and exercises are intended to be financial even if actual data is used or accessed. Any resemblance to, or use of real persons or organization should be treated an entirely coincidental.

Copyright Information

International Council of E-Commerce Consultants
67 Wall Street, 22nd Floor
New York, NY 10005-3198

http://www.eccouncil.org

Phone: 212.709.8253
Fax: 212.943.2300

CONTENTS

About This Course

Course Overview

Description

This course provides attendees with a perspective and technical knowledge base necessary for understanding, planning and implementing a CRM initiative in their respective organizations.

Audience

This course is designed for middle and senior level managers from marketing, e-commerce, sales and operations, strategic planning and general management; senior technology and information managers who support marketing, e-business and CRM programs; product, brand, e-marketing and advertising managers; finance managers responsible for customer profitability measurements and analysis and sales and service managers.

Prerequisites

This course requires that the attendees have some exposure to customer relationship management in their respective functional domains.

Objectives

At the end of this course attendees will gain a comprehensive knowledge of customer relationship management, the different core concepts that are fundamental to CRM, the various technology applications that facilitate CRM initiatives and managing the CRM project from concept to implementation.

Course Structure

The following structure is an estimate of the course layout. Your timing may vary.

Day 1

Start	End	Module
9:00	9:30	Introductions
9:30	10:45	Module 1: Overview of CRM
10:45	11:00	Break
11:00	12:15	Module 2: Developing a Customer Strategy (Section 1 and 2)
12:15	1:15	Lunch
1:15	2:30	Module 2: Developing a Customer Strategy (Section 3 and 4)
2:30	3:30	Lab Session 1
3:15	3:30	Break
3:30	5:00	Module 3: Customer Lifecycle Management and Lifetime Value

Module Description

Module 1: Overview of CRM

This module gives an overview of Customer Relationship Management (CRM). It discusses popular definitions of CRM, identifies the drivers behind this concept, introduces the technology involved and serves as a preview of the modules that succeed.

Module 2: Developing a Customer Strategy

This module covers in-depth, the core fundamentals that any functional manager should know before starting out on a CRM program. An understanding of this module is critical to the successful completion of this course.

Module 3: Customer Lifecycle Management and Lifetime Value

This module examines the stages involved in managing the customer lifecycle and means to assign a financial value to the estimated customer lifecycle.

Day 2

Start	End	Module
9:00	9:30	Day 1 Review
9:30	10:45	Module 4: CRM Technology
10:45	11:00	Break
11:00	12:30	Lab Session 2
12:30	1:30	Lunch
1:30	2:45	Module 5: Operational CRM (Session 1)
2:45	3:30	Lab Session 3
3:30	3:45	Break
3:45	5:00	Module 5: Operational CRM (Session 2)

Module Description

Module 4: CRM Technology

This module introduces and gives a preview of the technology applications involved in CRM. It categorizes these applications according to base functionality and establishes the course for further detailed learning.

Module 5: Operational CRM

This module covers the different technology applications that enable operational areas such as sales force automation, marketing automation and contact management. The module also discusses various key concepts related to the use of these applications.

Day 3

Start	End	Module
9:00	9:30	Day 2 Review
9:30	10:45	Module 6: Analytical CRM (Session 1)
10:45	11:00	Break
11:00	12:30	Lab Session 5
12:30	1:30	Lunch
1:30	2:45	Module 6: Analytical CRM (Session 2)
2:45	3:00	Break
3:00	4:15	Lab Session 6
4:15	5:00	Review

Module Description

Module 6: Analytical CRM

This module addresses the analytical side of CRM and its related applications. This is a critical aspect of any CRM technology implementation as disregarding analytics can impede an organization from deriving real value from its CRM initiative and from proactively pursuing its strategic objectives.

Day 4

Start	End	Module
9:00	9:30	Day 3 Review
9:30	10:45	Module 7: Collaborative CRM (Session 1)
10:45	11:00	Break
11:00	12:30	Lab Session 7
12:30	1:30	Lunch
1:30	2:45	Module 7: Collaborative CRM (Session 2)
2:45	3:00	Break
3:00	4:15	Lab Session 8
4:15	5:00	Review

Module Description

Module 7: Collaborative CRM

This module discusses the collaborative aspect of CRM. It delivers an insight into the various technologies available and popular architectures adopted by organizations in their CRM initiative.

Day 5

Start	End	Module
9:00	9:30	Day 4 Review
9:30	10:45	Module 8: CRM Project Management
10:45	11:00	Break
11:00	12:30	Case studies and Student project
12:30	1:30	Lunch
1:30	2:30	Module 9: Building a CRM Business Case
2:30	2:45	Break
2:45	3:15	Module 10: CRM Product Comparisons
3:15	4:15	Case Studies and Student Project
4:15	5:00	Course Review

Module Description

Module 8: CRM Project Management

This module discusses the various phases involved right from conceptualizing the project to its final implementation. It delves with various related issues that organizations have to confront with during a CRM initiative.

Module 9: Building a CRM Business Case

This module serves as a referential guide to building a business case for CRM. It deals with the various aspects to be dealt with in framing a business case to present to the senior management and includes an ROI methodology.

Course Details

Module 10: CRM Product Comparisons

This module serves as a reference resource to look up salient features of a select list of popular CRM products available in the market.

Document Conventions

Various icons have been used through out this courseware to draw the reader's attention. The icon legend is as given below:

Icon	Description
	Module objective
	Key Concept
	Exam Tip
	Reference
	Exercises
	Multiple Choice Questions

CUSTOMER RELATIONSHIP MANAGEMENT (CRM)

Introduction

Exam 212-16 - Certified e-Business Associate (CEA)

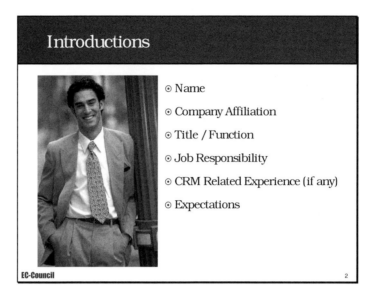

Introductions

- Name
- Company Affiliation
- Title / Function
- Job Responsibility
- CRM Related Experience (if any)
- Expectations

EC-Council   2

Introductions

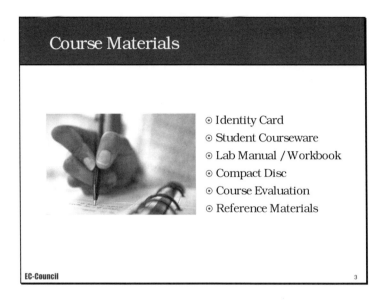

Course Materials

The following materials will be included in your kit:

> Name Card. Write your name on both sides of the name card.

> Student Courseware. The Student Courseware contains the material covered in the course

> Lab Manual and Student Workbook. The Lab manual and student workbook contains the hands-on lab exercises used during the course. It also contains review questions and multiple-choice questions to supplement the student courseware

> Student Materials Compact Disc. The Student Materials compact disc contains multimedia presentations, course related case studies, web links and additional readings.

> Course Evaluations. At the conclusion of this course, please complete the course evaluation to provide feedback on the instructor, course, and lab sessions. Your comments will help us improve future courses.

Course Outline

- ⊙ Module I : Overview of CRM
- ⊙ Module II: Developing a Customer Strategy
- ⊙ Module III: Customer Lifecycle Management and Lifetime Value
- ⊙ Module IV: CRM Technology

EC-Council   4

Course Outline

Module 1: Overview of CRM

This module gives an overview of Customer Relationship Management (CRM). It discusses popular definitions of CRM, identifies the drivers behind this concept, introduces the technology involved and serves as a preview of the modules that succeed.

Module 2: Developing a Customer Strategy

This module covers in-depth, the core fundamentals that any functional manager should know before starting out on a CRM program. An understanding of this module is critical to the successful completion of this course.

Module 3: Customer Lifecycle Management and Lifetime Value

This module examines the stages involved in managing the customer lifecycle and means to assign a financial value to the estimated customer lifecycle.

Module 4: CRM Technology

This module introduces and gives a preview of the technology applications involved in CRM. It categorizes these applications according to base functionality and establishes the course for further detailed learning.

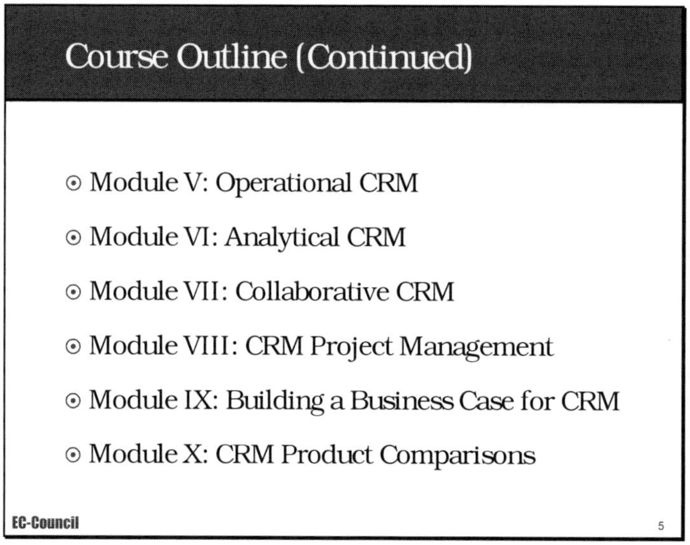

Course Outline (Continued)

⊙ Module V: Operational CRM

⊙ Module VI: Analytical CRM

⊙ Module VII: Collaborative CRM

⊙ Module VIII: CRM Project Management

⊙ Module IX: Building a Business Case for CRM

⊙ Module X: CRM Product Comparisons

EC-Council
5

Module 5: Operational CRM

This module covers the different technology applications that enable operational areas such as sales force automation, marketing automation and contact management. The module also discusses various key concepts related to the use of these applications.

Module 6: Analytical CRM

This module addresses the analytical side of CRM and its related applications. This is a critical aspect of any CRM technology implementation as disregarding analytics can impede an organization from deriving real value from its CRM initiative and from proactively pursuing its strategic objectives.

Module 7: Collaborative CRM

This module discusses the collaborative aspect of CRM. It delivers an insight into the various technologies available and popular architectures adopted by organizations in their CRM initiative.

Module 8: CRM Project Management

This module discusses the various phases involved right from conceptualizing the project to its final implementation. It delves with various related issues that organizations have to confront with during a CRM initiative.

Module 9: Building a CRM Business Case

This module serves as a referential guide to building a business case for CRM. It deals with the various aspects to be dealt with in framing a business case to present to the senior management and includes an ROI methodology.

Module 10: CRM Product Comparisons

This module serves as a reference resource to look up salient features of a select list of popular CRM products available in the market.

EC-Council Certified e- business
Certification Program

⊙ There are four e-Business certification tracks
under EC-Council Accreditation body:

1. Certified e-Business Associate
2. Certified e-Business Professional
3. Certified e-Business Consultant
4. E++ Certified Technical Consultant

EC-Council

6

EC-Council certified e-Business Certification Program

The International Council of Electronic Commerce Consultants (EC-Council) is a professional organization established in the USA, with headquarters in New York hosting members and affiliates worldwide.

The EC-Council certification is based on definitions of job functions and skill sets in the three key areas: technical, content management, and business management. These definitions have been developed by a broad coalition of industry and academic experts, and the skill set definitions have been adopted by the U.S. Department of Labor. In the technical area, skill sets include such topics as Customer Relationship Management, e-Procurement, Supply Chain Management, Business Process Re-engineering. Web business management includes principles of finance, legal issues, project management, and cyber marketing as they apply to E-Commerce web-related activities.

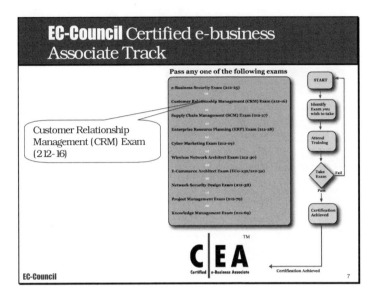

EC-Council Certified e-Business Associate Track

EC-Council, certification is designed to provide the foundation needed by every Electronic Commerce Professional. EC-Council curriculum provides broad range of skills and knowledge needed to build and manage an organization's E-Commerce web site and to coordinate with other inside and outside resources to accomplish that organization's electronic commerce goals.

The EC-Council certified e-business associate track could lead to an e-business professional certification by passing any two associate level exams. Each associate level track gives a comprehensive knowledge in the subject area and endorses the knowledge and skill competency of the certified associate.

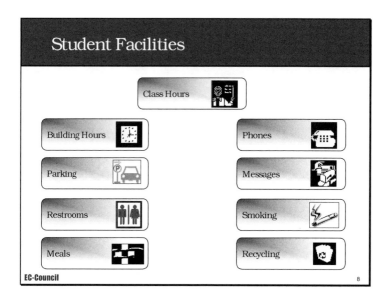

Student Facilities

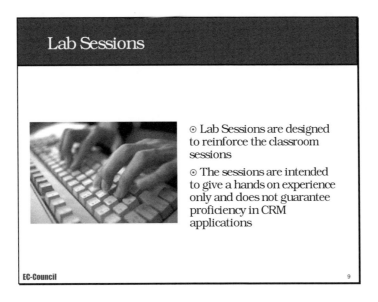

Lab Sessions

Participants may please note that the lab sessions have been designed to supplement the student courseware and reinforce the concepts learnt therein. The sessions are intended to let the students practically apply the concepts learnt and understand the workflow in similar applications. They are intended to give the students a feel of a working CRM application. This does not guarantee proficiency in CRM applications.

Prelude

It is quite likely that you have come across the quote "the customer is always right!!", some time, somewhere. While this looks good on a plaque in the store, this may not sound like a heartfelt sentiment always. In this era, when we are talking about customer relationship management, the question arises whether customer relationships can actually be managed? Is this a concept contrary to 'nurturing' a relationship? And above all, what is the need to focus on relationships when you can claim superiority in products and/or services?

As a prelude to this course on customer relationship management, we shall have a brief discussion on the scope of this course, what you can expect from it and what it can do for you. The focal aspect of this course and the ones in this e-business series is the e-business environment. By e-business, we do not restrict ourselves to transactions conducted over the internet. What needs to be highlighted is that there is a high degree of dynamism in the Internet enabled commerce scenario.

Today, the customer has a greater choice of goods, with access to a global marketplace, where the best deal can be just a mouse click away. This scenario presents various challenges to today's organizations.

Modules I, II, III

- It is more difficult to acquire a customer, while it is easier the cost involved.

- There is an inherent need to present a consistent view of the organization before today's discerning customer. This means, the customer must be able to interact with the organization in a consistent manner, irrespective of time or place.

- People across the organization and functional strata need 'relevant' information easily available and delivered in a 'useful' manner. This implies streamlining of processes and implementation of suitable technology.

Module I

The issues highlighted above form the foundation towards seeking an answer to the question 'why your organization must go in for CRM?'. These three fundamental aspects will be unraveled to you as you progress through the courseware, starting from CRM drivers in the first module and finally culminating in building a business case for CRM.

Modules V, VI, VII

The next aspect that needs to be addressed is the range of benefits that can be derived from CRM. Will there be a difference in terms of bottom line performance? Would the effort and resources expended for the cause be justified?

Modules IV, VIII

Readers need to understand that CRM initiatives take time to implement and also for fruition. CRM is not a stand alone technology implementation. It involves an enterprise wide change at some instances to departmental transformation at others. What will be the scope of a CRM implementation in your organization depends on several factors – primarily among them, your business strategy. As you complete this course, you will be guided towards making a judicial assessment about the possible scope of CRM in your organization. It is the endeavor of this course to let you assist your organization in its CRM initiatives by providing you with a comprehensive body of practical knowledge.

The benefits of CRM are both tangible and intangible. While the tangible benefits may be reflected in the bottom line relatively sooner, the intangible ones such as better service quality – leading to greater customer satisfaction and repeat business – will be reflected in the balance sheet only progressively. These will be highlighted as we lead you through the various CRM technologies. So, is there a way to expend resources such that the benefits derived have visibility and can help buy in more resources? This is often what organizations look for, when they go in for short term CRM campaigns. It is debatable whether this is the right approach. However, this can be one of the several approaches that an organization can strategically adopt in the greater plan.

Modules VIII, IX

What would be involved in implementing a CRM project? You will learn more about these in the CRM project management module and the financial analysis covered in the courseware. The related issue that arises often in this context is the cost factor. This is especially important for organizations that have just managed to keep off the red and would like to leverage the concept of CRM for improved performance - but, at what cost? Again, there is no one answer to this question. It will be influenced by your existing infrastructure, the extent of change required, the size of your organization and of course the CRM strategy adopted. This is covered in detail in the project management and business case modules.

Finally, nothing succeeds like success… You will learn about best practices that organizations have followed in deriving value from CRM. The accompanying workbook will detail small cases where you will see CRM in action and the resource material will highlight resources you can revisit to build a compelling case for adopting CRM in your organization. "

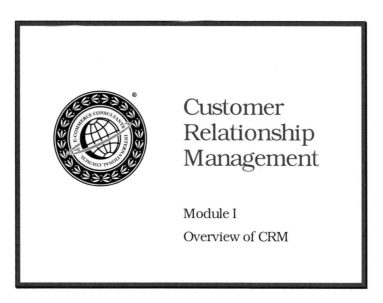

CUSTOMER RELATIONSHIP MANAGEMENT (CRM)

Module I – Overview of CRM

Exam 212-16 - Certified e-Business Associate (CEA)

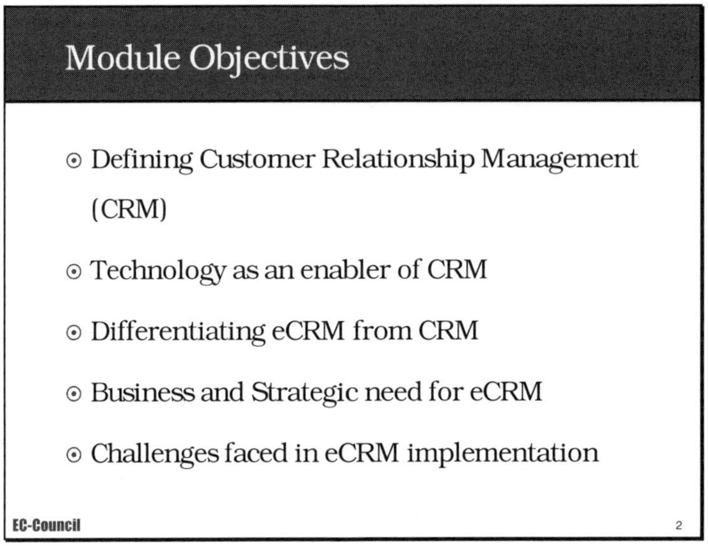

Module Objectives

⊙ Defining Customer Relationship Management (CRM)

⊙ Technology as an enabler of CRM

⊙ Differentiating eCRM from CRM

⊙ Business and Strategic need for eCRM

⊙ Challenges faced in eCRM implementation

EC-Council   2

Objectives

- **Module Objectives**

After completion of this module you will be familiar with:

➢ The concept of Customer Relationship Management (CRM)

➢ Technology as an enabler of CRM

➢ The difference between CRM and eCRM

➢ The Business and Strategic need for eCRM and

➢ Challenges faced in CRM implementations

The purpose of this module is to familiarize you with the core fundamentals that are essential for an in-depth understanding of the course. This module is structured as a combination of slides and explanatory notes.

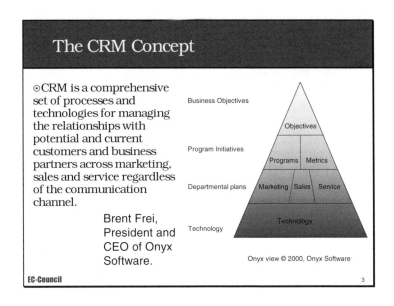

CRM Concepts

Definitions of Customer Relationship Management (CRM) are continuously evolving, as are new terminologies to describe it. What remains fundamental though is that CRM involves customers, suppliers, partners, and employees.

CRM is widely described as a "strategy", popularly as "processes and practices" or "methodology" and often *not* as "technology". However, CRM can be said to comprise of all the above. This note will give a concise compilation of the most popular and accepted definitions, leading to a discussion on what is considered to be a good CRM strategy.

CRM is a comprehensive set of processes and technologies for managing the relationships with potential and current customers and business partners across marketing, sales and service regardless of the communication channel. The goal of CRM is to optimize customer and partner satisfaction, revenue, and business efficiency by building the strongest possible relationships at an organizational level.

Brent Frei, President and CEO of Onyx Software.

Optimization of customer and partner satisfaction receives paramount importance, along with increasing revenue and improving business efficiency. The organization seeks to achieve this by adopting a holistic approach to every relationship.

How does an organization decide on a CRM initiative? This is shown in the figure given above. Business objectives form the apex of the CRM definition pyramid here, and are considered to be a two to five year strategic goal plan, clearly defined by the enterprise leadership. It may even be an abstract vision statement or a corporate style such as being a 'customer centric enterprise'.

Once the organization is clear about its business objectives, it can formulate its CRM program initiatives, which can include short-term CRM campaigns. These initiatives will be of shorter time frames of less than two years typically, and are intended to be stepping-stones on the pathway to achieving a long term CRM goal.

Examples of such initiatives are 'improve customer satisfaction by 'x' points', 'up sell to segment A customers' and 'build out an interactive virtual web store'. These program initiatives are measurable and captured through CRM metrics. They provide an indication of whether the CRM initiative is taking the right course or would require further fine-tuning.

Next in the strata come departmental plans. They comprise of processes and accepted norms of daily behavior. These plans can be providing live support on the website, automating email responses, guided call center processes and the like. Departmental plans can overlap several departments and have short time frames.

The last in the strata is technology. Technology enables coordination and integration of the above three layers of business processes wholly or partly. It is therefore an enabler.

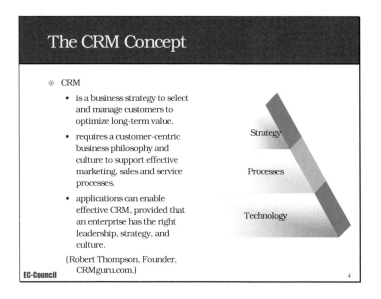

CRM – More definitions

Robert Thompson, founder, CRMguru.com, gives another popular definition of CRM. It states that:

> *Customer Relationship Management is a business strategy to select and manage customers to optimize long-term value. CRM requires a customer-centric business philosophy and culture to support effective marketing, sales and service processes. CRM applications can enable effective CRM, provided that an enterprise has the right leadership, strategy, and culture.*

This definition again shows the importance of starting with a business strategy, which will facilitate change management and rightly configure processes. This is supported by technology.

The need for technology arises as businesses expand and have many one to many employee customer relation mappings. The case for technology is to increase customer profitability due to improvements in the processes of customer acquisition, customer value maximization through cross selling and up selling, credit & risk and debt recovery, and customer retention.

Technology makes it possible to deliver improved level of services demanded by customers through integration of communication channels and function mapping within the organization.

Every organization that undertakes a CRM initiative has a set of strategic objectives that are to be met by the program. These initiatives may differ from organization to another. Inevitably, these objectives will involve processes that are critical to attaining success.

It becomes the responsibility of the organization to automate its processes to the extent possible, using appropriate technologies and subsequently integrate these vehicles of automation.

It therefore goes to indicate that CRM technology is not a single system or software. It is a collection of processes and technologies brought together to achieve the strategic objectives of the organization.

> *CRM is a business strategy to create and sustain long-term, profitable customer relationships. Successful CRM initiatives start with a business philosophy that aligns company activities around customer needs. Only then can CRM technology be used as it should be used—as a critical enabling tool of the processes required in order to turn strategy into business results.*

CRM Drivers

Sources of competitive advantage:

⊙ Location - a mouse click away

⊙ Size - Internet as level playing field

⊙ Product driven differentiation - Service

⊙ Technology - Internet, Automation

⊙ Customer - Awareness, Accessibility

EC-Council   5

CRM Drivers

Before taking a look at what constitutes a good CRM strategy, let us take a look at the drivers behind this 'process strategy'.

➢ **Location**: The best deals available to the customer are no longer restricted to his local geographical area. New market places have emerged from the 'e' economy and market distances are measured in mouse clicks.

➢ **Size**: Related to the earlier competitive advantage of location, size does not matter any longer as the Internet allows level playing field, and even better competitive advantage when combined with proper logistics. The visibility of a corporation can be engineered to stand out on the World Wide Web with the aid of supporting technology.

The product innovation cycle has become shorter, leading to faster commoditization thereby decreasing life spans and product advantages. The thrust is on the service linked to a particular product and how it differs from that of a competitor. Thus **service driven differentiation** acts as a competitive advantage.

➢ **Internet** in itself has brought about new business models, marketplaces, revolutionized the economy and has become an integral part of an organization's existence. With the proliferation of e-marketplaces over the Internet, technology has started pervading the organization through automation.

There is back office automation through enterprise resource planning (ERP), individual automations or 'islands of information' such as Sales Force Automation (SFA) that interplay along the CRM path in the organization.

➢ **Technology** has empowered the **customer** to possess a greater controlling stake in interactions with organizations. Today's customer is aware of his choices, skilled to access marketplaces / related information and places great expectations on the service providers.

The fundamental truth is that while organizations cannot control the pace of technology, its competitors or the economy, *it can still retain its competitive edge by controlling its interactions with the customer, using technology as an enabler.*

There remains no doubt about the fact that competitive differentiation depends highly on relationship management, both within and without the organization.

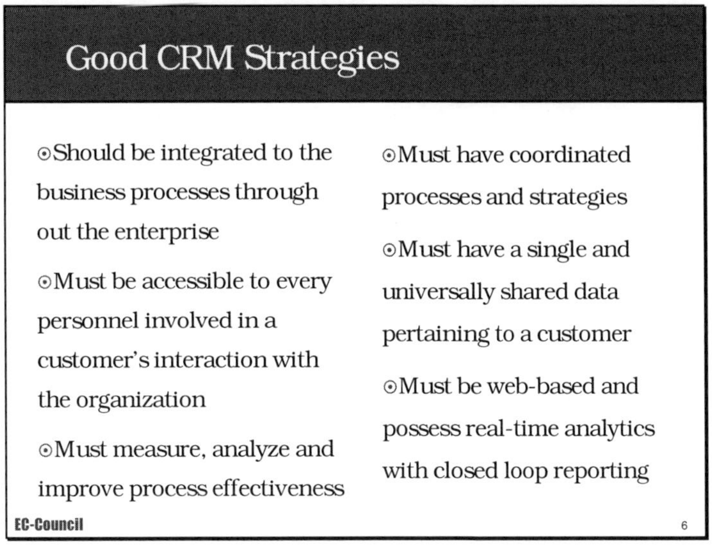

Good CRM Strategies

⊙Should be integrated to the business processes through out the enterprise

⊙Must be accessible to every personnel involved in a customer's interaction with the organization

⊙Must measure, analyze and improve process effectiveness

⊙Must have coordinated processes and strategies

⊙Must have a single and universally shared data pertaining to a customer

⊙Must be web-based and possess real-time analytics with closed loop reporting

EC-Council

6

Constituents of a Good CRM Strategy

Good CRM strategies essentially contain the following features.

A good CRM initiative

➢ Should be integrated to the business processes through out the enterprise.

➢ Must be accessible to every personnel involved in a customer's interaction with the organization to provide a consistent approach and enhance customer experience.

➢ Must measure, analyze and improve process effectiveness.

➢ Have a single and universally shared data pertaining to a customer.

➢ Must have coordinated processes and strategies.

➢ Must be web-based and possess real-time analytics with closed loop reporting features.

Best practices and further discussions on good CRM strategies are undertaken in later modules.

CRM and Technology Involved

⊙ Operational CRM

- Sales Force Automation (SFA), Enterprise Marketing Automation (EMA), Front Office Suites

⊙ Analytical CRM

- Data warehouses, Data Miners

⊙ Collaborative CRM

- Communication channels, Partner Relationship management (PRM), Customer Interaction Center (CIC)

EC-Council   7

CRM and Technology

CRM can be broadly categorized under three heads - Operational CRM, Analytical CRM and Collaborative CRM.

Operational CRM: The goal of operational CRM is to achieve the automation of horizontally integrated business processes including customer touch points, point of sales, ERP, SCM and the legacy systems integration. While ERP forms the back office automation, CRM covers the front office. Typical applications include sales automation, call center automation, channel automation, enterprise marketing automation and proposal generation. Operational CRM is capable of integrating with financial and HR suites of ERP, thus making it possible to have end-to-end functionality from lead management to order tracking.

Analytical CRM: Analytical CRM involves capturing, storing, extracting, processing, analysis and interpretation of customer data to the corporate user. It makes use of data mining models as front-end tools and builds a data warehouse at the back end by using both transactional data and market research data. These applications are capable of catering to changing decision-making needs in real time. The purpose of these tools is to draw inferences regarding customer preferences, attitudes, behavior etc. They allow corporates to differentiate and segment customers and gain competitive advantage.

Collaborative CRM: Collaborative CRM is the application of collaborative services to facilitate interactions between the customer and the organization. Examples are portals, partner relationship management (PRM) application, e-communities or customer interaction center (CIC). With the adoption of eCRM, collaborative CRM gains heightened importance as businesses strive to understand the customer and offer more personalized services. This will enrich the information and services available to the customer, thereby increasing the customer satisfaction equity.

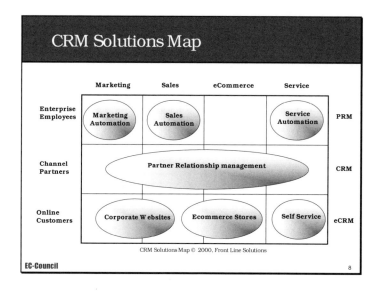

CRM Solutions Map

This figure depicts the various applications used in a CRM program. These applications are used in the management of customer relationship lifecycle.

➢ **Marketing**: Prospecting, Segmenting, Accurate targeting, devising appropriate customer acquisition strategies, campaign management, and lead distribution.

➢ **Sales**: Enabling effective Sales processes to ensure faster closure of deals, proposal generation tools, knowledge management tools, contact management and forecasting aids.

➢ **E-commerce**: Transforming selling processes into purchasing transactions seamlessly and cost effectively marks the Internet era.

➢ **Service**: Rendering support services through sophisticated call center applications, portals or customized web interfaces are increasingly important

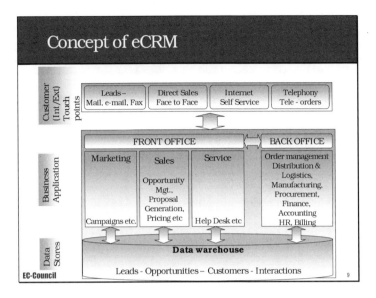

The Concept of e-CRM

eCRM is a combination of business process and technology that seeks to understand an organization's customer from a multifaceted perspective. It helps organizations to formulate enterprise wide business rules that ensure consistency of customer experience independent of the contact channel adopted by the customer.

It encompasses contacts, accounts, opportunities, activities, marketing, customer support, partner/channel support and other sales and service related processes.

---

eCRM vs. CRM

- eCRM is web integrated CRM.

- eCRM technology and architecture differs from conventional CRM.

- eCRM has heightened interactivity.

- eCRM renders an enterprise 'web experience.'

- eCRM is the CRM concept that tries to integrate multiple channels through a web access point.

EC-Council

10

---

e-CRM and CRM

➤ eCRM is web integrated CRM.

While traditional CRM tools provide a possible web interface, they are not ideally designed to give the customer the upper hand when it comes to accessing knowledge bases, personalization of web content, customization of product bundling or interaction with the enterprise as a first hand virtual experience. eCRM are designed primarily for web access, and seeks to offset customer service agent costs while improving efficiency and customer satisfaction.

➤  eCRM technology and architecture differs from conventional CRM.

From a technology perspective, eCRM involves capturing and integrating all customer data from anywhere in the organization, analyzing and consolidating it into information and then distributing the results to various systems and customer contact points across the enterprise.

➤ eCRM provides heightened interactivity.

eCRM offers Internet customers the choice to interact with the organization through their preferred channel of communication. An efficient eCRM application makes the organization portable and offers a consistent personalized interface to the customer, wherever he is connected.

➢   eCRM renders an enterprise 'web experience.'

eCRM is the customer facing web front of CRM.

It provides direct access to interfaces and functionality that traditional CRM tools do not provide, as the latter is designed largely for the corporate interfaces and in a client server environment. eCRM is the integration of all functions, external and internal, related to a customer, and is entirely web based.

➢   eCRM is the CRM concept that tries to integrate multiple channels through a web access point.

While eCRM offers better accessibility and control to the customer, lack of seamless integration with traditional CRM channels, is likely to frustrate the customer, decreasing his satisfaction and depriving the organization of the customer loyalty that it sought to gain in the first place. Therefore it would be prudent to state that eCRM encompasses the whole of CRM and CRM is evolving into eCRM.

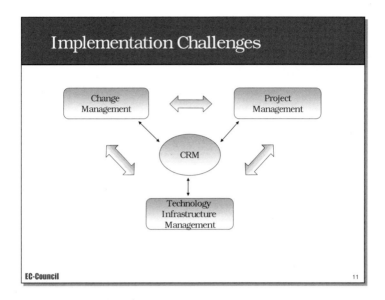

Implementation Challenges

Features of a good CRM strategy were discussed earlier. An eCRM implementation requires wide transformation of the enterprise.

An organization must define its business focus, organizational structure, business metrics, marketing focus and technology before embarking on a CRM implementation strategy.

A CRM implementation cannot be considered to be a quick and easy process. Furthermore, making changes to an implemented CRM is tougher.

CRM implementation initiatives require technology infrastructure management. It should be scalable, have a flexible tool set, and be compatible with existing legacy and Internet systems.

Change management warrants that personnel should be familiar with the working of the system, incorporate data generated through the system in their activities and diverse ways.

A good CRM implementation will integrate with the management practices and philosophy. Similar to any other technology initiative, CRM implementation also requires a well charted out **project management** methodology. Detailed project management issues are covered in a subsequent module.

Module Summary

- ⊙CRM combines strategy, processes and technology.
- ⊙Nurturing relationships is a source of competitive advantage.
- ⊙Good CRM strategies involve customer centric organizational initiatives.
- ⊙Technology is a CRM enabler.
- ⊙eCRM is web integrated CRM.
- ⊙eCRM offers greater interactivity to the customer.
- ⊙CRM implementation involves change management, project management and technology infrastructure management.

EC-Council

12

Module Summary

 Recap

➢ CRM combines strategy, processes and technology.

➢ Nurturing relationships is a source of competitive advantage.

➢ Good CRM strategies involve customer centric organizational initiatives.

➢ Technology is a CRM enabler.

➢ eCRM is web integrated CRM.

➢ eCRM offers greater interactivity to the customer.

➢ CRM implementation involves change management, project management and technology infrastructure management.

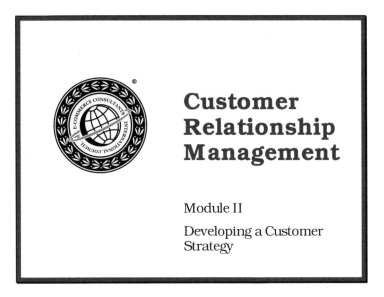

CUSTOMER RELATIONSHIP MANAGEMENT (CRM)

Module II – Developing a Customer Strategy

Exam 212-16 - Certified e-Business Associate (CEA)

Module Objectives

⊙ Fundamental Aspects of Customer Strategy

⊙ Evolution of a Customer Centric Enterprise

⊙ Seven Habits of Successful CRM companies

⊙ Mapping People, Process and Technology

EC-Council   2

Objectives

☛ Module Objectives

In the last module we discussed the concept of CRM and had an overview of the CRM landscape. In this module, we will move in a little more closer and see how an effective customer strategy is developed.

After finishing this module you will be able to:

➢ Comprehend the fundamental aspects of customer strategy

➢ Appreciate the need for corporates to evolve into customer centric enterprises.

➢ Understand the core of successful CRM initiatives

➢ Decipher the mapping of people, processes and technology.

This module is arranged into four sections. The first section gives insight into the fundamental aspects, which forms the basis of any customer strategy. The second section details the evolution of customer centric enterprises and takes a closer look at customer centric strategies. The third section highlights the core of any successful CRM initiative. The module ends with the mapping of the three critical components of CRM – people, processes and technology.

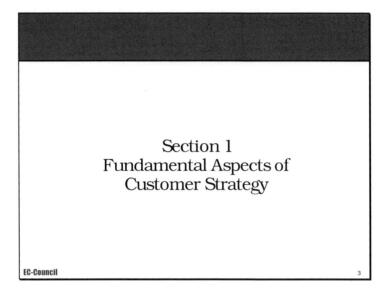

Section 1
Fundamental Aspects of
Customer Strategy

EC-Council   3

Section 1: Fundamentals of Customer Strategy

Basics

⊙ Linking Customer Strategy to CRM strategy

⊙ Introducing Customer Segmentation

⊙ Introducing Customer Profiling

⊙ Importance of Customer Strategy

EC-Council   4

Customer Strategy Basics

We have seen that **Customer Relationship Management (CRM)** is the science of developing a customer-centric organization. An enterprise with a CRM focus, capitalizes every opportunity to delight customers, foster their loyalty and build long-term, mutually satisfying relationships.

➤ Linking Customer Strategy to CRM strategy

One of the biggest sources of CRM failure arises when enterprises put CRM tools in place before forging a clear customer strategy. This section explores the underlying principles of a good customer strategy. Let us begin by trying to position it within the CRM strategy framework.

One facet of the CRM strategy framework requires the enterprise to segment its customer base concisely and contemplate on desirable means of doing business from a customer's perspective. To this end, the organization must have a clear insight regarding the benefits that a customer will amass by using its products and services.

The starting point of a new Customer Relationship Management initiative is to develop a customer strategy. The strategy should define the sort of customers the enterprise wants. This can be achieved through customer profiling and customer segmentation.

➤ **Introducing Customer Segmentation**

Customer segmentation refers to the process of dividing customers into mutually exclusive groups, presumably because customers within each group are more similar to each other than to others.

➤ Introducing Customer Profiling

Any organization has to determine the means and methods of acquiring its target customers. This can be achieved through customer needs assessment using consumer surveys or marketing plans. On acquisition, the organization has to render customer service in order to grow and retain these customers.

The customer strategy should also indicate what measures are to be adopted to handle customers who do not belong to the target profile. This involves using customer-profiling techniques.

The principle behind customer profiling is to gain customer loyalty at minimal cost by designing marketing plans that appeal to a larger percentage of target customers, and initiate them into taking desirable action.

Customer profiling can be demographically or behavior based. Customer behavior profiling is critical to a company interested in retaining customers and increasing their value.

➤ Importance of Customer Strategy

Apart from assessing the future needs of customers, organizations must also capture information regarding any of its shortcomings from the customer's perspective. An additional strategic information need of the organization is to know which services and products compete with those of the organization.

It is therefore clear, that without a proper customer strategy, a CRM strategy cannot succeed.

The underlying purpose of a customer strategy is to gain customer loyalty and achieve customer satisfaction. Customer strategy therefore forms the foundation of CRM strategy.

Customer Loyalty

- ⊙ Defining Customer Loyalty

- ⊙ Importance of Customer Loyalty

- ⊙ Components of Customer Loyalty

- ⊙ Measurement of Customer Loyalty

- ⊙ Creating Customer Loyalty

- ⊙ Brand Promise

EC-Council   5

Customer Loyalty

➤ **Defining Customer Loyalty**

The simplest definition of customer loyalty can be put as *repeat purchase of a product or service* offered by an enterprise. A more theoretic definition would describe customer loyalty as the degree to which customers are predisposed to stay with the enterprise and resist competitive offers.

➤ **Importance of Customer Loyalty**

The importance of loyalty in CRM strategy is highlighted by the fact that it has a rewarding impact on bottom-line performance.

To a business concern, having a loyal customer base translates into *lower costs, higher margins and greater profits* than businesses that fail to satisfy and retain their customers. Therefore it can be said that satisfied and loyal customers are the principal drivers of profits.

One of the strategic needs for CRM is to retain customers, as the cost involved in acquiring a new customer is almost five times that of retaining a customer. Not only do they continue to purchase products and services, but the value of satisfied and loyal customers increases exponentially as they refer new business.

There is a direct correlation between customer and employee satisfaction, as it has been noted that companies with loyal customers typically enjoy loyalty in the workplace as well.

Components of Customer Loyalty

The concept of loyalty can be portrayed as comprising of two different components: **perceptual** and **transactional**.

Measurements of perception are based on customer attitudes, opinions, and emotions, such as satisfaction. It indicates how closely the customer's perception of the company's performance matches his or her pre-purchase expectations.

Transactional measurements are based on the customer's intentional or tangible purchase behavior, such as the inclination towards making repeat purchases. Transactional measure gives an indication of the receptivity the customer is likely to have towards cross-sell and up-sell opportunities, and the frequency with which the customer makes repeat purchases.

This component is also likely to be influenced by perceived and actual barriers to switching to another provider, such as search costs, transaction costs, learning costs, and other forms of risk.

➤ **Measurements of Customer Loyalty**

The simplest measurement of customer loyalty is the concept of **wallet share**. Here loyalty is measured by calculating share of customer wallet over a time period. For any pre-existing customer, this is determined by dividing the total purchase of the corporate brand in a particular category by their total purchases in the specified category.

It is reasonable to assume that loyalty is repurchase **behavior**. We had stated earlier that, to realize CRM benefits, organizations must foster behaviours, implement processes and technology.

If loyalty is seen as a process, an evolving relationship, then it is clear that it cannot be introduced instantly. Loyalty needs to be designed and created systematically.

➤ **Creating Customer Loyalty**

Creating loyalty is about being intentional, consistent and different; it is also about creating **value**.

How does a corporate create value? The answer lies in creating a **customer experience** that is so distinctive and valuable that it goes beyond satisfaction and individual loyalty. It involves taking service to such a level that it becomes the primary engine for growth.

Building a brand experience requires absolute clarity about profitable customer segments, perceived brand value and how the organization can create and deliver on a brand promise that differentiates them from competitors.

A customer strategy that segments customers based on behavior will be more effective in keeping customers loyal and turning them into advocates who attract others who value the same things. To this end, an organization must create a brand promise.

➢ **Brand Promise**

A brand promise is an articulation of what target customers can expect from their experience with the organization. This describes the proposition and the value to the customer that the brand represents.

Where does the brand promise fit in the strategy map?

The brand promise drives all of the company's actions, including investments in people, processes, products, technology and delivery channels. Hence, the brand promise lies at the core of the customer strategy.

Loyalty depends upon how the customer views the competitors as well as the corporate brand. Customers are loyal because they believe it's in their best interest to be loyal, or they have to loose something in order to gain a new service. This can be time, effort, money or all of the three.

Therefore, the corporate brand has to solve customer problems and suit their needs better than competitors in the same price bracket.

When a brand raises the bar by improving quality or service or convenience or any other thing customers appreciate, then that brand will gain more loyal customers until another brand meets the challenge. This is where a customer relationship strategy matters.

In essence, customer loyalty is achieved when the customer believes that a particular brand is the best of the breed for him and he proves this by repurchasing the brand. Customer loyalty is therefore the result of well-managed customer retention programs.

When loyalty is considered an attitude, (as sometimes advocated), the customer not only advocates the brand after a one time purchase, but also endorses higher pricing, relating it to a higher perceived value.

Customer Satisfaction

- ⊙ Defining Customer Satisfaction

- ⊙ Linking Customer Satisfaction to Customer Loyalty

- ⊙ Correlation between Customer Satisfaction and brand value

- ⊙ Measuring Customer Satisfaction

- ⊙ Importance of Customer Satisfaction

EC-Council   6

Customer Satisfaction

➢ **Defining Customer Satisfaction**

Customer satisfaction results from a process of internal evaluation that actively compares expectations before purchase with perceived performance during and at the conclusion of the purchase experience.

The smaller the discrepancy between the customer's expectations and the perception of the purchase experience, the higher the resulting satisfaction level.

➢ **Linking Customer Satisfaction to Customer Loyalty**

Customer satisfaction and customer loyalty are not identical concepts. There is a fundamental difference between customer satisfaction and customer loyalty.

Satisfaction measures attitudes, which is a benign state for a customer, and looks at past impressions, rather than the current state.

A successful customer strategy will try to link these beliefs, inherent in performance, and the actions and behaviors associated with likely future purchase and recommendation, to formulate an effective loyalty program.

➢ **Correlation between Customer Satisfaction and Brand Value**

The link between customer satisfaction and corporate success is indisputable. Customer satisfaction results from the creation of value for the customer. We have discussed earlier the importance of brand value.

Customer satisfaction is directly proportional to the value a corporate creates for the customer. The value created can be perceived as 'functional value' and 'emotional value'.

A firm may add functional value to their value proposition through product improvements, added features, access, convenience etc. It may enhance the emotional value by providing superior customer service. This is the 'feel good' part of the total value proposition.

The emotional form of value is considered more valuable as customers who perceive this value are likely to recommend the firm to others, and give the firm a higher share of their business.

The customers who are functionally loyal are much less likely to remain a customer if a more functionally attractive alternative presents itself. They are much less likely to recommend and give the firm a smaller share of wallet.

Customer satisfaction can therefore be said to be a composite mix of different value components in the total value proposition. This is the reason why customer satisfaction surveys can be misleading or be misinterpreted.

➢ **Measuring Customer Satisfaction**

The scope of discussion here is to highlight the need for effective loyalty programs and customer satisfaction measurement. While surveys are popularly used to capture customer satisfaction, proper analytics are required to interpret the results.

This is covered in detail under analytical CRM.

Means of interpretation can be regression analysis of attribute ratings, framed in order to reveal which characteristics have the greatest impact on overall satisfaction. Other techniques such as multiple classification analysis reveals the benefit or risk associated with specific levels of customer satisfaction.

Therefore a customer strategy should also consider means and methods to improve response rates and generate more meaningful feedback.

➤ **Importance of Customer Satisfaction**

Customer satisfaction represents an important feedback mechanism for brands to determine how they have been received and where weaknesses exist among competitors that might be used to lure future customers.

A customer satisfaction measurement system must be built around a framework for understanding customer experience. No single event is responsible for customer satisfaction and loyalty. However, a single event can destroy the same.

Customer Profiling and Modeling

⊙ Overview of Customer Profiling and Customer Modeling

⊙ Customer Modeling explained

⊙ Customer Scoring and Scoring Methods

⊙ Introducing Customer lifetime value.

⊙ Role of Technology

EC-Council   7

Customer profiling and Modeling

➢ **Overview of Customer Profiling and Customer Modeling**

Once an enterprise has created a brand promise as a value proposition to the customer, it must have clear insight regarding who it's target customers are and what information does it need from the customer to evolve into a truly customer centric organization. This is where customer profiling and customer modeling comes into effect.

In the previous slide, we have touched upon what customer segmentation is and the essence of customer profiling.

The elements that identify the best customer profiles should be those that reflect the corporate business model, unique selling proposition and customer value statement(s).

An enterprise must be clear about which strategic objectives are to be optimized (cross selling, retention, credit risk, etc.) and for what products, to arrive at a sound basis for customer profiling and modeling.

➢ **Customer Modeling Explained**

The difference between a Profile and a Model is the element of time, making models more powerful predictors of behavior. Modeling involves profiling in order to elicit action.

Unlike customer profiles, models are not static in nature. Building customer models take into consideration customer behavior and seek to discover a commonality in them.

Models assume significance in constructing campaigns, designing marketing plans, offering new / better products and services to the target customers.

➤ Customer Scoring and Scoring Methods

Customer scoring is one of the means to develop a customer model. It attempts to score the whole customer base on a regular basis than have the corporate build specific models for each requirement.

This enables the corporate to assign each customer multiple product/service scores plus lifetime value, making it useful across multiple requirement areas such as campaign management, marketing departmental plans etc.

A popular scoring method is the **RFM** method. It captures **Recency, Frequency** and **Monetary** behavior of customers. Customers who had bought most Recently, most Frequently, and had spent the most Money will rank as the most economically viable customers with regard to future product / service offerings. RFM is closely related to another customer strategy metric: **LifeTime Value (LTV)**.

➤ Introducing Customer Lifetime Value

Customer Lifetime Value (CLV) is the expected net profit a customer will contribute to your business as long as the customer remains a customer. This indirectly serves as an indicator of the future profitability of a business. This concept is dealt in detail in the subsequent module.

➤ Role of Technology

In a dynamic environment that requires development and deployment of high quality models rapidly and reliably, a predictive model factory that automates and manages the entire predictive modeling process, from data preparation to model evaluation is desirable.

The contribution of technology in enabling these activities are databases, analytical tools such as data mining, statistical tools such as predictive modelers and the like.

The corporate needs to check the effectiveness of its customer model regularly. This is especially true where the model is a predictor. The basis for this inference is that customer dynamics change so rapidly that such a model would soon be outdated. Hence it is in the best interest of the enterprise to have challenger models that will test the effectiveness of the main model on a regular basis.

Understanding the customer and the type of relationship customers wish to have is key to CRM. This means not only customer profiling and a knowledge of customer behavior but also insight into customer motivations and attitudes. Through effective market segmentation companies can identify differences between customers and manage them flexibly.

Market research has a critical role to play, which, in combination with company held or other external intelligence about the customer, can provide a fully rounded view of the customer. Undertaken on an on-going basis, this process enables companies to adapt to market changes and to anticipate and cater for the specific needs and wants of individual customers, thereby consolidating customer loyalty.

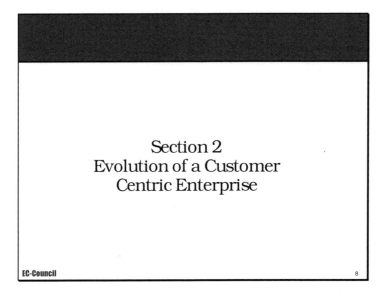

Section 2
Evolution of a Customer
Centric Enterprise

EC-Council

8

Section 2: Evolution of a Customer Centric Enterprise

Background

- *"...an enterprise-wide business strategy designed to optimize profitability, revenue, and customer satisfaction by organizing the enterprise around customer segments, fostering customer-satisfying behaviors and linking processes from customers through suppliers."* – CRM definition by Gartner Group
- to realize CRM benefits, organizations must
  - foster <u>behaviours</u>
  - implement <u>processes</u> and
  - implement <u>technologies</u> that

  support coordinated interactions through all customer touch points

EC-Council   9

Customer Centric Enterprise - Background

Any CRM initiative starts with a top management commitment to put customers first. The need to exceed and possibly anticipate customer needs drive most CRM strategy.

Corporates with successful CRM have been willing to trade off short-term profits for the benefits of longer-term, loyal relationships. They have shown determination to convert these relationships into drivers of profit.

The constant motivation for win-win relationships have seen corporates evolve into customer centric enterprises. Outstanding examples are companies like Amazon.com, Dell, Schwab, and Nordstrom.

➢ CRM definition revisited

The Gartner group defines Customer Relationship Management as an enterprise-wide business strategy designed to optimize profitability, revenue, and customer satisfaction by organizing the enterprise around customer segments, fostering customer-satisfying behaviors and linking processes from customers through suppliers.

Further, we have seen that this strategy involves fostering customer behaviors, implementing business processes and adopting technologies that support coordinated interactions through all customer touch points.

Corporates are therefore shifting from profit centric enterprises to customer centric enterprises. The underlying belief is that by becoming customer centric, corporates are investing in future returns and therefore meeting its objective to be profitable as well.

```
┌─────────────────────────────────────────────────────┐
│  ███████████████████████████████████████████████    │
│  █                                             █    │
│  █     Basics  Concepts                        █    │
│  █                                             █    │
│  ███████████████████████████████████████████████    │
│                                                     │
│      ⊙ Defining Customer Centricity                 │
│                                                     │
│      ⊙ Importance of Customer Centricity            │
│                                                     │
│      ⊙ Characteristics of a Customer Centric        │
│                                                     │
│        Organization                                 │
│                                                     │
│      ⊙ Achieving Customer Centricity                │
│                                                     │
│                                                     │
│  EC-Council                                    10   │
└─────────────────────────────────────────────────────┘
```

Customer Centricity - Concepts

Before we trace the evolution of product centric enterprises into customer centric enterprises, let us take a look at the basic concepts involved here.

➤ **Defining Customer Centricity**

Customer centricity can be said to be a set of disciplines and practices that allows companies to treat different customers differently, thereby gaining strategic advantage leading to expansion of revenues and increase in profitability.

These Organizations set customer loyalty/retention goals and then employ specific capabilities to meet or exceed these goals. These specific adaptations are discussed later in this section.

➤ **Importance of Customer Centricity**

A recent study by Deloitte consulting reported that customer centric enterprises were 60% more profitable than product centric corporates. These enterprises were also twice as likely to exceed their business performance goals.

➤ **Characteristics of a Customer Centric Organization**

A customer centric enterprise (CCE) addresses all customer issues fully and resolves them completely.

CCE employees adopt an external focus and possess the authority and tools to decide the right way to treat customers.

A CCE allows customers to interact across multiple channels and organizes itself around its customers.

The true mark of a customer centric enterprise is when the enterprise stays in touch with customers even when there is no immediate perceived need for the corporates' products or service.

In essence, a Customer-Centric Enterprise (CCE) is a company that focuses on customer satisfaction and places the customer at the center of the company's existence.

➤ **Customer Centric Enterprise – A Customer's Perspective**

A customer perceives an enterprise to be truly customer centric when it meets or exceeds most if not all of the customers' expectations. The customer expects openness, honesty, respect and integrity to be provided without compromise, in all its interactions with the enterprise in addition to receiving fair value at a fair price.

The enterprise is expected to provide the emotional support necessary to sustain and grow a relationship, which could imply putting the customer's needs and long-term relationship before personal short-term gain.

The customer seeks a consistent experience, which would require the corporate to deploy a knowledgeable and trained staff that believes that the customer is their priority.

This would imply that every employee is held accountable to the customer regardless of title or responsibility. To this end, the customer requires quick, easy, and convenient access designed to meet a cross section of needs.

The key is to understand customers (current and future status, the elasticity of customer behavior, relationships between customers, etc.), define value propositions (products, channels and service), and identify those customers to which we can afford to provide a truly customer centric environment, without forgetting that all customers deserve a certain level of customer centricity.

A customer centric enterprise has a customer strategy that projects a worthy brand promise, supported by superior products and services. These products and services are promoted through carefully designed marketing plans, targeting specific target customers, as determined through analytical customer profiling and segmentation. Efficient customer satisfaction measurement aids in predictive customer modeling to roll out effective loyalty programs and sales initiatives. A closed loop feedback reporting ensures that these enterprises constantly measure up to their customer expectations and provide consistent customer experiences.

Herein lies the practicality of the customer strategy that the enterprise develops meticulously to drive the organization through CRM initiatives successfully.

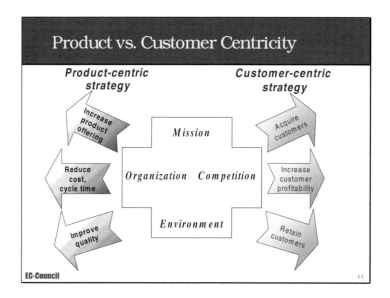

Product Centricity Vs. Customer Centricity

Traditionally, businesses have been differentially focusing in three major areas, namely customers, products (or services), and channels. However, there has been a progressive shift of focus towards customers, as markets have become more customer driven. This has been discussed along with the competition drivers of the new economy in the first module.

➢ **Increased Product Offerings => Customer Acquisition**

The earlier focus of enterprises to increase product offerings and thereby gain competitive advantage is slowly being replaced by a concerted effort to acquire customers. Innovative technology and shrinking market place distances have enabled easy reproduction and hence the emphasis on customer acquisition.

➢ **Reduced cycle times => Customer Probability**

Conventional strategy of mass production, reduced cycle times and cost differentiation are being rethought against increasing customer profitability primarily through service differentiation. Where enterprises could flood the market with their product(s), and look forward to improvements in their bottom line, are today strategizing means and methods to penetrate new customer bases and evolve an effective customer strategy.

> ## Quality => Support and services

Enterprises that positioned themselves as quality product providers are now determined to encompass their support and services with similar standards, in order to retain their customers.

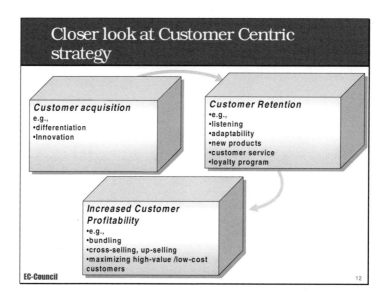

Customer Centric Strategy

Customer centric strategies can abound, as do organizations. However, the basic rudimentary framework of any customer centric strategy will include customer acquisition, customer retention and increasing customer profitability.

> ## Acquiring new customers

How does an enterprise go about acquiring customers in a competitive market place? While a judicious mix of product innovation and service differentiation may set the tone for the acquisition of business, the enterprise has to put forth a detailed plan of action to intrude and engage prospective customers.

It is evident that enterprise cannot survive without customers and that there is an inherent cost in acquiring a customer. Almost every company has to invest valuable resources in getting a prospective client to become a customer. Some of the costs include advertising directed to new customers, sales incentives and commissions aimed at new customer acquisition.

Though communication is one of the less obvious costs, the key to customer acquisition is to get the right message to the right target in the right manner. That makes communication crucial to a customer acquisition strategy. Enterprises can employ a combination of media strategies to drive business toward their companies. These strategies should be aimed at eliciting response that would mirror the profiles of the company's best customers.

> ## Retain Customers

On engaging and acquiring a customer, the enterprise has a more challenging task at hand – retaining the customer. Maintaining customers becomes more crucial, and it is essential to understand the complex relationship between the company, the brand, the channels of distribution and the customer. The competition now tries to disengage and migrate customers from the enterprise with incentives, service and product offerings. How does an enterprise manage to retain its customer?

According to Deloitte and Touche study, it costs five times as much to acquire a new customer as it does to keep an existing one.

The Loyalty Effect by Fredrick Reicheld reports that five percent retention in customers over their lifetime results in an 85 to 125 percent increase in company margin over that same time period.

Enterprises have to communicate product/service updates in a "just-in-time" basis. This implies use of a continuous stream of communications that depend on the customer's life cycle and tenure with the company.

The firm must utilize the knowledge gained from the customer's transaction history and behavior over their lifetime with the company and set up intelligent systems that identify when a customer is changing their patterns and then communicate with them appropriately. To this end, the company needs to be able to recognize a customer process and then set up the appropriate messaging activities to keep that customer coming back.

Enterprises should track the satisfaction level by cost-effectively generating customer feedback through various channels. Suggesting alternative ways to use the product or service to give it a more utilitarian purpose reinforces a customer's good purchase decision.

Loyalty programs should seek to increase the frequency and involvement (sometimes quantity) of the customer, thus deepening the customer's relationship with the marketer. The measurement for this stage is Lifetime value.

Lifetime value is measured both in terms of historical and projected lifetime. It allows the company to begin to allocate marketing resources by segmented group, and in the more advanced stage, by individual.

CRM Technology can help determine exactly how much money should be invested in a given segment based upon an expected longer-term return. Reactivation or retention is critical to the success of customer centric enterprises.

If a customer is perceived as profitable, the enterprise will require five kinds of information to be gathered. These include customer wants and needs, customer purchase cycle, customer interaction opportunities, customer profile and a customer life cycle.

➢ **Customer Needs and Wants**

Needs are defined as the pre-requisites that qualify customers to use a company's goods and/or services. Wants in this context is defined as desirable products and services.

The enterprise should be capable of anticipating the customer's next move and being there at the time they are ready to purchase or in need of a service or are ready to upgrade, or add an accessory to their original purchase.

➢ **Customer Purchase Cycle**

This is the time between a customer's repeat purchase of goods and services. The frequency and likelihood of additional purchases as well as the nature of those purchases depend on both the customer and the product.

➢ **Customer Interaction Opportunities**

Enhancing customer loyalty and capitalization of repeat business requires enterprises to explore the costs and benefits of customer interaction. This is where customer touch-points gain significance.

Enterprises must follow an appropriate channel integration strategy according to their business needs.

➢ **Customer Profile**

It is in the business interest of the company to allocate its customer support resources most efficiently. To facilitate this effort, the enterprise needs to know as much relevant information about the customer as possible. The concept of customer profiling as discussed earlier gains prominence here.

The customer profile can be limited to demographic statistics and product or service history. Some of this information can be industry specific and can be valuable in determining if industry developments would affect the customer behavior.

➢ **Customer Lifecycle**

For a customer centric enterprise, the customer lifecycle evolves in parallel with the product lifecycle as it traces it path from innovation and growth to maturity and decline.

The objective of the enterprise should be to predict the customer lifecycle evolvement, so as to be in a position to offer appropriate products and/or service offerings in order to prolong the customer-enterprise relationship.

The purpose behind evolving into a customer centric enterprise and incorporating customer centric strategies of gathering and predicting customer behavior is not restricted to driving profits.

This can also result in savings through increased effectiveness of the corporates internal processes. The internal processes, from product development to service allocation eventually affect the efficiency, effectiveness, and the return on investment of a CRM initiative.

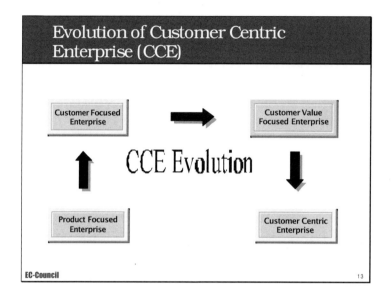

Evolution of Customer Centric Enterprise (CCE)

➢ **Product Focused Enterprise**

Traditionally, companies have been product focused.

A product centric enterprise concentrates on delivering products and services as efficiently as possible to provide large numbers of customers with the best deal.

This is largely achieved by adopting a hierarchical structure and formal, command-and-control culture, and with volumetric measures of performance.

These enterprises typically hold a lot of data about its customers. However, this is not structured or categorized data. In some cases, it is not meaningful data and even not required by the corporate.

➢ **Customer Focused Enterprise**

Transition through time and market place has made some of these companies aware of this state. These are the corporates that become customer focused enterprise.

They try to align with their customers and use their understanding to provide more relevant products supported by better service strategies. Their goal is to maximize customer as well as employee satisfaction.

These enterprises are characterized by the ability to manage end-to-end processes capable of adding value to specific customer segments. These enterprises may also have systems to support their initiatives especially service and customer support.

➢ Customer Value Focused Enterprise

Customer focused enterprises find the evolution to a customer value focused enterprise necessary in order to maximize the value of selected customers through maximizing the value they add to them.

The primary objective behind this phase of evolution is to minimize customer management costs by reducing wastage on servicing customers of lesser strategic value.

This is achieved by devising customer strategies that add value at each stage in the customer's lifecycle. This entails reflection of customer worth through personalized service, customized products and the like. The value added is delivered consistently across multiple channels.

The purpose behind this strategy is to manage information to ensure that it's in the right place at the right time. Being a customer value focused enterprise helps the corporate to maintain information in real time in order to encourage those interacting with customers to make decisions regarding customer interaction dynamically.

➢ Customer Centric Enterprise

An enterprise is called a truly customer centric enterprise when it holds its customers at the heart of the business. They consider their customers as stakeholders and having a stake in the business.

These enterprises consider their customers as innovators, and a new way to create value.

A customer centric enterprise looks to leverage the inherent ability of the customers to shorten the learning curve and provide innovative leads. The CRM initiatives of these enterprises can help reduce costs by encouraging customers to render service to each other in communities of interest, promote the enterprise to like-minded people known to them at low cost, seek redress willingly in the event of a shortcoming, be enterprising in taking up new products, and remain loyal for life.

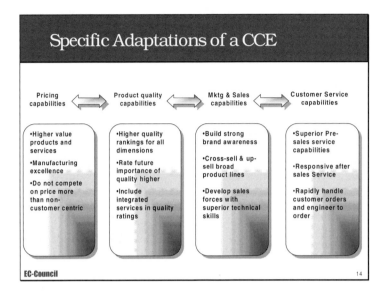

Specific Adaptations of a CCE

The exhibit above illustrates the specific adaptations that an enterprise adopts, as it becomes customer centric.

➤ Pricing capabilities

   ➤ Higher value products and services

   ➤ Manufacturing excellence

   ➤ Do not compete on price more than non-customer centric

➤ Product quality capabilities

   ➤ Higher quality rankings for all dimensions

   ➤ Rate future importance of quality higher

   ➤ Include integrated services in quality ratings

➤ Marketing & Sales capabilities

   ➤ Build strong brand awareness

   ➤ Cross-sell & up-sell broad product lines

   ➤ Develop sales forces with superior technical skills

➢ Customer Service capabilities

  ➢ Superior Pre-sales service capabilities

  ➢ Responsive after sales Service

  ➢ Rapidly handle customer orders and engineer to order

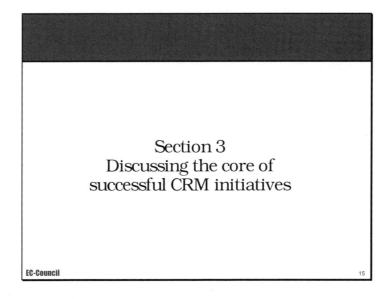

Section 3: Discussing the core of successful CRM initiatives

Core of any successful CRM initiative

⊙ To create a consistent customer experience:
- *Know the customer*
  - Who are they, how they want it, where they want it, when they want it.
- *Reach the customer*
  - Reaching the right customers with the right offer at the right time through the right channel.
- *Grow the customer*
  - Effectively execute Marketing strategy based on your knowledge of customer share and customer lifetime value.

EC-Council   16

Core of any successful CRM initiative

➢ **Know the customer**

This is about understanding the individual customer's value and needs. It involves collecting information that customers provide in their interactions with the company, in order to develop a 360-degree view of customer behavior across all touch points. This helps an enterprise gain an intimate level of understanding. As the enterprise initiates communication with the individual customer, it creates a learning relationship. Thereafter, each interaction develops into an opportunity to build and extend the relationship with the particular customer. The exit barrier is higher for a customer if the learning relationship is extensive and is the result of invested efforts. The final objective of CRM will be to raise the exit barriers.

➢ **Reach the Customer**

This is about reaching the right customers with the right offer at the right time through the right channel. Based on the knowledge developed for each customer, the enterprise will be able to reach specific customers with targeted offers, information, products, and services. The enterprise can therefore reach each customer with personalized messages based on his or her needs, behaviors, and value.

➢ **Grow the Customer**

This aspect of CRM refers to the enterprise's ability to effectively execute marketing strategies based on tactic knowledge of customer share and customer lifetime value. Increasing the total value of the customer base by retaining and growing the most prized customers significantly reduces the expenses than trying to generate the same amount of value by acquiring new customers. Enterprises need to re-examine and re-allocate total marketing and sales investments from less profitable customers and the acquisition of new customers to focus on its best customers.

Seven Habits of a Successful CCE

⊙ Determined to deliver value to customers

⊙ Focused on long-term business results

⊙ Backing of senior management

⊙ Committed to effective communication both internally and externally

⊙ Adopts suitable metrics to assess progress

⊙ Imparts training to its employees

⊙ Recognizes stakeholders inside and outside the enterprise

EC-Council   17

Seven Habits of a successful CCE

1. The firm is obsessed with delivering value to customers. This means elevating the customer experience, improving customer satisfaction, and paying close attention to customer feedback and attitudes. The firm consistently changes itself in order to deliver more value to customers. The firm might have one or more customer advisory boards in order to capture real data and suggestions. It's also likely to seek out customer insight through its quality-improvement initiative.

2. The firm is comfortable with long-term business results. It's careful not to allow the push for quarterly results to overshadow its business investment rationale or its internal operations. While a comprehensive CRM vision is likely to be shared among the executives of the firm, they are cognizant that the transition cannot occur overnight.

3. Senior executives sponsor the customer-based initiative. The firm will have a specific project manager accountable and responsible for executing the plan. And the customer-based initiative won't be the first set of process changes the firm has managed in this way, either.

4. The firm demonstrates a deep commitment to the initiative by communicating its launch plan both internally and externally. As the initiative moves forward, reporting capabilities and a vehicle to communicate successes are crucial for building and sustaining momentum.

5. The company is unafraid to assign a completely new set of metrics to assess the incremental progress and success of the initiative. It may even use a "balanced scorecard" or some other tool for explicitly assigning priorities to non-financial objectives.

6. The firm actively invests in training its employees. Companies that invest in training are much more likely to enjoy successful CRM implementations, particularly because these types of initiatives often require the firm's people to do business in a different way. But the training will take root easily in a culture that is centers on the concept of constantly seeking to provide more customer value.

7. The firm identifies internal stakeholders who can act as key disseminators of the CRM vision, and actively work to build support within the stakeholder group. The search for stakeholders will be carried out not just among the direct participants in the program, but among the program's clients and customers, and within the firm's own financial group as well.

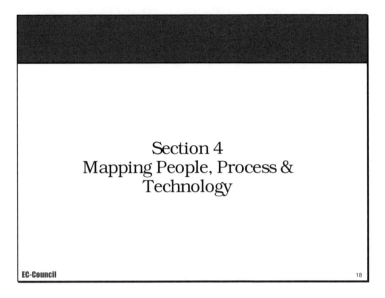

Section 4
Mapping People, Process &
Technology

EC-Council   18

Section 4: Mapping People, Processes and Technology

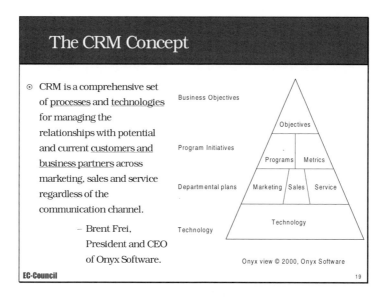

Revisiting the basic precepts

Definitions of Customer Relationship Management (CRM) are continuously evolving, as are new terminologies to describe it. What remains fundamental though is that CRM involves customers, suppliers, partners, and employees.

CRM is widely described as a "strategy", popularly as "processes and practices" or "methodology" and often *not* as "technology". However, CRM can be said to comprise of all the above.

This note will give a concise compilation of the most popular and accepted definitions, leading to a discussion on what is considered to be a good CRM strategy.

CRM is a comprehensive set of processes and technologies for managing the relationships with potential and current customers and business partners across marketing, sales and service regardless of the communication channel. The goal of CRM is to *optimize* customer and partner satisfaction, revenue, and business efficiency by building the strongest possible relationships at an organizational level. –(Brent Frei, President and CEO of Onyx Software.)

Scope of Discussion

- ⊙ Processes
  - activities dedicated to the running of the business.
    - – Sales, Marketing, Service & Support
- ⊙ People
  - organizational enablers to the CRM processes
    - – Organization, Human resources
- ⊙ Technology
  - technological enablers to the CRM processes
    - – Infrastructure, Applications
- ⊙ Relationships
  - relationship and customer value management
    - – Specific CRM processes

EC-Council   20

Discussing People, Processes and Technology

The scope of discussion here involves Processes, people, technology and relationships. A successful CRM initiative pre-supposes realignment of people, processes and technology around Customer. This forms the basis for discussing the transition from the traditional Product Centric approach to the new Customer centric way of organizational functioning

The term 'Processes' is used to describe activities dedicated to the running of the business. It encompasses the areas of Sales, Marketing, Service and Support.

Organizational enablers to the CRM processes represent the 'People' component here. It involves both organization and its human resources.

The technological enablers to the CRM processes include both technical Infrastructure and related Application systems.

The term 'Relationships' encompasses building and nurturing customer relationships and customer value management. These form the basis of specific CRM processes adopted by the organization.

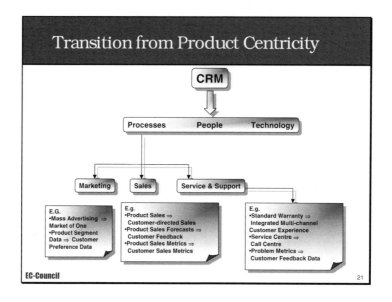

Transitioning from product centricity -Processes

In this context we look at Core CRM business processes. Irrespective of the maturity of the enterprise in the Customer centricity scale, traditional (product centric) or evolved (Customer centric), Marketing, Sales and Service/Support are the key processes, facilitating customer interaction with the organization. It is essential therefore, to comprehend the changes that are happening within these business processes as the customer gains significance over the product/service.

> Marketing: For instance, in the traditional make up of the enterprise, advertisements addressed masses, where as one-to-one campaigns show more effect in the new scheme of things. Similarly Customer preference data has more business value in the customer centric enterprise as compared to product segment data in the traditional set up.

> Sales: In a customer centric enterprise, sales pitches are more centered on the customers' needs than product strengths. Similarly we can also see that in the new enterprise Customer feedback had a stronger influence in the forecasting process as opposed to the traditional enterprise.

> Service/Support: In the Customer service / support arena there are clear differences as in a standard warranty from a traditional enterprise transforming to a multi-channel customer care establishment which intents to enhance the customer experience. Similarly a problem metrics in the traditional enterprise has paved the way for a customer feedback based metric.

Therefore it is clear that as the enterprise evolves a from product centric strategy to a customer centric strategy, the underlying processes evolves accordingly.

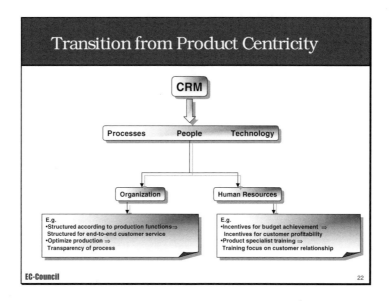

Transitioning from product centricity -People

Here, we look at People issues pertaining to the transition. There are two dimensions that we scrutinize for this purpose, viz. the Organizational structure and the Human resources management.

> Organization: In the traditional scheme organization was structured around production functions, where as in a customer centric enterprise, the organization is structured around customer service. In the first case production optimization was at the center stage, which gave way to process transparency in the new scheme.

> Human Resources Management: Here again the traditional incentivisation based on production targets transformed to ones based on customer centric targets as customer acquisition, customer retention, customer profitability. Similarly training rooms, which teemed with product specialists, began churning out executives with exemplary customer relationship management skills.

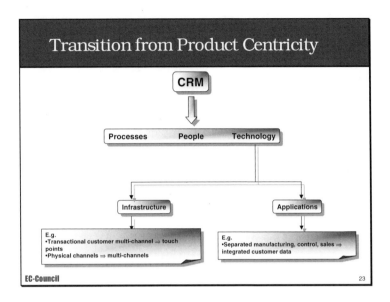

Transitioning from product centricity -Technology

Technology issues pertaining to transition from product centric to customer centric enterprise is worth checking out. We shall scrutinize the technology infrastructure evolution as well as the technical application evolution for this purpose.

➤ Infrastructure: Transactional infrastructure as used by the traditional enterprises proved to be inadequate as the customer centric enterprise evolved. Customer wanted to transact using multiple touch points and therefore infrastructure needed a revamp to enable customers to transact using multiple touch points.

➤ Applications: Traditional enterprises ran Application programs, which discretely took care of various functions within the enterprise as in manufacturing, finance, Sales and distribution etc. As the customer centric enterprise evolved customer information got integrated into this multiplicity of applications.

Summary

- Customer Strategy is the core of a successful CRM initiative
- Enterprise are evolving into customer centric enterprises (CCE)
- There are four stages in a CCE evolution
- Adaptive CRM is the core of a successful CRM program
- CRM is about mapping people, processes and technology

Module Summary

Recap

➢ Customer Strategy is the core of a successful CRM initiative

➢ Enterprise are evolving into customer centric enterprises (CCE)

➢ There are four stages in a CCE evolution

➢ Adaptive CRM is the core of a successful CRM program

➢ CRM is about mapping people processes and technology

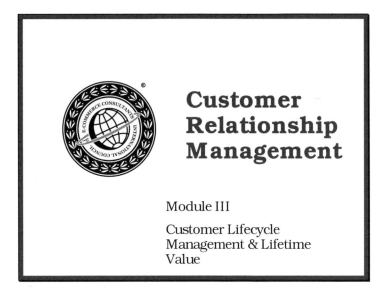

CUSTOMER RELATIONSHIP MANAGEMENT (CRM)

Module III – Customer Lifecycle Management and Lifetime Value

Exam 212-16 - Certified e-Business Associate (CEA)

Module Objectives

- ⊙ Concept of Customer Lifecycle

- ⊙ Discussing Customer Lifecycle Management

- ⊙ Using CRM Technology to manage Customer Lifecycle

- ⊙ Concept of Customer Lifetime Value

- ⊙ Deriving Customer Lifetime Value

EC-Council   2

Objectives

☞ **Module Objectives**

On completion of this module you will:

- ➢ Understand the concept of Customer Life Cycle

- ➢ Learn how customer life cycle is managed

- ➢ Be able to correlate CRM technology to customer lifecycle

- ➢ Comprehend the concept of customer lifetime value

- ➢ Derive Customer Lifetime Value

This module assumes significance in this course, as any CRM initiative must be based on a sound understanding of the customer life cycle involved.

Enterprises need to strategize their offerings and initiatives in alignment with the best practices in customer lifecycle management. Customer lifetime value is an essential concept that guides any CRM initiative.

Concept of Customer Lifecycle

- ⊙ The customer life cycle is a means of defining and communicating the way in which an enterprise interacts with its customers and prospects.

- ⊙ The purpose of the customer life cycle management is to define and communicate:
  - the stages through which a customer progresses while considering/purchasing/using products

  and

  - the associated business processes an Organization uses to move the customer through the customer life cycle.

3

Concept of Customer lifecycle

The customer life cycle is a means of defining and communicating the way in which an enterprise interacts with its customers and prospects.

The purpose of the customer life cycle is to define and communicate the stages through which a customer progresses when considering, purchasing and using products, and the associated business processes an enterprise employs to move the customer through the customer life cycle.

The customer life cycle is a vehicle for defining and communicating the stages a customer goes through when purchasing and using products/services. It also aids in understanding the associated business processes that an organization might use to move the customer through the customer life cycle.

The customer life cycle begins with reaching the target market and progresses toward an established loyal customer base. Along the way, it is necessary to acquire, convert and retain customers.

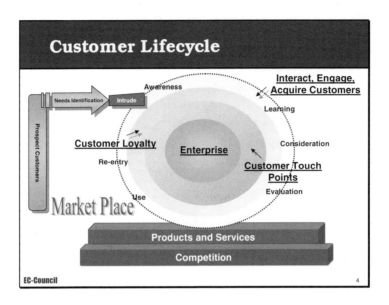

Customer Life Cycle stages - Illustrated

In the illustration presented above, the customer life cycle is depicted as a circle or ellipse to represent that it is truly a cycle, one that the organization would want its best customers to move through over and over again.

This concept of customer life cycle shown here is generic. The stages shown represent thought processes for typical customers and companies. While these stages may or may not change, it is possible that the business processes that map to these stages will differ from company to company. Differences will also exist based on the product under consideration.

The enterprise *assesses* the needs of a potential customer and *intrudes* into the marketplace with marketing initiatives.

When a customer is considering the purchase of a product or service, he or she is termed as a prospect.

As a prospect, he or she goes through a predictable series of thought processes. These processes are shown in the outermost circle on the customer life cycle diagram.

These can be distinguished as under:

> Identifying needs that may be filled by a product or service available for purchase from the enterprise.

> Developing awareness of the organization's existence and its ability to fulfill the identified need.

> Gaining insight about the organization and the products and services that may fulfill the need.

> Considering how the products and services offered by the organization do or do not satisfy the identified need.

> Evaluating the suitability of the products and services against the competition to fulfill the identified need.

> Deciding to purchase the product or service, go to a competitor or not fulfill the need.

The last phase is often termed as the customer moment. When the prospect decides to purchase the product or service on reaching the customer moment, he or she is termed as the customer.

The organization then changes its focus from customer acquisition to customer retention. This is marked by a shift in focus from the customer's purchase decisions to a focus on customer satisfaction and relationship nurturing as the customer uses the product or service he or she has acquired. The organization is now in a position to influence the customer either positively or negatively.

Inaccurate or untimely fulfillment and poor service can result in a decision not to purchase additional products or services on part of the customer. On the other hand, satisfied customers can become customers for life, owning many products and services and generating much profit. This is the objective of customer lifecycle management. During this stage the customer acquires the product or service and utilizes it. This may last for the life of product ownership and sometimes beyond.

If the customer is satisfied and positively influenced by the organization, the customer will re-enter the customer life cycle to do additional business with the organization.

The outermost circle (dotted lines) represents the flip side of the customer stages described earlier. Here, a negatively influenced prospect may be lost or a hard earned customer may exit the lifecycle and the organization faces customer attrition.

There are two ways a customer or prospect can drop out of the customer life cycle. The first is termed "loss" and is the capture of a prospect by a competitor at or before the customer moment. Losses are a fact of doing business. While losses are not desirable, if the loss occurs on the prospect's first trip through the customer life cycle, it is at least acceptable. These prospects have just entered the competitor's customer life cycle.

The second way for a customer to leave can be more severe than a simple loss; this is attrition. Attrition is the erosion of customer loyalty after the customer moment leading to their capture by a competitor. These are customers – not prospects. Frequently, the company has made a significant investment in the relationship.

An organization can lose a valuable customer due to its inability to provide acceptable service. These lost customers may influence prospects to avoid contact. Like the lost prospects, these lost customers enter your competitor's customer life cycle.

The Competitive Environment

Competition is another factor that influences the customer life cycle. While the customer life cycle activities sit upon the foundation of products and services, the customer life cycle itself is driven by the principle of competition.

A competitor is any enterprise that offers products and services that rival the organization. The need for (and value of) CRM is influenced by the amount of competition faced by an organization or industry.

The competitive environment as the driving factor in CRM is represented in the customer life cycle by the position of competition in the figure shown above.

The Customer Touch Zone

A customer touch-point is any interaction between the customer and the enterprise. Either the company or the customer can initiate customer touches.

The customer touch zone illustrates this in the figure. This zone is where all interactions with the customer happen. Every interaction occurring in the customer touch zone is a tremendous opportunity to build trust and reinforce the relationship.

Customer loyalty depicts the customer trust in the customer life cycle and illustrates the key role it plays. Trust plays such a role because it can be gained or lost anywhere in the customer life cycle, and the loss of trust is detrimental to CRM strategies. Trust is fragile. It can take a long time to build trust, but only a moment to destroy it.

The objective of learning about the customer lifecycle is to understand the basis of CRM business strategies adopted by organizations.

   The final goal of CRM is to raise the exit barriers so that prospects are not easily lost to competitors and attrition of hard earned customers is prevented.

The use of CRM technology is to enable organizations to provide consistent and desirable customer experience. This is important, as customer acquisition is a costlier proposition as well as a time consuming one as we have seen in the customer life cycle.

Successful organizations are able to maximize the customer lifecycle value (explained later in this module) and match the customer life cycle with that of the organization.

Customer Lifecycle Management (CLM)

- "...mapping customer data to define customer behavior so that the processes of a company are fully occupied in acquiring, selling to, and maintaining a long term relationship to a customer." – Gartner Group
- "...engage, transact, fulfill, service." – Meta Group
- The purpose of CLM is to envelop the customer so deeply in the corporate mesh that they are retained for a lifetime, optimally.

EC-Council   5

Customer Life Cycle Management

The business processes conducted by the organization fall into the following general categories:

Intrude and Engage: This includes the efforts of the organization to get a prospect's attention, increase the prospect's awareness about the organization and engage the prospect in a dialogue intended to move him or her into the customer life cycle.

Transact and Fulfill: Awareness about the organization does not guarantee purchase of products or services. The organization must work towards educating the prospects about itself and maintain the prospects' attention and interest as they continue with their buying decision in order to acquire them as customers.

Retain/Service and Expand: After a prospect buys your products or services and becomes a customer, the real work begins. Many of the cross-functional business strategies designed to increase customer satisfaction and foster customer loyalty are conducted in this segment of the customer life cycle.

In a properly defined customer life cycle, the organization's processes map clearly to the customer stages, and a relationship that complements both the customer and the organization can be established.

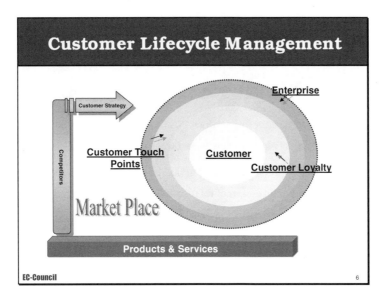

Managing the Customer Life Cycle in a CCE

In managing the customer lifecycle, the organization employs customer centric strategies towards retaining and growing the customer base. In the figure shown above, the customer is held at the heart of the enterprise.

The trust that the customer places in the organization, as expressed through customer loyalty strengthens the relationship. This loyalty is built upon by providing a consistent customer experience that has been proven as desirable.

This may also involve alterations in the service provided as the customer needs evolve over the lifecycle. The organization exploits these changes through cross selling and up selling activities.

The customer touch points are used to ensure that the customer has a satisfying experience and this counters the competitor's influence on the customer in the market place.

An organization that is not vigilant about changes in its customer lifecycle may have to face customer attrition. As mentioned earlier, the final goal of CRM is to raise the exit barriers so that prospects are not easily lost to competitors and attrition of hard earned customers is prevented. Towards this the enterprise can deploy customer relationship management initiatives and gain competitive advantage.

Concept of Customer Lifetime Value (CLV)

- ⊙ Customer Lifetime Value (CLV) is a measurement of what a customer is projected to be worth over a lifetime.

- ⊙ The purpose of CLV is to allow the corporate to allocate a weighted version of its resources and focus on specific customers depending on the projected CLV of that customer

- ⊙ The application of CLV is to design specific programs to escalate the customer-type's CLV.

EC-Council   7

Concept of Customer Lifetime Value

Customer Lifetime Value or CLV provides the "purposeful" analysis required to integrate and coordinate disparate functions within a company to operate as a customer asset portfolio manager, maximizing the value of the firm by maximizing the value of customer assets.

By calculating CLV, a business can measure the expected financial benefits from customer retention investment to build customer loyalty. Customer relationship building is a long-term commitment.

It is possible to measure the lifetime value of a customer the profit that the enterprise makes over the lifetime of the customer relationship.

This calculation has two main components: 1) the lifetime cost of the customer, including acquisition cost, operating expense and customer service; and 2) the sum of the expected lifetime revenues of a customer.

Maximizing the "lifetime value" equation requires maximizing the rate of new customer acquisition, the conversion rate of prospects to buyers and the repeat frequency of existing buyers.

The costs of acquiring new customers are substantial. This means that existing customers are responsible for near-term profits, and new customers will only contribute in the future. It is not economical to build the business only on first time buyers. A continued customer relationship is therefore critical to short and long-term profits.

In a traditional model, profit is measured by balancing the revenues from the sale of a product against the costs of making, selling and servicing the product. In this model, customer service is a cost to be minimized.

By contrast, using the lifetime value model, it is possible to weigh the value of customer service against the lifetime value of the customer. It is often worthwhile to provide additional services that maximize the customer's value over time.

In short, the Customer Lifetime Value (CLV) is a measurement of what a customer is projected to be worth over a lifetime.

The purpose of CLV is to allow the corporate to allocate a weighted version of its resources and focus on specific customers depending on the projected CLV of that customer. The application of CLV is to design specific programs to escalate the customer type's CLV.

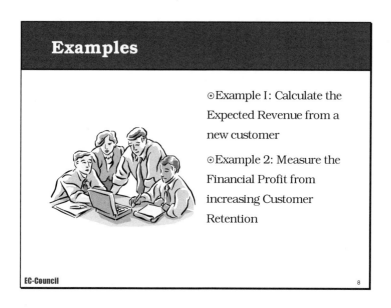

Customer Lifetime value assessment

The following examples are taken for the purpose of illustration from the pioneering work of Mei Lin Fung, who is considered a subject matter expert in the area of customer lifetime value measurement.

Example I: Calculate the Expected Revenue from a new customer

Let's look at the two-year history of revenue from customers. Suppose we find that 60% of customers come back and make a purchase the next year, while 40% of new customers never return. On average, how much revenue do you get from 1000 new customers over 2 years?

	Year 1	Year 2
New Customers	1000	
Expected number of Customers = 1000 x Retention Rate of 60% or		600
Average size of sale for each customer	$1,000	$1,000
Revenue	$1,000,000	$600,000

Expected Revenue from 1000 New Customers Cumulative	$1,000,000	$1,600,000

Average Revenue from each of the 1000 initial customers = Expected Revenue by Year 2 divided by 1000 = $1.6M / 1000 or		$1600

Note: If Retention rate were 70%, Expected revenue from each new customer would be $1,700

Example 2: Measure the Financial Profit from increasing Customer Retention

The Customer Value Model can be used to value Customer Retention. Customer Lifetime Value is defined as the profit you earn from a customer over their lifetime. This is the net present value (NPV) of the Expected value of the profits the enterprise earns on sales to that customer in each of the years the customer remains a purchaser. Assume each customer delivers $1,000 in profit for each year that they are retained. We'll use Expected value to project the expected profit from a new customer.

Customer Retention Rate	50%	
NPV Discount Rate	20.0%	
	Year 1	Year 2
New Customers	1000	500
Average profit for each customer	$1,000	$1,000
Profit	$1,000,000	$500,000
Discount Rate 20%: Factor	100%	80%
NPV Profit	$1,000,000	$400,000
Expected Profit from 1000 New Customers Cumulative	$1,000,000	$1,400,000

Average Profit over 2 years from each of the 1000 initial customers = $1,400
Expected Profit by Year 2 divided by 1000 = $1.4M / 1000 or

Customer care activities can change the retention rate. If activities increase retention rate, profits will go up. If activities decrease retention rate, profits go down. The model can be used to determine how much should be spent to achieve a specific increase in customer retention.

Summary

⊙ The Customer life Cycle must be linked to the Enterprise life cycle

⊙ Customer life cycle management involves distinct phases - Engage, Transact, Fulfill, Service

⊙ Customer profiling, modeling and scoring aids customer life cycle management

⊙ Customer life time value enables measurement of expected financial benefits from customer retention.

EC-Council 9

Module Summary

 Recap

➢ The Customer life Cycle must be linked to the Enterprise life cycle.

➢ Customer life cycle management involves distinct phases - Engage, Transact, Fulfill and Service phases.

➢ Customer profiling, modeling and scoring aids customer life cycle management.

➢ Customer lifetime value enables measurement of expected financial benefits from customer retention.

"There is only one boss - the customer. And he can fire everybody in the company, from the chairman down, simply by spending his money elsewhere."

- Sam Walton, late founder of Wal-Mart stores

CUSTOMER RELATIONSHIP MANAGEMENT (CRM)

Module IV – CRM Technology

Exam 212-16 - Certified e-Business Associate (CEA)

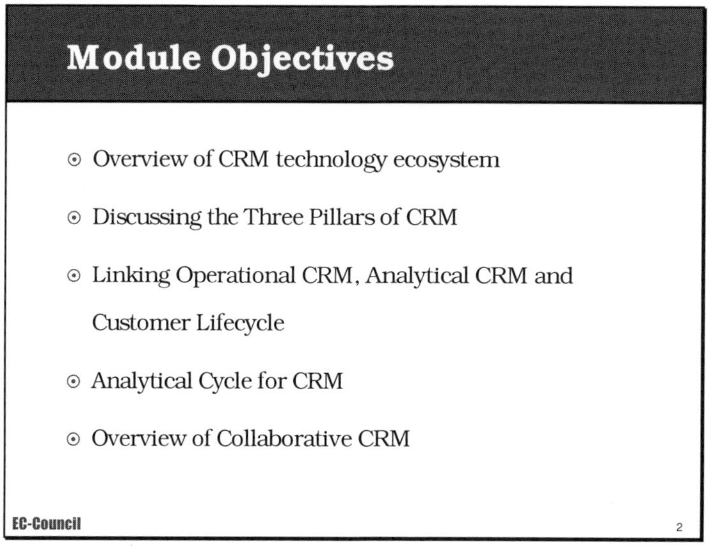

Module Objectives

⊙ Overview of CRM technology ecosystem

⊙ Discussing the Three Pillars of CRM

⊙ Linking Operational CRM, Analytical CRM and
Customer Lifecycle

⊙ Analytical Cycle for CRM

⊙ Overview of Collaborative CRM

2

Objectives

👉 Module Objectives

The strategic aspects of CRM have been discussed at length in the previous modules. We have seen that technology acts as an enabler in optimizing CRM strategies. This module introduces CRM technology and lays the foundation for the subsequent modules where this is discussed in depth.

After the completion of this module you will:

➢ Have an overview of CRM technology ecosystem

➢ Discuss the three pillars of CRM

➢ Be able to link Operational CRM, Analytical CRM and Customer Lifecycle

➢ Understand the analytical cycle for CRM

➢ Comprehend an overview of Collaborative CRM

The objective of this module is to give an overview as detailed treatment of the different categories is carried out in subsequent modules.

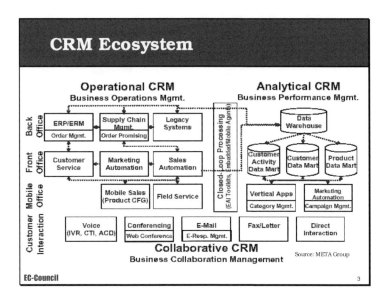

CRM Ecosystem

We have defined CRM as first and foremost a business strategy for realizing higher profitability and enhanced competitive advantage.

Enterprise CRM strategies focus on the automation of horizontally integrated business processes to provide end-to-end coordination among sales, marketing, customer service, field support and other vital customer touch points.

CRM seeks to integrate people, process and technology in order to optimize relationship management across the full customer spectrum — including consumers, business partners, and other distribution channels.

The CRM application architecture must combine operational (transaction-oriented business process management) technologies and analytical (data mart-centered business performance management) technologies. Besides these, the enterprise also needs to cater to the interaction needs of its customers across multiple channels using various collaborative technologies.

A balanced CRM approach requires that all three sides of the equation be implemented to form the CRM backbone.

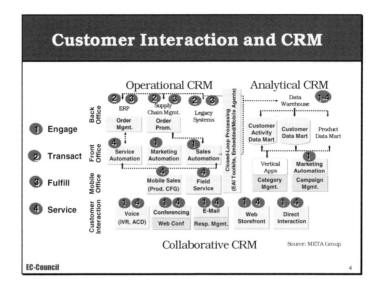

Customer Interaction and CRM

In the previous module we have discussed the customer life cycle and the stages involved in managing the customer life cycle. The illustration here maps the various stages with the three different categories of CRM technology.

As is evident, no single application can deliver the capability to address all the life stages of the customer. There is also a significant level of resource sharing between the various applications. Most CRM vendors are trying to position their suites as complete CRM solutions. It may be noted that almost all these vendors began with the basic sales force automation.

The operational side of the CRM equation consists of customer facing applications integrated among the front, back, and mobile offices: sales automation (SA), enterprise marketing automation (EMA), customer service/support, and miscellaneous components.

The operational CRM components are called customer facing, as they are mostly involved in transacting and fulfilling customer requirements. Hence, it is imperative that they have both front office and back office integration capabilities.

Data created on the operational side of the equation must be analyzed for the purpose of business performance management. This side of the architecture is inextricably tied to the data warehouse (DW) architecture, and is most often manifested in analytical applications that leverage data marts.

A significant portion of analytical applications available is oriented towards EMA (e.g., campaign management). However, DW and EMA (and outsourced-style database marketing) initiatives are typically at odds from an IT architectural perspective, as these marketing applications typically come with their own embedded proprietary database and data model.

Collaborative CRM is defined as the communication and coordination model across the ETFS life cycle between channels and customer touch points.

It includes establishing cooperative partner networks (e.g., affiliates, portals), management of customer interactions (e.g., e-mail, Web, CIC) and channel alignment strategies that enable consistent collaboration between customers and business organizations.

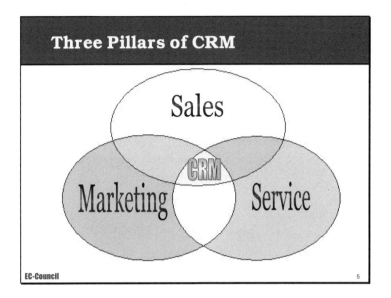

Three Pillars of CRM

 Sales, Marketing and Service are considered as the three pillars of CRM.

CRM technology has also followed a similar path in its evolution. Most CRM product suites began as sales force automation and added higher functionalities as markets and technology adoption changed.

The significance of discussing this aspect here is that the three categories of CRM technology – namely operational, analytical and collaborative CRM addresses each of these areas through various applications.

While operational CRM constituents have enhance visibility, analytical CRM components address the needs of the marketing function by rendering enhanced decision making abilities. Collaborative CRM helps bind all the three functions with the customer and is essential for the smooth functioning of the organization's internal departments.

With the escalating emphasis on quality service and the quality of customer interactions, the concept of collaborative CRM plays a pivotal role in the evolution of corporate service delivery.

In the rest of the module we shall discuss the various aspects of these technologies and their relevance to these primary functions of sales, marketing and service.

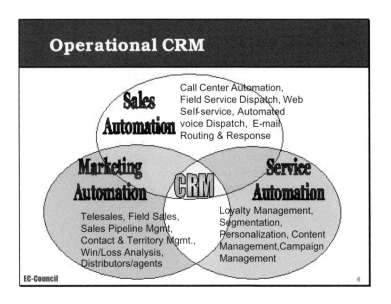

Operational CRM

 Operational CRM is covered by customer-facing applications that integrate the front, back, and mobile offices, including sales-force automation, enterprise marketing automation, and customer service and support

Operational CRM focuses on processing transactions or accessing information for a specific task. This mostly affects those processes associated with sales such as sales force automation, telesales, call center management and sales campaign management.

Operational CRM can hold transactional level data on individual products, customers and transactions. They provide support for customer facing process done by direct mail, phone, the Internet, third party agents or field sales.

The business requirements of operational CRM include

➢ Sales Automation caters to the automation of sales processes.

➢ Marketing Automation includes campaign execution.

➢ Service Automation has three basic components – agent based service, self-service and field service. Agent based service includes call centers etc.

e-business impact of CRM cannot be decoupled from other ebusiness components such as commerce chain, adaptive infrastructure.

Operational CRM should integrate commerce chain, adaptive infrastructure

On the operational side of the business, interaction with the customer can take a number of forms: personal contact, post, fax, telephone and Internet. This is relevant to the sales, marketing and commercial and technical customer service departments.

A call center or a customer service center can serve as a communications portal or as a point of interaction.

Operational CRM Systems integrate the various channels of contact with the various departments, to create a complete front-office service instrument linked to a fully functional back office. In addition, the sales force can have access to constantly updated information via mobile terminals.

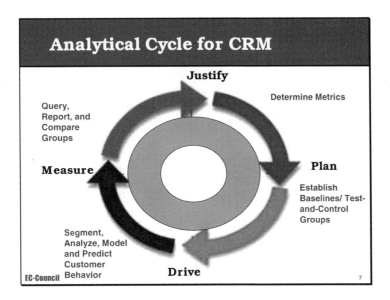

Analytical cycle of CRM

Analytics play a crucial role in each phase of the CRM program. They are not just for segmenting and targeting customers, but must be used to help justify, plan and measure CRM initiatives.

Justify

Analytics can be used to justify new initiatives or to generate ongoing support for initiatives by executive management. One of the first steps in the development of the CRM vision and strategy should be to determine the metrics by which CRM success will be measured.

Such metrics include assessing customer profitability, customer satisfaction, customer retention and sales and service delivery efficiency and effectiveness. Expected benefits to be gained must be well thought out, clearly explained and presented to executive management.

Plan

CRM initiatives should be prioritized based on an evaluation of the organization's biggest problems and greatest opportunities. Profitability analysis by product, channel and customer is an essential part of the planning process to make decisions regarding resource allocation, product development and for identifying pockets of opportunity.

Increasingly, planning solutions will need to take into account budgetary allocations so that trade-offs can be made, priorities established and resources allocated appropriately for specific initiatives.

Drive

Analytics drive CRM initiatives through enhanced customer insight that enables better customer segmentation and targeting. Customer analytics enable organizations to segment their customer bases across a variety of characteristics including life stage, profitability, products, demographics and lifestyle. Information on customers within each segment can be analyzed to model and predict customer behavior.

Predictive modeling is essential to effectively targeting customers. Many campaign management vendors are combining segmentation and predictive modeling into a single solution, which Gartner has termed relationship optimization. Profitability information from profitability systems can also be placed into the marketing system so that it becomes a dimension for segmentation and analysis. Over time, analysis must be performed in real time and compared to customer profiles.

Measure

CRM initiatives must be measured on an iterative basis to refine initiatives and to justify initiatives, continuing the CRM analytic cycle. Organizations must measure against pre-defined metrics determined during the justification and planning phase, making comparisons to established baselines or between test and control groups.

Such metrics enable decision makers (e.g., product, channel, segment, district and region managers, and marketing managers, as well as the heads of business lines) to make business decisions by enabling them to understand customer behavior, guide business strategy, better manage resources, optimize channels, improve products and maximize customer profitability. To do this effectively requires query, reporting and group comparison capabilities.

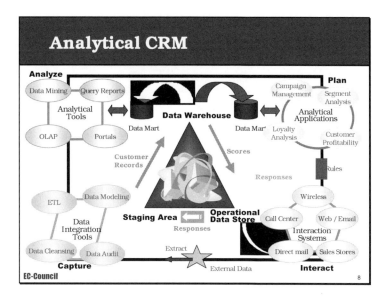

Analytical CRM

Successful CRM solutions adhere to a customer intelligence lifecycle. This is a closed loop business process that has four steps: Capture, Analyze, Plan and Interact.

Capture: The capture phase extracts the customer interaction data from operational systems, then integrates and stores the data for quick retrieval.

Analyze: During the analysis phase, business analysts create reports of customer behavior, define customer segments, and create predictive models that determine what recommendations or offers to make to customers.

Plan: The planning phase leverages the knowledge gained from analyzing customer information to create rules for optimizing customer interactions. These rules enable the business to deliver the right offer to the right customer through the right channel at the right time.

Interact: The interact phase involves executing these rules in various touch-point systems, such as web or contact center. Here, action is taken to optimize customer interaction across all channels. They then capture the results, and repeat the cycle, refining their plans based on experiences.

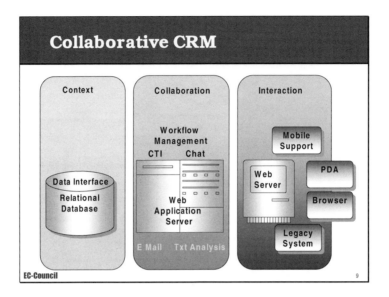

Collaborative CRM

Collaborative CRM facilitates interactions with customers through all channels (personal, letter, fax, phone, web, e-mail) and supports co-ordination of employee teams and channels.

Collaborative services such as personalized publishing, E-mail, communities, conferencing, and Web-enabled customer interaction centers that facilitate interactions between customers and businesses.

Collaborative CRM is used to establish the lifetime value of customers beyond the transaction by creating a partnering relationship.

A people centric collaborative environment achieves its true value addition from the cumulative value of internal and external users working in an integrated and collaborative fashion.

The interactions between a multiplicity of users, accessing applications and data that are inside and outside their respective departments, can significantly enhance the value of internal and external business processes and technology.

This is not just a matter of people-to-people interaction, however people-centric collaboration also requires that applications and services interact automatically with one another, without human intervention, in order to facilitate people to people collaboration. This requirement for system-to-system interaction is a key behind-the-scenes element in any people-centric collaborative environment.

The benefits from establishing a people-centric collaborative environment can be seen in three potential ways.

➢ The first is the most obvious: these environments bring with them the promise of streamlined operations that offer lower transaction costs, lower error rates, and other operational efficiencies.

➢ The second is the improvement in customer and partner relations that come from building tight links between technology and business processes. When done right, collaborative environments greatly enhance customer and partner satisfaction and help leverage all partners' investments in technology and business processes.

➢ Finally, a people-centric environment provides a platform for changing products, partnerships, and business processes in support of dynamic businesses and industries that require "first-to-market" rapid response. The capability of handling second sourcing, product or personnel substitution, alternative routings and services, and other just-in-time requirements can enhance the value of the entire value chain, and improve the effectiveness and efficiency of all participants.

➢

Collaborative CRM enables an organization's internal customer facing and support staff, mobile sales people, partners and customers themselves to access, distribute and share customer data/activities.

The unique part of this enablement is that the customer data/activities can be structured, unstructured, conversational, and/or transactional in nature.

True collaboration is not only based on having discussion threads and web access, but that it needs to incorporate business processes, rules, workflow and messaging as defined by the customer.

The bottom line is greater efficiency, a better return on human and technological assets, new business opportunities, and a closer and more fruitful working relationship between supply chain or value chain partners, be they buyers, sellers, administrators, or service providers.

Summary

- Three pillars of CRM are sales, marketing and service automations
- CRM technology can be broadly divided into operational, analytical and collaborative technologies
- Achieving CRM goals require integrating disparate technologies

EC-Council

10

Module Summary

Recap

➢ Three pillars of CRM are sales, marketing and service automations

➢ CRM technology can be broadly divided into operational, analytical and collaborative technologies

➢ Achieving CRM goals require integrating disparate technologies

We have seen the benefits of CRM as reducing the cost of service through merging and removing redundant processes and elimination of unnecessary touch points. CRM delivers more efficient use of technology, enables enterprises to provide more convenient services, thereby delivering enhanced customer interaction and experience.

Good CRM technology ensures customer information security and protection, placing customers at the centre of the departmental mission and service strategy, facilitating self-service where appropriate, and recognizes that each customer is unique.

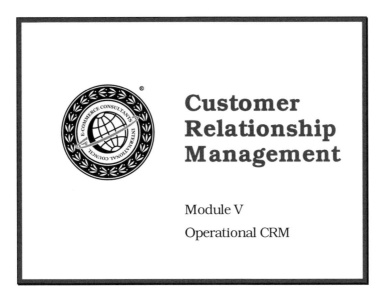

CUSTOMER RELATIONSHIP MANAGEMENT (CRM)

Module V - Operational CRM

Exam 212-16 - Certified e-Business Associate (CEA)

Module Objectives

⊙ Understanding Operational CRM technologies

⊙ Discussing operational CRM constituents

⊙ Illustrating various functionalities

2

Objectives

☞ **Module Objectives**

In the earlier modules we had introduced the three categories of CRM tools viz. operational, analytical and collaborative. This module intends to provide gainful insights into the domain of operational CRM.

At the end of this module you will:

> Have a clear comprehension of operational CRM

> Be able to identify and relate to the different constituents of operational CRM

> Gain a visual appreciation of operational CRM tools through the illustrations accompanying this module.

A company's CRM operational systems are at the heart of effective interactive customer relationship architecture.

In addition to providing operational capabilities for contact centers, SFA, field service and marketing, these systems provide the company's foundation for customer information architecture.

The goal of operational CRM is to achieve the automation of horizontally integrated business processes including customer touch points, point of sales, ERP, SCM and the legacy systems integration. The screenshots used in this module does not endorse any vendor product and is used for the sole purpose of illustration.

Sales Force Automation

- ⊙ Sales force automation is not CRM
- ⊙ Sales force automation products typically include:
  - Account Management
  - Opportunity Management
  - Sales Forecasting tools
  - Sales Pipeline Management
  - Lead Management

EC-Council   3

Sales Force Automation

Quite often, CRM has been confused as comprising solely of automated sales applications. While sales force automation applications are an integral part of CRM, they do not encompass the entirety of CRM functionality.

Sales force automation tools automate the collection and distribution of all types of sales information. They allow for the design of sales teams based on defined criteria.

Calendar management, activity management, sales reporting and forecasting, lead distribution, and tracking sales contacts with customers and prospects are some of the myriad of capabilities offered within these solutions.

Many also provide access to internal and competitive product information as well as the automated collection and distribution over the Internet of relevant external information such as breaking industry news and customer-specific events. Sophisticated pricing and product configuration engines and third-party channel management capabilities are also available.

Sales Force Automation (SFA) mainly involves enabling the sales force with some software tools.

The benefits derived from sales force automation is:

➢ Increased efficiency of the sales force

> ➢ Timely sharing of data
>
> ➢ Shortened sales cycles
>
> ➢ Field reporting
>
> ➢ Access to useful customer information.

Implementing SFA may or may not involve the re-configuration of the sales force.

The strategic objective of implementing SFA is to provide the sales force with ways to leverage technology to achieve operational efficiency. An indirect benefit of SFA is that it can lead to easier and more in-depth reporting.

A general flow of an SFA Module includes Lead, Opportunity / Proposal and Order Capture sub-modules. The Lead stage can be understood as the initiation of the sales cycle.

Here Lead management could include:

> ➢ Capture of Lead information like:
>
> ➢ Contact details
>
> ➢ Area of Interest
>
> ➢ Lead source
>
> ➢ Lead rating parameters
>
> ➢ Capture of details of all prospect interaction at the lead stage, like:
>
> ➢ Phone calls
>
> ➢ Email
>
> ➢ Meetings
>
> ➢ Lead Qualification based on some pre-determined rules.
>
> ➢ Lead allocation or assignment within the sales team or to resellers.

In effect, the flow of operations becomes Lead -> Opportunity -> Order Closure. The above is a generic view of a sales cycle and each business would have its own processes as to what best suits it product/service profile. SFA supplements the general sales cycle with built in tracking mechanisms and tools.

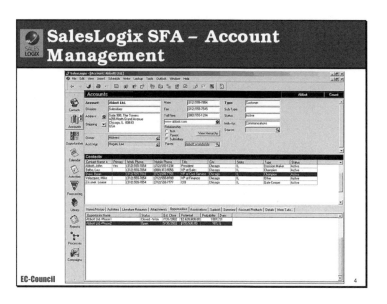

Account Management - Illustrated

We have seen that SFA increases productivity by automating key aspects of the selling cycle.

Account management is a standard feature of any SFA. It facilitates the salesperson or sales manager to handle individual corporate accounts. While this can be achieved with the help of a database as well, the difference here is in the customer view.

Each account has multiple links to other information that are relevant or have the potential to enhance business value. These may include corporate name, address, grouped by corporates or opportunities. The views generated can be general or highly detailed according to the requirement of the user. The data generated here is designed to work with sales departments that have account managers or that want corporate information.

In the areas of sales and account management, an integrated approach to CRM can provide the ability to link disparate sources of account information, customer purchasing patterns and forecast demand to create more complete and accurate sales forecasts to drive business planning efforts

Opportunity Management -Illustrated

We have seen that lead management and opportunity management are important functionalities of a sales force automation product.

Lead Management deals with the generation of leads based on multi- channel marketing campaigns to introduce new products or target specific customer segments.

The challenges in lead management revolve around providing the right content to the right customers at the right time with the right product.

Once the Lead is qualified and a financial implication can be attached to it, it can be moved to the opportunity level. This is where it comes into the sales funnel.

The main points associated with opportunity are financial details, decision dates, proposal and probability of closure. As a result, opportunity management is perhaps a longer time in the sales cycle in most cases.

Opportunity management can entail:

> ➢ Pipeline management to track the opportunity life

> ➢ Proposal management

> ➢ Capture of multi channel interactions with the prospect

> ➢ Milestone management for sales processes

> ➢ Managing the sales forecast depending on the decision date, etc

The objective at the opportunity level is to close the sale as soon as the opportunity has been identified. The goal of opportunity management is to collect any and all information about the customer/prospect and utilize this information to close the deal.

Opportunity management deals with leads identified. This may be an outbound call center waiting to be qualified, or a qualified lead being worked by a representative in the field or on the phone, or by email.

The application should be able to forecast the concerned opportunity to the sales organization accurately and provide all of the information the customer/prospect needs to make a decision.

Opportunity management spans all enterprise applications, as the enterprise would need information about the customer/prospect from the front office applications as well as credit or financial information from the back office. It may also be necessary to extract information from a data warehouse for past transactions or purchase history.

The most successful sales organizations all have very well defined and well structured rules about what is an opportunity, when it gets added to the system as an opportunity instead of just a prospect, and how it moves from stage to stage throughout its life.

Another feature that can be seen under opportunity management is competitive information. An enterprise can know who is competing with it for the opportunity in hand and assess competitor threat.

Advanced applications also offer competitive product matrix that a salesperson can use to present a valuable selling point. These applications can also provide information on customer preferences with regard to product functionality, support services, pricing, availability, differentiation etc. This gives the sales edge in closing the deal for the given opportunity.

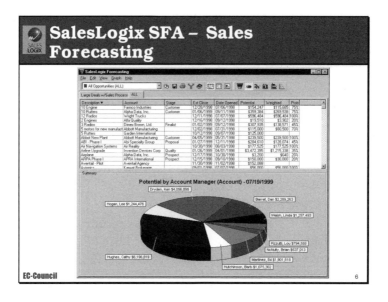

Sales Forecasting

Forecasting provides accurate, timely forecasts of revenue and customer demand, enabling managers and executives to help the sales organization close more deals, bring higher profits to the company, and align expenses with revenue growth.

Sales forecasting is another standard functionality of sales force automation software. It provides the enterprise sales force with a comprehensive view of the sales potential. Besides providing relevant information in customized views, graphical interpretation is also provided for ease of comprehension.

In the illustration shown here, the forecasting screen takes into consideration the different accounts, description of the sale involved, the stage in the sales cycle, potential of revenue, weighted revenue and probability of closing the deal.

The graphical view shows the potential grouped according to each account manager.

Sales forecasting provides a system for customers and sales people to list their projected needs so these can be accounted for in the manufacturing process.

Forecasting usually is one of the very top requirements by sales executives and senior management, especially in large and/or public companies.

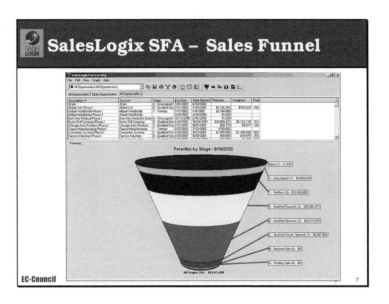

Sales Funnel management

A sales funnel offers a bird's-eye view of sales opportunities and gives managers sales forecasting information.

The lead management functionality and the opportunity management functionality are closely related to the sales funnel approach.

Leads that have financial potential are classified as opportunities and assigned an estimated time frame for closure of the deal. Sales funnel uses time and territory management to qualify the leads as suspect, prospect and sponsor.

The advantage of having sales funnel functionality in the SFA is that at any given time, the sales force has access to information (not just data) regarding the stage of each lead generated, specific details of the account facilitating strategic planning and informed decision making.

The other benefits derived include efficiency, timeliness and consistency arising out of having single view across the organization.

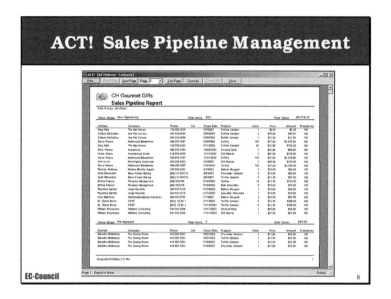

Sales Pipeline Management

Predicting demand is probably the largest benefit of CRM, but it's also often the least understood.

Sales pipeline is used to describe established sales processes. Each organization has its specific criteria with regard to what constitutes its sales process. The SFA application can be customized to cater to a firm's established sales processes. This typically includes prospecting, potential lead, qualification, opportunity, building vision, short list, negotiation and closure.

At a high level, the best practices in sales pipeline forecasting come down to two components:

> Removing bias and subjectivity from the forecast

> Using a time-series of past actual sales to determine the current forecast.

Objective statistically based forecasts are always more accurate and predictable than forecasts that are manipulated with subjective weightings or probabilities from sales reps, management, or executives.

Pipeline management extracts data from sales forecast and then plans sales activities to align with the forecasts. The benefit from sales pipeline functionality inclusion is again that derived from having a different view than traditional statistical applications.

Marketing Automation

- Enables end to end automation of marketing tasks
- Typical constituents of marketing automation are:
  - Campaign Planning & Management
  - Workflow Automation
  - Loyalty and Retention Programs
  - Communications / response management

Marketing Automation

Marketing automation encompasses designing, executing and measuring marketing campaigns.

Marketing automation applications aid in the selection and segmentation of customers, tracking contacts made with the customers, measurement of the results derived from these contacts and sometimes, in modeling those results to efficiently target customers.

"Campaign management" is the term used to refer to segmenting customers and executing marketing campaigns

Enterprise Marketing Automation (EMA) is the technology of end-to-end marketing. Campaign management is the core component of EMA and is often complemented with analysis tools.

Marketing automation is a subset of operational CRM that focuses on the marketing aspect.

This involves capture of customer information, analysis, customer segmentation and strategy, campaign management, tracking, etc. It usually does not refer to the advertising aspect and agency relations, which are far from being automated.

Marketing automation applications enable automating marketing campaigns and tracking of the results. Typical functions include generating lists of customers to receive mailings or telemarketing calls, scheduling automatic or manual follow-up activities and receiving third-party lists for incorporation into the campaigns.

Internet personalization tools are also being deployed to track behavior on corporate web site and allow tailoring of the contact experience, or generation of specific cross-selling opportunities, based on customer behavior. Inbound and outbound e-mail management capabilities are also being seen in marketing automation suites.

Desirable Features of Marketing Automation Software:

> Flexibility

The desired solution should work with a flexible data model that fits the business. At the same time, it should run on an operating system and platform that the IT team can support. Not only will this reduce the initial project implementation times but it will also free the enterprise from the technological barriers that can arise from acquiring external data, managing collaborative marketing projects and the data sharing problems of future mergers and acquisitions.

> Adaptability

The solution should adapt to the way the business wants to work, not the other way around, if the greatest and fastest possible return on investment is desired.

> Integration

CRM runs right across the enterprise. Therefore, a Marketing Automation Solution, either as a precursor to or part of a CRM system, must be capable of integration with all of new media channels such as Web, e-commerce and email as well as more traditional channels such as direct mail and advertising.

It is also desirable to integrate with complementary systems such as analytical and reporting tools, call centres and so on.

> Reporting and measurement

The chosen solution needs to be able to record and report on the success of various campaigns in a variety of ways. Depending on particular business requirements, these could include cost per lead, cost per order, repeat and additional sales, response rates by customer profile or segment, and others.

It should also give the ability to predict response rates (and therefore return on investment) and give the opportunity to fine-tune campaigns before they go live by performing 'what if' queries and analyses.

> Targeting and profiling

Good marketing automation software should make it easy for non-technical people to segment and target an audience for any campaign, from one-off marketing activities through to complex event-triggered and multi-stage campaigns.

Ideally, it should give users a simple, easy to understand graphical representation of the mapped database, providing them with a logical view of all customers, prospects, and product data, for the rapid analysis and definition of campaign strategies, selection and output.

Moreover, it should be easy to define and implement rules and priorities, both at system level and campaign level, and define conceptual entities by using an array of filters to accurately segment contact data.

➢ Automated responses

Apart from recording inbound responses from whatever channel, the solution should also automate the process of responding to enquiries, sending the fulfillment and processing the sales leads.

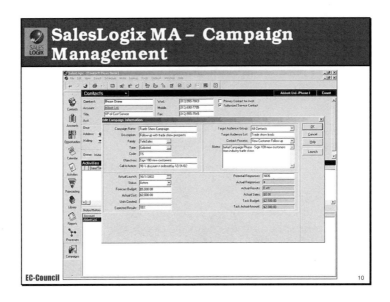

Campaign Management

Tracking is critical to the success of campaign marketing, as campaign performance can be understood and evaluated. It also provides a basis for justifying past marketing investments, and can help in optimizing future investments.

Tracking the success of the campaign and subsequent leads determines the return on the campaign, allowing the enterprise to change the campaign or reuse a proven one. It also helps in processing leads and making sure they are passed to the right people (Territory Management) with the right skills to handle the response.

Segmenting customers, generating targeted marketing campaigns for these segments and tracking results are important parts of CRM analysis. Most integrated marketing automation tools provide these analytical capabilities.

These analytical applications can provide campaign offers and results directly to the customer sales and support processes. Integrated campaign management software can incorporate offers and solicitations into the common contact repository and prompt contact agents to follow-up on campaigns.

Some of the common features seen in campaign management software are:

➢ Planning marketing activities and developing campaign hierarchies.

- ➢ Outlining marketing campaign objectives.
- ➢ Defining campaign success measurements.
- ➢ Coordinating multiple channels and event triggers to automate response actions.
- ➢ Building and testing sample campaigns.
- ➢ Storing and reusing content from previous marketing campaigns.
- ➢ Measuring campaign effectiveness by linking directly to call center, front-line employees and sales force.
- ➢ Importing third-party target lists.
- ➢ Tracking customer inquiries.
- ➢ Tracking sales force closures.
- ➢ Resource Allocation with reference to personnel, budget and time.

Analyzing, Learning, Listening and Responding Management

- Criteria for evaluating campaigns
- Tracking reports, new selling opportunities
- Developing a base for future campaigns
- Differentiating between components that work and that don't
- Modifying customer experience
- Choosing the right tools

EC-Council 11

Analyzing, Learning, Listening and Responding

How does an enterprise evaluate the effectiveness of its campaigns? The criteria adopted may vary from campaign to campaign based on the strategy behind the campaign and the objective sought. The concept of closed loop reporting is significant here, as campaigns need to be altered according to the analysis of the results of the campaign.

When planning a campaign and projecting response and conversion rates, it is useful to know how similar campaigns have fared in the past. This knowledge can be used to project the return on investment (ROI) from a campaign, and compare that to other alternative campaigns.

Without a system to track and store campaign results, and feed these back into planning, campaigns become one-time exercises with no long-term value to the business. A system that addresses this need is a closed-loop system. An effective campaign management ensures that this aspect is built into the system.

The main objective of measurement is to understand at a reasonably detailed level what component worked and what did not.

Most marketing activities are measurable at least at the aggregate level, if not at the individual level.

For instance, the evaluation criteria for a media campaign can be customer awareness. This can be measured through customer surveys. More targeted tactics, such as direct marketing, can be measured by the quantity of responses, leads or qualified leads generated. One-to-one marketing tactics, such as direct mail or e-mail can be measured at the individual level, with such metrics as response and conversion rates.

Here, the most important factor is being able to link the tactics with customer response. Another important factor in tracking responses is that prospects are exposed to multiple marketing messages in any given period. Moreover, a campaign can have a lingering or residual impact over time.

Resolving multiple campaign influences to determine which one had a greater impact is difficult, but important. Enterprises can capture first hand the impact of campaigns by asking its customers which marketing stimuli prompted the desired response.

Tracking needs to be carried out over varied time periods as the results or responses may be skewed depending on the tactic followed. For instance, if a campaign has several phases, with mass-market advertising followed by more targeted communications; the impact can last over several months.

Developing a sound base for future campaigns involves closing the loop. There are two major aspects to closing the loop:

The first is to pool the learning obtained from all the tracking that was done.

The second is to apply this accumulated learning in planning the next round of activities.

The enterprise needs to evaluate the effectiveness of the campaign in reaching the intended target and achieving its intended purpose — be it awareness generation or lead generation.

The metrics should give insight about the conversion of responses into qualified leads and into opportunities and sales closures.

Efficiency of the campaign can be ascertained by measuring the cost per response, qualified lead / opportunity / sale. This will also indicate partly the return on the investment.

Every campaign should have its metrics compared with previous campaigns, and to budgets and expectations. When planning and budgeting activity takes place, the resource allocation should be in proportion to the historically measured effectiveness of similar campaigns, and to the business need for this campaign given the current market situation. This will also help in identifying campaign components that worked from those that didn't.

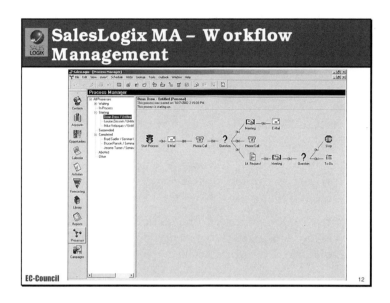

Workflow Management

The objectives of workflow management feature included in the marketing automation applications are:

➢ Streamlining marketing and sales campaigns by automating standard tasks

➢ Visually configuring campaign workflows such as calls, mail, or meetings

➢ Assigning custom processes — such as 'Trade Show Lead' — to campaign target groups

➢ Adding decision points and conditional requirements before events are triggered

Workflow automation reduces the time required in doing routine tasks. Another important benefit from workflow automation is propagation of well-defined business processes across the marketing department. This helps in delivering consistent customer experiences across multiple channels.

Successful CRM initiatives integrate applications across the enterprise to get a 360-degree view of the customer. Workflow automation is an enabling feature in enterprise application integration.

Marketing Communications - Illustrated

The illustration shown above depicts an Email marketing campaign.

E-mail management capabilities are used in two ways in marketing automation - inbound and outbound.

Inbound e-mail management capabilities assist organizations in handling inbound inquiries from customers.

While on the surface this would seem to be a purely service-oriented activity, organizations are linking these facilities to their personalization technologies and thus tuning the resulting communications on the basis of CRM analytics. Benefits of this can be quite high as it offers a chance to extend personalization techniques to multiple communication types.

Outbound e-mail management capabilities provide the ability to construct and execute permission-based marketing campaigns (where the dialog has been started with a customer via e-mail communications) and are said to be up to twenty percent more successful than traditional direct marketing at a fraction of the cost.

We have discussed campaign management in detail in this module. One important aspect of campaign management is to listen, interact and communicate with customers / prospects according to the needs analyzed.

While communication channels vary, email is emerging as a popular communications channel. Most businesses therefore, use e-Newsletters as part of the marketing mix. The response and conversion rates associated with email marketing have been on the rise and also found to be an effective method for customer acquisition and retention

Sales and lead generation are the popular criteria used in evaluating the effectiveness of Internet related marketing activities. The marketing edge is gained by getting the right message across to the right target at the right time.

E-mail campaigns are noted for their cost effectiveness, high ROI – Email marketing campaigns are capable of generating at least three times the cost of the campaign in new business.

Email Management programs usually possess the following capabilities:

> Automation of the targeting and sending of mass e-mails.

> Automation of mass e-mail responses.

> Use of decision engines to parse information from incoming e-mail correspondence.

> Crafting responses to incoming e-mail without human intervention

One aspect that has been discussed with regard to email management is that of personalization. There has been speculation about the utility of mass customization when the focus of CRM initiative is 'relationship' enhancement. This is addressed through analytical CRM components, where specific data about the customer is transformed into useful information.

Contact Management

- ⊙ Contact management is not CRM

- ⊙ Differentiating contact managers from CRM applications

- ⊙ Features of contact managers

- ⊙ Benefits derived from contact managers

EC-Council

14

Contact Management

Contact Management is often confused for CRM. Popular applications such as Goldmine, ACT! started out as contact managers. As the needs of the user have increased to accommodate more integrated information into daily operations, contact managers have been supplemented with limited CRM functionality.

A contact manager is a critical component of CRM functionality. However, it differs from a CRM application in that these applications cannot be customized and has fewer sales processes inbuilt in them. The other differences are limited data synchronization, lack of integration with legacy systems and limited scalability.

The goal of contact management software is to provide views that are limited to contact history and channel, and exclusive of the transactional system. The benefits derived from contact managers is the ability to track complete contact information including name, company, phone numbers, address, website, e-mail address, and much more.

It can double as a storage management for keeping track of important conversations, commitments, and meeting notes.

Contact Management - Illustrated

Contact management solutions improve the sales efficiency and the quality of customer service, by:

➢ Enabling access to all relevant customer data available across the enterprise to facilitate informed customer service and sales.

➢ Designing and implementing new contact or commerce channels such as websites, Portals, WAP, and integrating them with the customer database;

➢ Designing and implementing call centers with an integrated access to a customer database.

Contact management software is used to track contact information such as name, phone number, and customer interaction history across multiple channels. They also include calendars to organize hectic schedules and can act as E-mail clients.

Return on investment is obtained from contact management solutions when the solutions are specifically designed to support customer selection, acquisition and retention processes; interfaces with central Customer Database and delivers all relevant information to each contact channel.

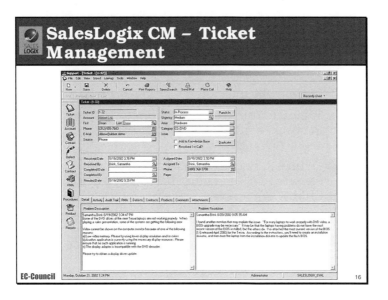

Ticket Management

We had discussed the three pillars of CRM as sales, marketing and service and support.

Ticket management forms part of the service and support functionality – primarily help desk.

It enables organizations to track reported service requests on items under account-specific service level agreements. This group of functionality can also provide tracking of affiliate and user-defined warranty programs for inventoried items.

Automation ticket management facilitates automatically routing and escalation of reported service tickets based on user-defined rules, and search for problem resolutions.

This increases customer service productivity as maintaining a ticket history in one location can enable employees to easily share and assign tickets. The ticket history can be quickly accessed to make sure that previous incidents are resolved.

The department can get a single view of ticket owners, priority weightings, and notification requests. This way, the enterprise can deliver consistent customer experience as each employee involved in support and service is in the knowledge of the customer's previous interactions and thus contributes to the customer relationship building process

Summary

- Operational CRM seeks to automate horizontally integrated business processes
- Typical technology applications include sales force automation, marketing automation, contact management
- Campaign management and opportunity management are critical functionalities for CRM
- Operational CRM should be integrated with collaborative technologies and analytical applications for effectiveness

EC-Council

17

Module Summary

Recap

➢ Operational CRM seeks to automate horizontally integrated business processes

➢ Typical technology applications include sales force automation, marketing automation and contact management

➢ Campaign management and opportunity management are critical functionalities for CRM

➢ Operational CRM should be integrated with collaborative technologies and analytical applications for effectiveness

Sales productivity can be realized immediately if the enterprise can provide the data that is relevant to requests for information. Information such as current sales pipeline, sales forecast, planned versus actual quota attainment, competitive landscape, previous customer sales history, and outstanding service requests is extremely helpful in developing a sales rep's call plan and reporting. When this information is combined with demographic data (address, phone, email, contacts, and partners) it can provide the sales force a detailed snap shot of their current sales related activities and give them a selling edge.

Marketing department can enhance their efficiency in planning and delivering strategic marketing tactics when information collected through the sales cycle is analyzed. Segmenting customers, generating targeted marketing campaigns for these segments and tracking results are important aspects of CRM.

Sales and Support form the third pillar of CRM. Support applications such as contact management, ticket management can help an organization increase the quality of its customer service thereby retaining the customer for longer time.

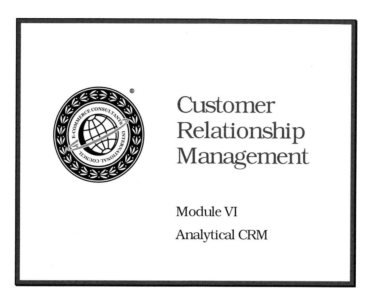

Customer
Relationship
Management

Module VI

Analytical CRM

CUSTOMER RELATIONSHIP MANAGEMENT (CRM)

Module VI - Analytical CRM

Exam 212-16 - Certified e-Business Associate (CEA)

Module Objectives

- Understand the critical components of customer centric strategies
- Define Analytical CRM
- Comprehend the CRM Data warehouse Architecture
- Discuss Analytical CRM components
- Understand the application areas of analytical CRM
- Discuss the requirements from an Analytical CRM application

EC-Council

2

Objectives

🖙 **Module Objectives**

In the previous module we have discussed operational CRM, as the automation of customer-facing business processes, whose traditional applications include sales force automation, customer service and marketing.

This module sets the tone for assigning ways of measuring CRM metrics. Once an organization has its CRM strategy drawn out, it strives to achieve the critical requirement of having a single view of the customer throughout the enterprise. Almost every organization has collected and stored a wealth of data about their customers, suppliers, and business partners. The differentiating factor of a successful progressive enterprise is its ability to discover valuable information hidden in this data and transform this data into knowledge.

A customer-centric database provides the critical technology among other enabling technologies such as real-time event management to allow companies to customize customer interactions based on knowledge obtained from the customer. The business need is, therefore, to extract valid, previously unknown, and comprehensible information from large databases and use it for profit. This is where analytical CRM comes into play.

Analytical CRM components can align the entire organization and the marketing and customer service processes to support CRM. Among enterprises that deploy analytics in their CRM strategy, those that apply the information gleaned in innovative ways to optimize customer relationships thrive best.

The intent of CRM is to create a dynamic environment of continuously improving customer relationships. The component to enable this is analytical CRM.

After completing this module you will be able to:

➢ Understand the basis for Analytical CRM based on the critical components of customer centric strategies.

➢ Define Analytical CRM

➢ Comprehend the CRM Data warehouse architecture

➢ Discuss the components of Analytical CRM

➢ Understand the application areas of Analytical CRM

➢ Discuss the requirements from an Analytical CRM application.

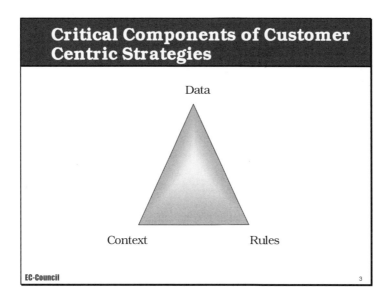

Critical Components of Customer Centric Strategies

Data

Context　　　　　Rules

Critical components of Customer Centric Strategies

The objective of a customer centric organization is to have an integrated view of the customer. To achieve this, organizations have to consider three vital components that produce the value and speed today's customer-centric business strategies require:

➢ **Data**: This includes the information required about the customer to extend CRM solutions across contact channels or product lines within the enterprise.

A wide variety of data is required to drive CRM value and provide an integrated view of the customer. This is to foster the ability to deliver the right data to ensure the desired customer experience across channels.

Customer data should be properly organized to drive customer interactions, such as demographic updates. The data required for generating customer insight also will need to be accessed by data mining and analytic tools.

Timing is another important consideration. For example, some businesses would find significant value in receiving real-time updates as customers log complaints. Complaint data would help drive real-time analytics and effect customer treatments applied in real time at the point of interaction.

Another area where real time availability is critical is when information is shared between two customer contact channels. This is important a customer may use both a call center and a Web site within minutes of each other. In addition, the quality of data and privacy issues must be considered.

➢ **Rules**: These are the instructions for using the data to shape the next interaction with the customer.

Rules define what the enterprise does with the information after it is captured and stored or warehoused.

The rules required for achieving an integrated view of the customer come in two primary forms - personalization and data transformation.

The enterprise needs to consider these rules as a manifestation of business objectives, decisions and requirements rather than technical implications of those requirements.

Personalization rules shape each customer interaction. They provide for consistent, timely and relevant individualized interactions across multiple customer touch points. Personalization rules govern what information is "pushed" to customers and how customer information is collected.

Data transformation rules, on the other hand, govern non-customer-facing activity. They provide for a similarly important business function: merging customer data from source systems or third parties.

Both forms of rules - personalization and transformation - are most effective when they address the broadest possible set of scenarios.

➢ **Context**: This is the translation of the enterprise's customer strategy into rules meant to deliver that strategy. Context is typically the missing piece for many CRM implementations, yet it has the most impact of all three components discussed here.

Two facets of context are especially important:

o Firstly, the rule should provide a holistic understanding of all the potential customer interactions within an organization, the events that make up those interactions and how the outcome of each interaction affects subsequent interactions or the overall customer relationship.

o Secondly, the reason why a rule is being implemented or a decision is being made. The purpose of each rule needs to be determined. The objective is the manifestation of context, which governs which of these rules, should take precedence at any given time.

Analytical CRM defined

⊙ Analytical CRM is the use of customer data for analysis, modeling and evaluation to create a mutually beneficial relationship between the company and the customer.

⊙ CRM (customer relationship management) analytics comprises all programming that analyzes data about an enterprise's customers and presents it so that better and quicker business decisions can be made.

EC-Council   4

Analytical CRM defined

Analytical CRM is a group of applications that utilize the data gathered from core CRM systems to enhance understanding of Customer behavior. This business objective is aided through providing reports, segmenting and classifying customers based on purchase patterns, and similar analytically focused functionality.

Analytical CRM is the use of customer data for analysis, modeling and evaluation to create a mutually beneficial relationship between the company and the customer. CRM (customer relationship management) analytics comprises all programming that analyzes data about an enterprise's customers and presents it so that better and quicker business decisions can be made.

Analytical CRM creates focus on creating and communicating rich, relevant personal content to customers. Therefore, it differs from its fraternal twin, operational CRM functionally.

CRM analytics include segmentation studies, customer migration analysis, cross-sell/up-sell analysis, new customer models, customer contact optimization, merchandising analysis, customer attrition and churn models, credit risk scoring, lifetime value (LTV) modeling and much more.

Operational CRM refers mainly to touch point- focused interaction systems.

CRM analytics can be said to comprise of special-purpose data warehouses and business intelligence applications that, instead of sustaining inventory analysis or financial reporting alone, are designed to draw content from the CRM core systems (the data sources), restructure and streamline that content as necessary, and support customized reporting, analysis, and data mining.

These can range from simple one-to-one data marts (e.g., data is extracted from a single SFA application into a separate database, where segmentation, profiling, and other analysis occurs) to more complex environments. In this case, the source database for CRM analytics may derive its data from multiple SFA applications and call centers.

Business Intelligence (technical realization) encompasses a range of tools that include query and reporting, business graphics, online analytical processing (OLAP), statistical analysis, forecasting, and data mining. These tools are often packaged into cohesive groups.

Some commercial software packages that support CRM analytics support more than just statutory reporting and analysis needs. They might perform customer segmentation and then, based on targeted marketing directives and company strategy, provide capabilities to support *campaign management* functions such as (1) mailing, faxing, or e-mailing offers (e.g., special promotions) to targeted customers or prospects, or (2) initiating and managing a program to reacquire former customers.

CRM analytics increasingly feed the results of the analytical processes into other transactional business processes, unlike traditional data warehousing and business intelligence in which the reporting and analytic activities tend to be ending points with regard to online activity.

Another business objective sought from investments in analytical CRM is the capability to manage customer value.

Customer value management (CVM) is a process that refines and leverages the benefits of customer relationship management. In a broad context it encompasses customer identification, contact management, campaign management, advanced data modeling and customer scoring.

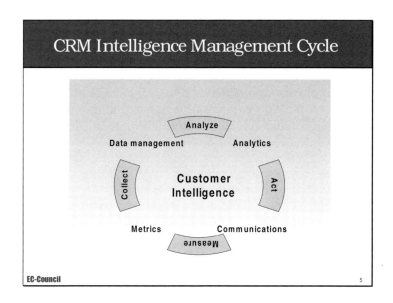

CRM Intelligence Management Cycle

A four-step process illustrates the CRM intelligence management cycle: collection (of data), analysis (plus modeling), action (with personalization and optimization) and effective measurements

➢ **Collection**: As the enterprise-class customer data warehouse foundation evolves and grows, the organization must evaluate and establish a robust infrastructure to cater to all the customer data throughout the enterprise. This entails collecting all customer interaction data, including transactions to manage the complete customer relationship.

Key operational and financial data such as channel capacity and profitability drivers (activity-based costs, transfer prices, etc.) also need to be captured to facilitate analysis of the organization's ability to meet customer demands and understand the financial implications of current and future behavior.

Customer data profiles need to be selectively appended to gain greater customer insight and make various operational decisions.

➢ **Analysis**: The logical sequence to any data collection exercise is data analysis. It should be noted that CRM data analysis differs from common data analysis, as it is more specific and complex in nature. The purpose of analyzing data include:

o Customer behavior and preferences: The more complete the view of each customer, the better the relationship can be conducted and fortified. This will provide the enterprise with the capability to enact effective customer based strategies that meet customer needs within organizational abilities and constraints.

o Operational factors such as channel capacity and design, sales effectiveness across Web, kiosk, and direct and indirect channel effectiveness.

o Financial factors such as customer profitability, cost allocation, consumption of resources to sell/service the customer, etc., in order to determine the key opportunities for improving profitability, and relate them to customer-related activities or operational activities.

This requires a set analysis and modeling tools. Analysis tools can provide the ability to evaluate customer profiles and behavior, and identify communication potential. In most cases they also enable evaluation of customer responses and event behavior.

➢ **Action**: Analysis forms the basis for the course of action opted. Customer communication tools to plan and execute communications based on analytical intelligence are crucial in this context. Enterprises need to avail the ability to plan and automate all types of customer communications from prospecting to multi-channel interactions over time.

However, it should consider the uniqueness of the customer and the need for personalization. This refers to the manner of treatment the customer has shown preference for through his past behavior.

A critical factor for success in CRM strategy is to deliver consistent customer experience across multiple channels.

Optimization capabilities can prioritize communications across all channels and ensure effective communication.

Optimization should be based on the priority of the message and the availability of resources to act within a particular time window. This should encompass all touch points such as direct mail, kiosks, POS, call center, Web, e-mail, ATM, store/branch and sales contacts. Optimization is intended to reduce the conflicts that may occur in channels.

➢ **Measurement of results**: The organization must measure the effectiveness and impact of its CRM activities on a regular basis to ensure meeting of its objectives. Performance can be evaluated in a number of ways.

A few measurement indicators can be:

o Campaign costs

o   Marketing campaign gross margin and revenue

o   Total customers in database showing real profitability

o   Revenue and gross margins per customer in the database

o   Revenue and gross margin from targeted customers

o   Percent change in CRM-related revenue and costs year to year

The genuine value of analytical CRM is its ability to identify a customer at a point of need. This has been seen in financial services industry where timely customer interaction has reduced customer attrition by over 40 percent.

The enterprises ability to accurately determine the point of need through analytics can facilitate relevant personalized communications. These communications when delivered through the right channel, enhances customer relationships leading to increase in marketing success and customer loyalty.

It is safe to imply that with analytical CRM, an enterprise-class data warehouse and a disciplined knowledge creation process, an enterprise is on the right path to increase both shareholder value and stakeholder goodwill.

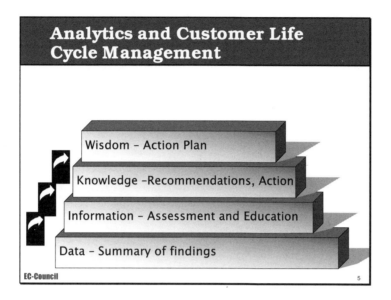

Analytics and Customer Life Cycle Management

Before we delve upon the interaction of CRM analytics with the customer lifecycle, let us recall the definition of customer touch points.

A customer touch is any interaction between the customer and the organization or someone representing the enterprise. We have also seen that a key success factor of any CRM strategy is the ability to utilize the available information on customers to understand the characteristics of the customer base and to influence the ways in which customers and the organization interact.

Data when seen in the relevant context and with supporting facts becomes information. Information transforms into knowledge when decision makers are educated about the information and begin to use it. Ultimately, corporate wisdom is gleaned from the information processed, when the business community takes action by consistently using and enhancing this knowledge.

The primary technology systems and processes within the enterprise that facilitate this conversion from data to wisdom are the business intelligence components.

Business intelligence components consist of the data warehouse, data marts, exploration warehouses, mining warehouses, the decision support interface and the processes for data acquisition and data delivery.

All analytical CRM capabilities have a robust customer centric data warehouse, at its foundation. This component contains detailed, static, enterprise-wide and integrated source of historical data and is a significant contributor to the overall intelligence of the CRM initiative. It acts as the collection point for the detailed, historical data garnered from both the operational systems as well as the operational data store (ODS).

Obviously, the quality of the data garnered from the customer touch points will greatly influence the success of the CRM initiative.

Unlike the operational systems, the data warehouse is primarily mapped to the customer life cycle in terms of information, not business functions:

- o Prospect information is integrated with customer information so that correlations can be found in the downstream data marts.

- o Customer interaction history is captured.

- o Competitor information is collected and integrated.

- o Point-of-sale information is stored.

- o Product history is captured.

- o Key performance indicators that reflect the health of customer relationships are retained.

From the data warehouse we can build a variety of analytical capabilities such as OLAP data marts, exploration warehouses and data mining warehouses. Each of these forms of analytical capability requires its own data, its own data design and its own set of access tools specific for the business problem at hand.

There are also two different orientations for data marts.

- o Departmental data marts usually satisfy requirements for the departments who pay for them.

- o Application data marts usually satisfy requirements for multiple departments or the organization as a whole and are funded within enterprise level budgets.

Neither type of data mart is necessarily better than the other, although each has its own ramifications.

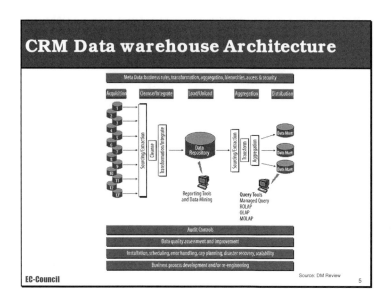

CRM Data warehouse

Customer-centric data warehouses are simply data warehouses that require complete, accurate views of customers, with their associated data, to solve important business problems.

The value of the customer-centric data warehouse or data mart is due to its integration, or consolidation, of customer data. The warehouse integrates customer data that is fragmented across multiple sources within your organization.

The sources often include various business line systems that support the following functions:

➢ Order processing

➢ Customer support

➢ Inquiry systems

➢ Marketing

➢ Various transaction systems.

Central to CRM data warehouse architecture is a customer-centric data repository. Ideally, the repository is part of an enterprise data warehouse as the volume of customer data can be staggering. Data can be sourced from customer interaction centers, customer touch points etc. Data from back- office systems is necessary to create a complete picture of customer value. Often third-party data such as psychographic and demographic information is relevant as well. Therefore, for consolidation and management of the customer data, a data warehouse is usually warranted.

Processes managed by an analytical CRM environment include data acquisition, cleansing/integration, loading/ unloading, aggregation and distribution.

Analysis of customer data essentially takes two forms -predictive and retrospective. One form enables companies to predict or forecast future behaviors or values of customers while the other provides a multidimensional view of customer activity.

➢ Predictive analysis uses historical customer data to uncover customer patterns, behavior and relationships. The use of data mining and predictive analysis enable a company to focus on high-value customers and create actions for cultivating potential high-value lifetime customers.

➢ Retrospective analysis provides capabilities such as online analytical processing (OLAP), query and reporting. When companies need to understand existing customer data by transaction, location, product and time, retrospective analysis is a good solution.

In the architecture shown above, the customer centric data warehouse forms the core of the architecture with data marts to supplement the various business area requirements. Query processing tools such as OLAP can extract data from these data marts and derive the results sought. Reporting tools and Data Mining Tools can extract data from the central data repository and do further processing.

Most of the CRM solutions available in the market have inbuilt analytics for different modules such as marketing automation. These let the modules interface with high-end analytical systems as per the requirements of the organization.

The organizations need to identify the data captured in existing systems and assess the data gaps while putting an Analytical solution in place. They also need to identify the potential sources for filling them such as transaction systems, customer call center history, web portals etc. The technology needed to develop an analytical CRM solution is discussed in detail in this module.

The key questions an enterprise needs to answer while addressing its data are:

➢ Where does all the customer data reside? Is information residing in the right places?

➢ What information is duplicated in multiple databases? How many databases?

➢ Is information easy to access for CSRs, marketers and others who need to use it?

> Of the shared information available, how much is being used? For example, are CSRs using the data available?

> When the shared information is used, how are revenues affected?

> Addressing these issues are critical to the success of any Analytical CRM initiative.

The key project tasks associated with designing and implementing data warehouses are:

> **Requirements gathering:** refers to the process of identifying the business needs and defining the key elements and relationships important in solving the problem in hand. Understanding the business is necessary so that the data and relationships identified may be validated as representing the business process or logical model and providing the infrastructure to respond to the business need.

> **Designing the Schemas** or the physical implementation of the data models. This is critical as designing an elegant business model that meets all requirements is not always sufficient. It has to be implemented effectively from a physical viewpoint; so that queries are completed in the desired time frames.

> **Create Extraction Transformation Loading (ETL) templates:** This refers to the process of developing and implementing the data transformation/ loading programs. These define the source to target, mapping and transformation rules to be applied as data is extracted from their respective source locations as the target data warehouse is populated.

> **Building queries for Analysis** that provides examples of how to access and use the models effectively. Queries are typically designed to address a set of key questions that will assist the user of the data warehouse in understanding the value of the data available. They are meant to equip the decision maker for exploration of the information domain, rather than the more predefined, static user interface generally associated with packaged operational applications.

> **Implement and Test** the data warehouse before it is deployed. Iteratively refine or customize the solution to more accurately meet the customer needs, and undertake the testing for compliance. This process associated with building and maintaining a data warehouse is usually referred to as the Iterative Development process.

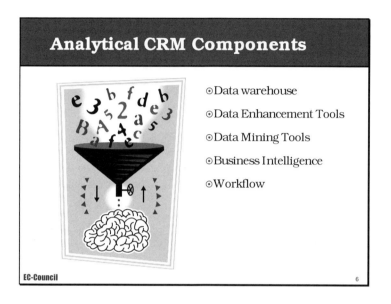

Analytical CRM Components

- Data warehouse
- Data Enhancement Tools
- Data Mining Tools
- Business Intelligence
- Workflow

EC-Council   6

Analytical CRM Components

> **Data warehousing** – Data warehousing technology and a comprehensive customer data warehouse are keys to making Analytical CRM work. Ideally, there should be a single customer repository for all transactions, behaviors, preferences, customer profitability and valuation, and segmentation treatments.

> Data warehousing technologies include the ETL or Extract, Transformation and Load functions to move data in and out of legacy systems and disparate data marts into the comprehensive customer data warehouse.

> **Data Enhancement** – This is a broad category consisting of data cleansing, data enhancement, and customer profitability. Data cleansing include 'cleaning' up, standardizing and linking the data as it is loaded from the legacy systems. Data enhancement involves adding external data such as demographic or spatial information.

> **Data Mining, Personalization and Segmentation** – These solutions are related but are sometimes perceived as vastly different because of how they arrive at their answers. Ultimately, they are performing the same task – using various modeling techniques to predict, tailor and present customers with better messages and increase the odds of acceptance.

➢ **Business Intelligence** – Often Analytical CRM is confused with Business Intelligence. Business Intelligence is a discipline on its own. While we discuss the term in the context of CRM, Analytical CRM, delivers most of the business intelligence capabilities. Its applications are not limited to CRM functionality.

Business Intelligence solutions range from ad-hoc query and OLAP analysis to portals, standardized reports and balanced scorecards.

Business intelligence provides users with access to the customer information and will be different for different types of users. Business Intelligence is the window into understanding the Analytical information.

➢ **Marketing Management Tools**– The Marketing or campaign management application is generally seen as the link between the Analytical and Operational worlds.

The Marketing application manages the marketing process by creating, executing and tracking offline-batch and real-time offers to customers. The execution of marketing offers is the link into the Operational or customer-facing CRM solutions.

➢ **Data Movement, Workflow and Integration into Other CRM Applications** – This last category is the glue that will connect the Analytical and Operational solutions into a cohesive and 'seamless' total solution. Workflow and business-rule driven capabilities are also key.

CRM suites often have built in capabilities to minimize the integration issues. Analytical CRM gives CRM system, the ability to collect metrics, as it is here that disparate data are analyzed. The closed loop reporting often advocated in CRM gains its basis here. Both operational and collaborative CRM gains from the information obtained from analytical CRM.

Analytical CRM enables feedback to be incorporated in meaningful ways into the business systems so that the objectives of the business are met.

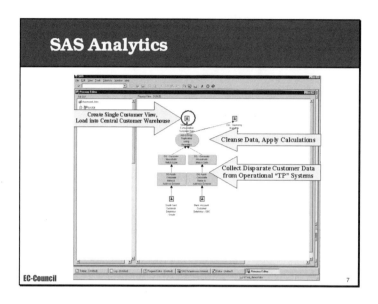

Benefits from CRM Analytics

This exhibit from SAS shows how the disparate components of Analytical CRM are arranged.

As discussed earlier, data collection and analysis are viewed as a continuing and iterative process and ideally over time business decisions are refined based on feedback from earlier analysis and consequent decisions.

Here, collection of customer data from disparate operational transaction processing systems is highlighted along with data cleansing, application of rules (calculations) and final culmination in the central customer data repository.

While applying calculations, the organization needs to analyze if the rules are consistent across multiple channels. This needs to be matched with the ability to deliver a consistent message across multiple channels.

The organization also needs to decide how many systems store rules that govern customer interactions, as well as identify those systems that store rules to unify customer data.

The benefits derived from CRM analytics are:

➢ **Customer retention.** Sophisticated customer-retention programs begin with modeling those customers who have defected to identify patterns that led to their defection. These models are then applied to the current customers to identify likely defectors so that preventive actions can be initiated.

➢ **Sales and Customer Service**. In today's highly competitive environment, superior customer service creates the sales leaders. When information is properly aggregated and delivered to front-line sales and service professionals, customer service is greatly enhanced. If customer information is available, rule-based software can be employed to automatically recommend products.

The programs like market-basket analysis (analysis of transactional databases to find sets of items that appear frequently together in a single purchase) have already shown phenomenal gains in cross-selling ratios, floor and shelf layout and product placement improvements, and better layout of catalog and Web pages.

➢ **Marketing.** Marketing depends heavily on accurate information to execute retention campaigns, lifetime value analysis, trending, targeted promotions, etc. Indeed, only by having a complete customer profile can promotions be targeted, and targeting dramatically increases response rates and thus decreases campaign costs. Direct mail costs are directly proportional to the completeness and accuracy of customer data.

➢ **Risk Assessment and Fraud Detection**. An accessible customer base significantly reduces the risk of entering into undo risk. For example, a mail order retailer can identify payment patterns from different customers at the same address, identifying potentially fraudulent practices by an individual using different names. An insurance company can identify its complete relationship with a client who may have different kinds of policies totaling more than an acceptable level of exposure.

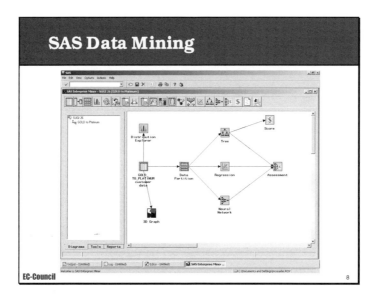

Customer Centric Data Mining

Customer-centric data mining is a collection of techniques and methods that enable businesses to engage and retain their share of the market. The goal of data mining is to provide the ability to convert high-volume data into high-value information.

Data mining accomplishes two things: it discovers enterprise knowledge from historical data and combines historic enterprise knowledge with current conditions and goals to reduce uncertainty about enterprise outcomes.

Thus, data mining is conceived of as a process having two components:

➢ *Discovery*, during which meaningful patterns are detected in data and characterized formally (descriptive models); and

➢ *Exploitation*, during which meaningful patterns are used to create useful applications (predictive models).

Model development entails developing a single or series of models, with each attacking a specific aspect of a complex problem.

Data mining provides a programmed method of discovering patterns in data. Data mining applications ingest and correlate data comprehensively. Data mining tools can identify the relationships that are exactly present in historical data.

Data mining provides the tools and techniques that are vital for optimization of customer relationships. Data mining enables organizations to use data actively for very powerful impacts, rather than just passively storing it.

Data mining is central to optimizing return-on-investment (ROI), because it offers objective, quantifiable insight. Data mining can identify high-potential customers in each market. It can help determine which customers are most likely to make significant and collateral purchases.

Data mining can extract "profiles" of these customers, which can be used to identify business opportunities.

Data mining can help by answering two questions:

➢ Which of my high-profit customers are most likely to leave? Be proactive to retain them.

➢ Which of my low-profit customers are least likely to leave? Raise their price and make them more profitable.

Common to all users is the need to maximize the amount of useful information extracted, while minimizing the loss of productivity that results from the information retrieval effort, prohibitive access, communications difficulties, or retrieval of meaningless, incorrect, or corrupted data.

In order to satisfy the needs of analysts, data mining systems can be designed to represent associations in large data sets, extract and transmit material across a distributed multi-user network, and analyze, interpret, and display information in a variety of meaningful ways.

Combining discovery-driven analysis with the more pervasive assumption-driven methods will ultimately produce the most comprehensive analysis for the greatest business benefit.

Operational efficiency is the key to keeping costs under control. Business forecasting is fundamental. Estimation of lifetime value of customers is a high-return activity. This forecasting is more than planning and developing cash-flow models. It includes market projections grounded in real business history.

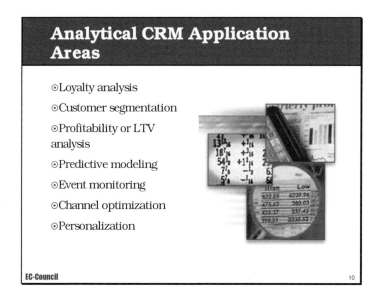

Analytical CRM application areas

➢ **Loyalty Analysis:**

This area of analysis provides answers to questions such as average defection rate, defection rate by cohort class, customer segment, sub-segment, geography, other attitudinal, demographic and behavioral attributes, total cost of defection, ratio of acquisitions versus defections, effectiveness of defection intervention techniques etc.

CRM analytics help organizations decide how quickly to detect customer defection and know about who are customers defecting to and how frequently. Competitive advantage is gained from knowing about new customers and the competing product are they defecting from and the frequency.

Customer Loyalty programs are based on the analysis of RFM Model. Recency is the length of time since a customer's last purchase, frequency measures the number of times a customer has made purchases and monetary value is the dollar amount of those purchases.

➢ **Customer Segmentation:**

Segmentation is the act of breaking down a large consumer population into segments in which those consumers within the segments are similar to each other, and those that are in different segments are different from each other.

The consumers within the segments may be similar to each other for a variety of different reasons. They may be similar in terms of where they live or their income, or they may be similar in the way that they think and behave. Or, they may be similar to each other based on some other factor that is important to someone else. For instance, people who respond well to the postcards that a direct marketing firm mails versus those who will respond to telemarketing.

The objective of customer segmentation in CRM Analytics is to segment the customers by business value.

> **Customer Profitability**

Customer profitability deals with identifying historical, current and projected value of the customers and then using it to improve segmentation and to implement customer strategies. Customer profitability analysis is one of the most important and under-appreciated components of Analytical CRM.

The understanding of customer profitability is critical to the way that a company runs its business. Understanding current customer profitability based on current known customer information is hard, and often requires the collection of much important external information as well as pointed data mining.

Beyond that, however, is the need to go to the next step to perform data mining to predict customer lifetime value, and ideally potential value and lifetime value. The difference between actual value and potential value is simply the difference between the value the customer will bring to the company if things are maintained at the status quo versus the value the customer could bring if he or she is well taken care of.

One of the best ways to increase the usefulness of strategic analyses is to perform a Customer Understanding/ Profit Link study. This process establishes empirical links between the primarily intangible qualitative measures of customer understanding (e.g., customer satisfaction, brand perception/strength and customer loyalty) with the critical business outcomes or quantitative data (e.g., market share, profitability or lifetime customer value.

Analytical and forecasting techniques can be used for determining customer revenue and predicting future receipts. Data mining offers this kind of capability, and it starts from understanding customer profiles and behavior, thus determining responsiveness towards certain supplier strategies like cross selling or up selling, retention, etc. Data mining allows assessment of different predictive models and the subsequent selection of the best fit.

> **Predictive Modeling**

Predictive modeling is a system that aids an entity in predicting what one of their users will do next. Multiple actions by the user are considered in determining the eventual outcome.

> **Event Monitoring**

Event monitoring triggers information or action-based recognition of specific patterns of data within or among application systems. Data mining can be used to identify the patterns of interest for each event. Such data patterns can result from customer behaviors or other processes.

The event monitoring can implement notification via a variety of means, such as e-mail messages or submitting actions to customer service queues. Event monitoring can be useful in a variety of selling, service, and retention activities.

Event modeling enables business organizations to deliver more accurate and successful marketing campaigns and treatment strategies. Event modeling takes advantage of statistical tools to build models that "explain" the behavior of customers and predict the response of customers and prospects to future marketing promotions.

Event modeling enables organizations to understand which events in a customer's life—birthdays, purchase of a new car or house, birth of a child—can lead to opportunities that add value with the organization's products and services. These events, which can be ascribed to market segments, are also powerful tools to evaluate customer and prospect profitability.

Event modeling seeks ways to reduce the number of promotions, manage the costs of business strategies, and increase the percentage response rates to promotions—all of which ultimately boost profits.

> ## Channel Optimization

Channel optimization has always been a critical success factor for business. Just by moving through their product maturity curves, companies have had to alter their distribution strategies and deploy new channels.

The principle behind channel optimization is to continuously evaluate ways to drive sales and service activities to the lowest cost channel that can successfully execute the desired value proposition.

A customer within a defined segment can buy a product or service with its buying requirements being delivered or met by various channels. A company can plan this process based on segment requirements and use CRM technology to ensure that the necessary information sharing takes place and that performance can be measured and customer satisfaction and cross-selling maximized.

> ## Personalization

The personalization process involves getting to know the customer through data gathering, creating a profile for the customer and extrapolating from past histories, segmenting the customer based on his profile, extrapolating predictions based on the customer's data, as well as his peers in the customer segment, delivering customized content, offers, etc. to the customer and finally allowing the consumer to log in/access the customized content directly.

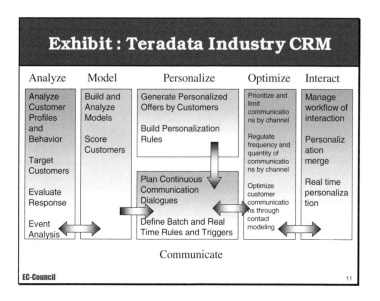

Exhibit : Teradata Industry CRM

Analyze	Model	Personalize	Optimize	Interact
Analyze Customer Profiles and Behavior	Build and Analyze Models	Generate Personalized Offers by Customers	Prioritize and limit communications by channel	Manage workflow of interaction
Target Customers	Score Customers	Build Personalization Rules	Regulate frequency and quantity of communications by channel	Personalization merge
Evaluate Response		Plan Continuous Communication Dialogues	Optimize customer communications through contact modeling	Real time personalization
Event Analysis		Define Batch and Real Time Rules and Triggers		

Communicate

EC-Council   11

Teradata Industry CRM

This exhibit above depicts the teradata CRM approach.

> The **Analysis tools** enable enterprises to track and analyze customer-buying behavior over time, and create profiles. This can be achieved by defining, analyzing and targeting segments by behavior, demographics, location, product/service usage and affinities, market basket, customer rankings, groups of transactions over time and scoring results. The tools can help realize opportunities based on new links discovered between customer segments and attributes as well as measure and report profitability at the account and transaction level.

> The Modeling tools help build models from multiple types of data sources, including campaign-based or ad-hoc analytic data sets. They can measure, model and report customer lifetime value (LTV) with the ability to take immediate action on this information for business advantage. Some of these tools can also mine the entire database to discover hidden patterns that are not obvious to human observation or to OLAP technology tools and take rapid business action to capitalize on the insight.

> The personalization components equip the enterprise with the ability to define rules-based, customized personalization variables for each individual customer, e.g. customer's name, individual offer with highest response probability, and most appropriate discount reward.

> ➢ The communications tools help determine, plan and implement the best communication tactics for each opportunity. The enterprise can also plan multimedia events including TV, radio, newspaper, direct mail, Internet and point-of-service.

> ➢ The optimization tools help deliver the most effective mix of messages and offers exclusively for each customer based on priority and the availability of resources to act within a particular period of time. Leads can be selected, filtered and then prioritized based on specified business rules. This set of applications helps the enterprise in optimizing customer communications by managing the frequency and number of messages and offers by individual, seamlessly manage communications across all channels and prioritize leads and channels based on capacity and existing workload.

> ➢ Lastly, the interaction tools enable personalized inbound and outbound customer interaction. This facilitates dynamic merging of variables specified in the e-mail personalization wizard for more effective interaction with web customers and allows marketers to respond to each customer contact with appropriate follow-up communication as well as capture the results of all communications for later analysis.

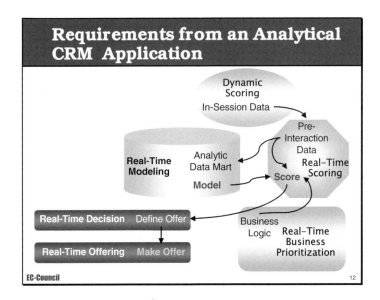

Requirements from an Analytical CRM application

The true test of an analytical application is its ability to deliver information in real time.

As illustrated above, an analytical CRM application allows for dynamic scoring using in-session data from various touch points. This is grouped along with pre-interaction data before being stored in the data warehouse to facilitate contextual analysis. The pre-interaction data in itself can be used to assign a score.

When scoring is done in real time, the inputs come from the model in the analytical data mart, pre-interaction data and in-session data. This is then combined with business logic (based on real time business prioritization) to define the most suitable offer to the customer. Once a decision is taken, the offer is made in real time to the customer. Examples include real time customer discounts, cross sell / up selling activities.

To qualify as a CRM analytic application, software products must demonstrate business process support, the separation of function, and use time oriented, integrated data from multiple sources.

The requirement of time orientation exposes a major stumbling block for real time analytics because true analytics require the integration of historical information. As CRM analytics become more integrated and distributed beyond the traditional technical analyst department, it becomes more important to assure the continuity of the experience from the user's point of view.

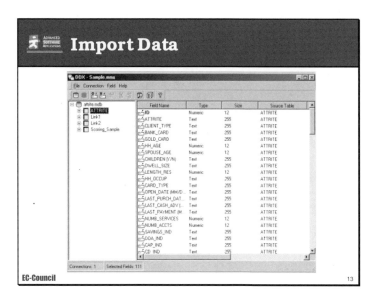

Data Extraction - Illustrated

Once an enterprise-class customer data warehouse foundation in place, it will evolve and grow. The organization must evaluate and put in place a robust infrastructure of all the customer data throughout the enterprise. This means collecting all customer interaction data as well as transactions to manage the complete depth and breadth of the customer relationship.

The organization also needs to collect key operational and financial data such as channel capacity and profitability drivers (activity-based costs, transfer prices, etc.) in order to analyze the company's ability to meet customer demands and understand the financial implications of current and future behavior.

It is also desirable to selectively append customer data profiles to shed further light on each customer and make various operational decisions, including credit authorization. The importance of this step to CRM success in the rest of the process cannot be overemphasized. Here, data import in ADS ModelMax Plus software is shown as an illustration of how customer attributes are defined and relevant data imported from disparate sources.

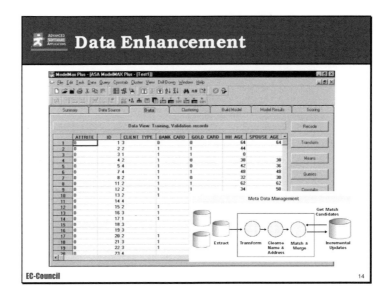

Data Enhancement - Illustrated

 Data enhancement means adding additional intelligence to an existing customer database for more in depth analysis. Data quality is of critical importance in any successful CRM initiative.

Key data elements to be included are:

➢ Names and addresses from all sources (internal and external), merged and reformatted into a single file that contains both customers and prospects, de-duplicated and enhanced

➢ Named contact information

➢ Profile information

➢ Financial information, usually summarized

➢ Product order and purchase information

➢ Other transactional information

➢ Service and support information

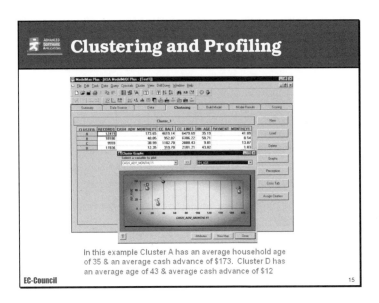

In this example Cluster A has an average household age of 35 & an average cash advance of $173. Cluster D has an average age of 43 & average cash advance of $12

Clustering and profiling

Customer profiling is the process of identifying consistent patterns within customer or prospect data that provides information, which can be used to make business decisions and take appropriate actions.

For example, customer profiling might be used to identify which prospects are most likely to respond favorably to a certain type of selling campaign or offer. It is a very useful technique that can be applied in all phases of the CRM life cycle. Customer profiling may use advanced data mining capabilities, or less sophisticated methods.

Advanced customer profiling applications utilize powerful data mining techniques to build predictive models based on common profiles within a customer base. This approach requires adequate historical data

Typically, the number of attributes used for customer profiling models is reduced to those key attributes that are most effective in identifying the differences between profile groups.

Customer acquisition profiling utilizes predictive patterns to identify which prospects are most likely to make a particular type of purchase. It is useful in identifying the best prospects (some may consider this to be an aspect of lead generation) and in determining which marketing programs will be most effective to reach the customers that conform to particular profiles.

Customer **purchase profiling** is similar to customer acquisition profiling in that purchasing patterns are used to identify additional selling opportunities for customers or prospects that are already in a buying mode. Similar profiles can be used to identify or optimize cross-selling opportunities and processes.

Customer **retention profiling** is similar to customer acquisition profiling in that predictive patterns are utilized to identify which customers are likely to remain loyal to the business and which ones are in jeopardy.

The clustering technique finds out what attributes make customers different. These attributes could be RFM measures, demographic characteristics or other attributes. In reality, the organization cannot create campaigns for every individual in the customer base – that's where clustering helps by targeting campaigns to as many groups as there are clusters.

The clustering algorithm assigns customers to different groups, depending on how similar their attributes are. Clustering models focus on identifying groups of similar records and labeling the records according to the group to which they belong. For instance, customers can be clustered into three - with the first cluster being clustered as those with high income levels; second cluster made up of those who are students; and the third cluster is those who work in the construction industry. Clusters enable the organization to tailor specific campaigns for different customers.

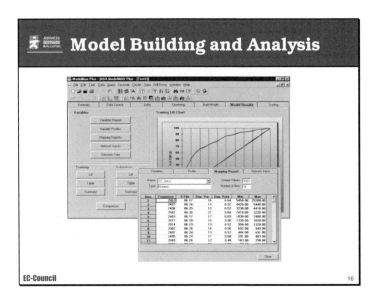

Model building and Analysis

The difference between a Profile and a Model is the element of time, making models more powerful predictors of behavior. Modeling lends an understanding of the fundamental preferences that individual customers have for product and service features, and of the process by which those preferences are transformed into purchases over time as the market evolves. Unlike traditional approaches, analytical modeling can provide accurate, flexible forecasts for customers across multiple channels, and under different market conditions.

Modeling and analysis can measure individual customer values for the features and pricing of the offer, and capture the richness, dependencies, and diversity of individual customer preferences. This measurement can give an in-depth understanding of customers, or potential customers, in specific markets through customized primary research, both qualitative and quantitative.

Models can also be used to capture the dynamics of the marketplace:

- ➢ Customer loyalty and inertia
- ➢ Untapped market segments
- ➢ Distribution channels
- ➢ Customer awareness

➢ Advertising impact

➢ Technology substitution

➢ Potential competitive moves

➢ Timing of product introductions

➢ Changes in customer needs and values as the market and competitive landscape evolve.

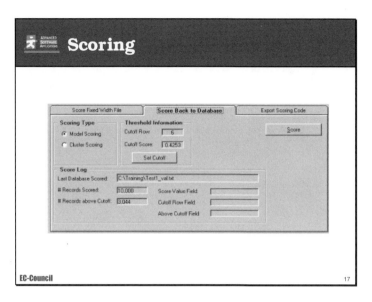

Scoring

Advanced data analysis will produce a collection of predictive and other models. These models, which are functions of a reduced set of variables (predictors) and are derived on a sample of customer data, have to be executed for the entire customer base.

The execution of models (scoring) results in assigning each customer a predictive or other score, expressing, for example, the likelihood of a customer to react in a certain way to a particular offer.

Data mining builds models by using inputs from a database to predict customer behavior. This behavior might be attrition at the end of a magazine subscription, cross-product purchasing, willingness to use an ATM card in place of a more expensive teller transaction, and so on. The prediction provided by a model is usually called a score.

A score (typically a numerical value) is assigned to each record in the database and indicates the likelihood that the customer whose record has been scored will exhibit a particular behavior.

For example, if a model predicts customer attrition, a high score indicates that a customer is likely to leave, whereas a low score indicates the opposite. After scoring a set of customers, these numerical values are used to select the most appropriate prospects for a targeted marketing campaign.

Sample Vendor Options for CRM Analytics

- ⊙ **Build**
  - CRM Analytics could be built using BI tools available off the shelf viz. **Business objects, Micro strategy, Cognos, Hyperion, Proclarity** etc

- ⊙ **Buy**
  - CRM analytics suite could be procured and implemented viz. **Quadstone**

- ⊙ **Integrate**
  - Analytics could be embedded into the operational CRM that's being run in case of suites like **AMDOCS, Chordiant, Onyx** etc.

EC-Council   19

CRM Analytics – Sample vendor options

Getting the required analytics up and running from the CRM application is an activity to be viewed seriously. Enterprises can go about implementing CRM analytics by way of any of the three approaches presented viz. Build, Buy or Integrate Analytic packages into the CRM system.

Buying analytic tools and customize them to the enterprise's unique needs was the traditional approach. As operational CRM applications developed, they continued to embed relevant analytical capability to support and report the operational processes.

The recent approach offers stand-alone CRM analytic suite that shares tools' ability to work in a very heterogeneous application environment with the expertise of the embedded analytics with respect to operational CRM solutions.

The benefits of building are:

➢ Flexibility

➢ Ability to choose from best-of-breed solutions

➢ Achieving a truly enterprise solution.

The benefits of buying are:

➢ Shorter implementation times

➢ Adaptors for common back office systems

➢ Inbuilt analysis tools and most often pre-defined metrics for most businesses.

Real-time analytics offer the speed and depth to provide more detail-oriented applications. Real-time reporting tools produce immediate reports for sales and marketing; real-time analysis updates data as it occurs with the customer; and marketers typically use real-time modeling to manage unstructured data, such as untested marketing campaigns.

Businesses that need to respond to customers immediately—such as those in financial services, telecom and retail—should use real-time analytics. Another trend used in association with real-time analytics that helps to sort through mounds of data, is the use of lifestyle trigger alerts. Triggers represent a shift in the marketing metaphor, which is to push out a long marketing campaign.

The business that knows its customers best will serve them best. Customer-centric data mining provides insight into customer attributes and behaviors. This understanding is the basis of any sound business forecast.

Suppliers that are leading the delivery of enhanced data analytics, include SAS and Epiphany, which provide real-time engines for trigger alerts; SPSS, which offers a statistical workbench tool; Unica, a maker of analytical direct-marketing software; and Kana, which offers Web-based analytical tools.

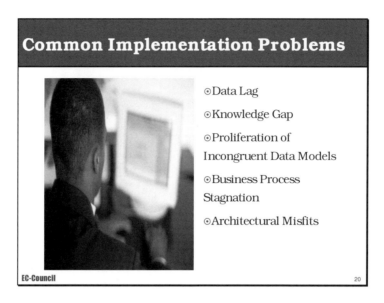

Common Implementation Problems

Customer relationship management analytics can deliver a unified platform for analysis, but there are inherent problems companies must deal with and overcome. Those problems include:

> **Data Lag.** The data from the transactional system must be extracted, transformed and loaded into the analytic database. This implies that there is always a gap in the availability of the most relevant data. This impacts not only market plans and future actions, but also may impact day-to-day operations as users must search multiple data sources to get a complete picture of the customer.

> **Knowledge Gap.** Even when the analytic platform can provide illuminating results, there is usually no guarantee that the results of the analysis will be distributed to the customer-facing employees when they need it or that they will leverage the information at the time and place most likely to impact the customer relationship.

> **Proliferation of Incongruent Data Models.** Disparate analytic and transactional systems lack a centralized repository to unify Meta data and models about the customers. This can create confused and inaccurate representations of customer analysis.

> **Business Process Stagnation.** Most analytic and CRM systems are designed to automate the best practices available to the software designer. Revising the business processes and metrics underlying those systems is sometimes impossible and often costly and difficult. The result is CRM systems that essentially lock companies into a way of looking at customers and interacting with them.

➢ **Architectural Misfits.** Because the data structure of most CRM databases is typically not optimized for online analytical (OLAP) processing, the customer-facing systems lack the ability to aggregate and analyze historical information. Today companies solve this problem by consolidating all data in a data mart and imposing a "star schema" in the data mart to enable visibility of the effects of time. However, few CRM systems today are designed to effectively leverage data marts.

A CRM analytics program that meets expectations must deliver a unified platform for CRM and analysis.

Module Summary

 Recap

➤ Analytical CRM helps organizations have closed loop reporting

➤ Components of Analytical CRM include data warehouse, data mining tools, query and reporting tools, and business intelligence.

➤ Analytical CRM helps in Loyalty analysis, Customer segmentation, Profitability or LTV analysis, Predictive modeling, Event monitoring, Channel optimization and Personalization

Organizations that identify their most valuable customers are able to prioritize their activities so that they spend their own scarce resources on customers and prospects in order of their *value*.

The value of analytical CRM—capturing and analyzing customer information to offer targeted marketing solutions and products. Analytics is becoming the business driver for companies. The reason: data mining and analytics tools dig deeper into large databases to deliver important insights, such as accurately determining customer acquisition and retention rates, segmenting customer values, and finding ways to meet the needs of high-valued customers.

Customer
Relationship
Management

Module VII
Collaborative CRM

CUSTOMER RELATIONSHIP MANAGEMENT (CRM)
Module VII - Collaborative CRM

Exam 212-16 - Certified e-Business Associate (CEA)

Module objectives

⊙ Overview of collaborative CRM

⊙ Collaborative CRM architecture

⊙ Customer Interaction Centers

⊙ Evolution of Contact Centers

⊙ Portal Management

EC-Council

2

Objectives

☞ **Module Objectives**

More than ever, companies are increasingly relying upon external organizations to help maximize sales, deliver superior customer service and reduce costs. In order to deliver on customer expectations and retain customers, organizations at times, need to operate as virtual enterprises integrating internal business units and partners.

As the business environment becomes increasingly complex due to globalization, mergers, acquisitions and strategic partnerships, the enterprise must focus on remaining competitive and profitable by building a cost-effective collaborative enterprise.

After completion of this module, you will:

➢ Have an overview of collaborative CRM

➢ Understand collaborative CRM architecture

➢ Learn about Customer Interaction Centers

➢ Gain insight into the evolution of Contact Centers

➢ Comprehend Portal Management

Collaborative CRM

⊙ Collaborative ebusiness is the

- strategies and technologies that enable

- multi-enterprise business process integration
  and content management, with the

- goal of creating, growing, and retaining
  profitable networks of customer and partner
  relationships.

EC-Council   3

Collaborative CRM

Collaborative ebusiness is the strategies and technologies that enable multi-enterprise business process integration and content management, with the goal of creating, growing, and retaining profitable networks of customer and partner relationships.

Collaborative CRM focuses on providing business solutions to meet the complex and dynamic environment of today's enterprises. It focuses on giving visibility into enterprise sales, service, marketing, and product development to support customers better.

By understanding the heterogeneous environment of most enterprise application portfolios, Collaborative CRM provides a framework that sales, service, marketing, and product development organizations can work together, but yet still maintain their unique way of doing business.

A collaboration platform needs to address challenges and capabilities including:

➢ Need for structured process tools that can manage simple as well as complex methodologies, in addition to the repeatable process.

➢ Account for multiple time zones and shared roles within the workflow.

➢ Provide easy management interface (driven by business needs).

- ➤ Status reporting of the overall process from start to delivery. Provide full functionality over the Web (Web-native architecture) to all users, with status reporting.

- ➤ Allow flexibility to be specific -- for well-defined vertical applications -- and a suite of common capabilities -- for generic applications.

- ➤ Embrace emerging technologies like Voice over IP (VOIP), video, secured file sharing, etc. with open architecture.

As technology barriers dissolve, enterprises become increasingly enabled to build, integrate, and extend processes to customers, employees and business partners, to improve customer satisfaction and loyalty while driving increased revenue.

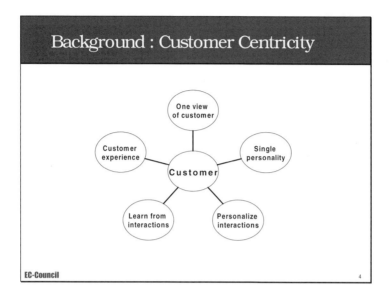

Customer Centricity revisited

The above slide illustrates the requirements from a customer centric enterprise, as we have discussed in earlier modules.

At its most basic, people-centric collaboration requires that the greatest number of users, both inside and outside the enterprise, have access to a wide variety of functionality – which spans the enterprise and its IT environment – according to their specific role or job function.

A people-centric collaborative environment achieves its true value-add from the cumulative value of internal and external users working in an integrated and collaborative fashion.

The interactions between a multiplicity of users, accessing applications and data that are inside and outside their respective departments, can significantly enhance the value of internal and external business processes and technology.

This is not just a matter of people-to-people interaction, however people-centric collaboration also requires that applications and services interact automatically with one another, without human intervention, in order to facilitate people-to-people collaboration. This requirement for system-to-system interaction is a key behind-the-scenes element in any people-centric collaborative environment.

The bottom line is greater efficiency, a better return on human and technological assets, new business opportunities, and a closer and more fruitful working relationship between supply chain or value chain partners, be they buyers, sellers, administrators, or service providers.

Ideally, a people-centric collaboration permits any user to access any relevant data on any system, internal or external, as long as that access will enhance that user's job performance or function.

The different users and the applications they use must be able to interact or collaborate with one another. The external client, having a problem with a self-service screen at the service provider's site, may contact a customer service representative, who can view that customer's service agreement and even replicate a particular problem found by the customer on the Web site.

The benefits from establishing a people-centric collaborative environment can be seen in three potential ways.

➢ The first is the most obvious. These environments bring with them the promise of streamlined operations that offer lower transaction costs, lower error rates, and other operational efficiencies.

➢ The second is the improvement in customer and partner relations that come from building tight links between technology and business processes. When done right, collaborative environments greatly enhance customer and partner satisfaction and help leverage all partners' investments in technology and business processes.

➢ Finally, a people-centric environment provides a platform for changing products, partnerships, and business processes in support of dynamic businesses and industries that require "first-to-market" rapid response.

The capability of handling second sourcing, product or personnel substitution, alternative routings and services, and other just-in-time requirements can enhance the value of the entire value chain, and improve the effectiveness and efficiency of all participants. When well designed and well implemented, people-centric collaboration will significantly impact the bottom lines of the enterprise involved.

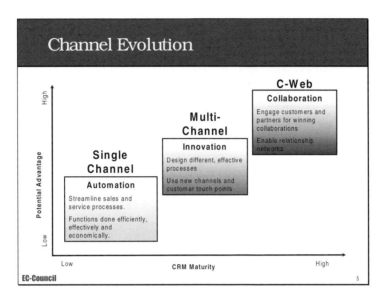

Channel evolution

An access paradigm starts by understanding when and how customers touch the organization.

The three primary methods of access to most companies are the bricks-and-mortar storefronts, the telephone, and the Web. Each of these access channels has its subset of methods and components as available tools for handling customer contacts.

The most effective companies will offer their brand through any combination of all three access channels in an integrated way. This will require that the technology, people, and processes be aligned to support the whole customer experience. This is not just buying the latest in technology and increasing the efficiency of the contact channel. It is rethinking the entire customer experience from the customer point of view and creating single mindedness in the people and processes that apply to the total customer experience.

Collaboration is a matter of degree, and the quantity of the software and services used for collaboration only defines how comprehensive the collaboration will be. Collaboration has its price - the cost to the enterprise increases as the number of collaborations grows, particularly when other applications are involved. While collaboration can and should be implemented in a "build-to-fit" manner, the more collaborations an enterprise wishes to enable, the more critical the vendor's support for both system-to-system interaction and heterogeneity.

The illustration shown here depicts how the single channel strategy with its focus on automation through sales force automation and call centers have been replaced by multi-channel strategy encompassing the whole of CRM functionality through customer interaction centers.

The multi-channel strategy focuses on innovation with differentiation in design aspects and improving process efficiency. The next step in this evolution is the collaborative business networks.

Here the focus is true collaboration. It is about the ability to engage customers and partners for mutually synergistic relationships and to facilitate many-to-many relationship networks.

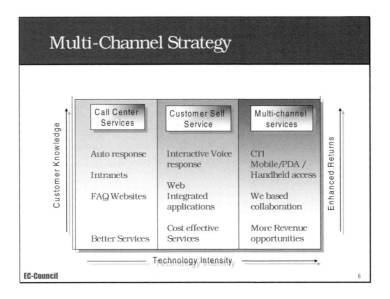

Multi-channel Strategy

> ### Phase I: Enhanced Call Centre Services

First phase marks the genesis of a multi-channel strategy and places emphasis on increased service. The characteristics of this phase are marked by components such as Intranet, Static Website (no interactivity), and Automated attendant and combines technology with a superior business information system.

The Automated Attendant is probably one of the most recognized applications in the Computer Telephony industry. Working alone or in conjunction with a live operator, the auto attendant answers the incoming call usually before ringing an extension.

At that time, prerecorded voice messages are played to the caller offering them a menu of choices for directing their call. Once the caller has made their choice, the call is routed to the appropriate ringing extension, where they will be connected to the called party, or presented with yet another series of choices.

Intranet can be used for providing necessary employees and departments' secure access to the customer intelligence system. Enterprises can push customer intelligence reports to customer service, sales, marketing and executive staff over the Intranet and regularly publish customer intelligence reports.

➢ **Phase II: Automated Self-service**

The next phase focuses on reducing costs and increasing uptake. Here components such as integrated websites, intelligent IVR and speech recognition play an important role.

Intelligent interactive voice recognition (IVR) combines the key decision-making attributes of expert systems and traditional IVR technology. Integrated websites provide a certain extent of interactivity to facilitate self-service.

The speech recognition system allows either full or partial automation of telephone transactions that would otherwise be performed by an operator or attendant. These automated transactions are known as applications.

Each application is designed and developed to meet a specific customer need. An application script is a set of instructions written for the system that informs it how to carry out the automated transaction. Scripts define the flows of calls and determine what callers hear and how callers respond to the system.

➢ **Phase III: The last phase is deploying multi-channel services.**

Here, web collaboration through portals, computer telephony integration (CTI), WAP and PDAs (to enable mobile services), kiosks (for heightened interactivity) are deployed for increased choice and revenue.

In its purest form, CTI is middleware that associates an application with an incoming service request, regardless of the media in which the request is received (chat, e-mail, Web collaboration).

It then presents the information to either a live or electronic agent to satisfy a customer need. For complex customer interaction center (CIC) implementations, CTI represents a core investment.

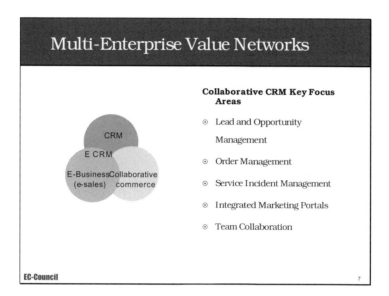

This illustration depicts the typical value networks seen in an enterprise / extra enterprise scenario. Collaborative CRM seeks to integrate these networks to benefit the customers, partners as well as the internal employees.

The areas where collaborative CRM comes into focus are:

➢ **Lead and Opportunity Management.**

These tools help deploy sophisticated systems to target leads to the most qualified partners, based on certification, geography, or other business rules. These leads can then be accessed via a secure extranet by the targeted partner. Next-generation systems will allow vendors and partners to exchange leads and lead status information through process integration, rather than forcing visits to yet another portal.

➢ **Order Management.**

Distributed e-commerce systems allow customers to visit a vendor's Web site, do some research, then fill a shopping cart. The vendor's site helps the customer pick the appropriate partner, based on geography, price or other factors, and the shopping cart is electronically transferred to the selected partner's site. This is great collaborative e-business, leveraging the strengths of each party.

> **Service Incident Management.**

Post-sales service and support is a costly fact of life in any business. Collaborative service systems help glue customer service processes together across multiple organizations. A customer service request can be tracked across departments or companies using a single Web page.

> **Integrated Marketing Portals.**

Effective portal tools use XML to aggregate content streams from multiple parties, then syndicate this information in a consumer-facing portal. If the content changes at the source, it's changed in the portal automatically without requiring a slow and costly traditional Web publishing process.

> **Team Collaboration.**

Even with robust relationship management systems, people still need to interact using e-mail, desktop documents, project plans, etc. Collaboration tools allow companies to manage this unstructured information via shared workspaces that can be used by customers, partners and employees. Using such systems can help an enterprise rapidly form teams and enable people to work faster and smarter.

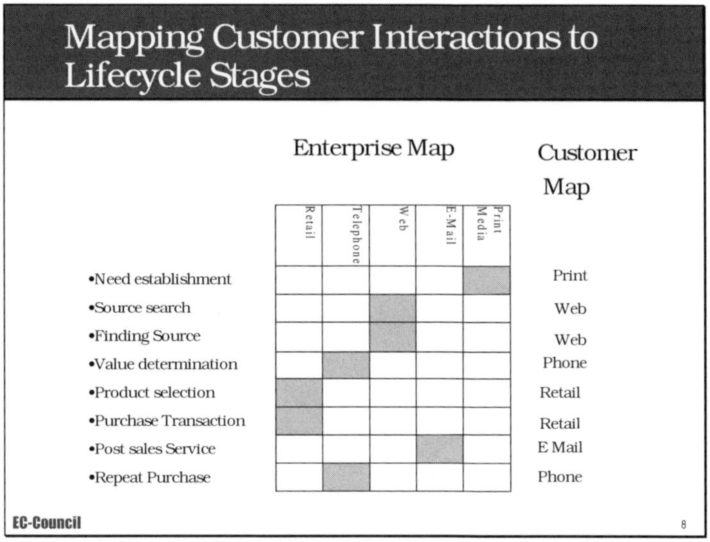

Mapping Customer Interactions to Lifecycle Stages

Enterprise Map

Customer Map

	Retail	Telephone	Web	E-Mail	Print Media	
•Need establishment					▓	Print
•Source search			▓			Web
•Finding Source			▓			Web
•Value determination		▓				Phone
•Product selection	▓					Retail
•Purchase Transaction	▓					Retail
•Post sales Service				▓		E Mail
•Repeat Purchase		▓				Phone

EC-Council

8

Mapping Customer interactions into Life Cycle stages

CRM activities in most industries are a combination of structured data about a customer or a prospect (sales orders, service requests, lead requests) and unstructured data (e-mails, sales notes, Web chats, proposals).

This data flows from planned events such as marketing campaigns or in reaction to ad hoc events such as proposal negotiation, problem escalation, up selling and cross selling. They are usually performed by a variety of disparate CRM staff and increasingly include channel partners and customers themselves.

The illustration shown above depicts the use of interaction channels by the customer as he or she progresses through the customer lifecycle.

Customer view of interaction channels is found to be linear and research shows that customers recollect the communication method of service and sales contacts 87% of the time.

While considering collaborative technology adoption enterprises need to consider scalability as well as the adoption of an open architecture for facilitating interactions both internal and external to the organization. Interactions over the web and through the call center / contact centers are gaining prominence as customers seek both convenience and prompt attention from enterprises.

Customer Interaction Centers

⊙ Single channel strategies are not viable

⊙ Point of interaction (POI) vary throughout the customer lifecycle

⊙ CIC gains prominence as hybrid channel strategies are increasingly adopted

⊙ Critical Issues
- Managing and prioritizing POIs
- Optimizing Process and Information Flows
- Ensuring service consistency
- Aligning applications and infrastructure

EC-Council

7

Customer Interaction Centers

Enterprise demand to accommodate "any point of interaction" (voice/Web/chat) is the basis behind investment in customer interaction centers. It is critical for enterprises to secure business-savvy managers/agents who can influence customer experience and establish valued-based performance metrics.

The proliferation of new points of interaction (POIs) within CICs has increased inbound interaction volumes by 10 percent to 20 percent. To address this demand, enterprises must align operating budgets for maintaining service-level expectations and leverage technology for higher transactional efficiencies (e.g., skills-based routing) and effectiveness (i.e., first-call resolution), thereby increasing productivity with current CIC professionals.

CIC key performance indicators (KPIs) must be anchored to corporate customer value statements. Metrics supporting customer value will better justify operating budgets and uncover infrastructure or operational inefficiencies needing improvement.

Consequently, CICs should increasingly seek to implement performance management systems to obtain KPI metrics across all POIs, eliminating time consuming and error-prone manual consolidation efforts.

CICs must fund performance management systems annually to implement, optimize, and further develop KPI metrics to support business operations. Ultimately, these will provide the baseline for future growth or transformation efforts and reflect the organization's commitment to customer service (e.g., costs, customer satisfaction, service-level adherence).

An emerging KPI metric directly affecting CIC operational performance goal is CIC infrastructure consistency (e.g., POI-specific response times remain the same for every working shift).

Establishing CIC infrastructure consistency will enhance customer experience and eliminate variables that affect staffing forecasts, that can result in shift(s) understaffing (i.e., risk not meeting service levels) or overstaffing (i.e., paying too much to meet service levels).

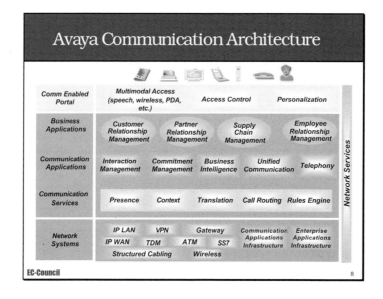

Avaya Communications architecture -Illustrated

The illustration here depicts Avaya's vision of converged communications. The purpose of discussing this here is to illustrate a real world example of a collaborative CRM architecture that is popular and widely adopted.

The Avaya Communication Architecture is an architectural framework for solution delivery that separates enterprise communication needs into three independent layers.

These three layers are:

➢ **Communication Enabled Portal**

The Communications Enabled Portal enables personalized communications preferences and supports multimode access and service delivery for anytime, anywhere, any mode communication.

This layer represents a user-centric gateway to the enterprise that gives individuals secure access to applications, information and people. This is the access layer, providing the separation of presentation from the underlying content and services. This decoupling makes access and presentation independent of the underlying business and communication applications. It illustrates how customers, partners, suppliers and employees communicate with each other using the devices of choice, over the network of choice, from a location of choice. For example, any application becomes accessible from any access mode—be it web, speech based or a mobile device. Examples of components in the communications-enabled portal include multimode access, access control, personalization and enterprise portal. These components provide the means to establish a common access mechanism.

> ## Applications and Services Layer

The Applications and Services layer enables the seamless integration of communication and business processes to increase employee productivity and power faster and better decisions among businesses, their suppliers and partners. These communications applications easily integrate with automated business applications (such as billing, supply chain management, sales force automation, customer sales, services and inventory), resulting in seamless interoperability among multi-vendor products and supporting anytime, anywhere, any mode communications. The business applications and communication services layer is composed of three sub-layers:

- o Business applications: The business applications sub-layer consists of the back-office applications typically deployed by the enterprise to manage its operations more efficiently. Examples include sales force automation, partner relationship management, supply chain management and employee relationship management. An enterprise value chain usually requires that business context and data be shared across these applications.

- o Communications applications: The communication applications sub-layer defines the communication capabilities necessary to provide more efficient, timely, competitive and productive responses. This sub-layer is composed of several components, including multimedia contact center, operational excellence, self-service, proactive contact, unified communication and telephony applications.

- o Communication services: The communication services sub-layer contains basic modules that can be reused by multiple communications applications. An example is call routing. Having a single call routing module means there is more consistent behavior across communication applications that require the same elements. In addition, taken together, these services can provide a flexible platform for the rapid and dynamic creation of new applications.

The real value of this layer is its ability to communication–enable business applications (i.e., integrate communication services with business applications) and to business–enable communication applications (i.e., integrate business rules and contexts with communication applications).

> ## Network Infrastructure

The Network Infrastructure layer provides the necessary converged networking for the evolution of enterprise communications. The layer provides the underlying multi-vendor infrastructure required to deliver the quality of service and reliability needed for enterprise-class communications. The importance of the underlying network infrastructure increases as enterprises link mission-critical business processes across dispersed stakeholders in the value chain.

The network components include LAN switches, secure VPNs, caching gateways, data and telephony servers, WAN access devices, routers, web and applications servers, data storage servers and communication applications infrastructure.

Together, these three layers form a flexible framework for addressing business communication needs from access to infrastructure.

The architecture seeks to:

➤ Integrate communication applications and business applications.

➤ Provide any device, any mode, and any network communication capabilities in real-time and non-real-time.

➤ Use a common converged network and applications infrastructure for both communication applications and business applications.

This convergence can result in the following benefits:

➤ Improved productivity for end users due to intelligent, efficient, and managed communications that are delivered according to user needs and with business context.

➤ Increased revenue due to timely communications that enable higher quality business decision making and that increase customer loyalty by integrating communications capabilities with business context.

➤ Reduced cost due to the standardization on common platforms and leveraging of existing infrastructure investments.

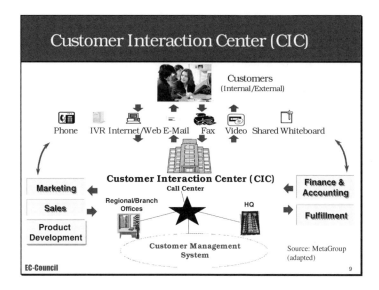

Customer Interaction Center - Detailed

The evolution of customer interaction centers is an acknowledgment that there is a need to manage the customer, separate from managing the "call" or the "case" or the "interaction" itself.

Companies are realizing the importance of multi-channel customer support. Sales and marketing functions are taking the lead in developing multi-channel centers that support Web and e-mail customer contacts.

This elevates the importance of the contact center within the organization, since the contact center has become a multifunction center for lifetime customer care.

The need to deliver personalized access, and enable transactions at anytime and anywhere drives the investment in contact centers. Enterprises are becoming largely virtual with globally distributed ecosystems, collaborating communities and interconnected processes. This coupled with increased demand for business performance and heightened security needs, calls for greater interaction technology being deployed at contact centers. The purpose of this illustration is to portray the CIC infrastructure and its linkages.

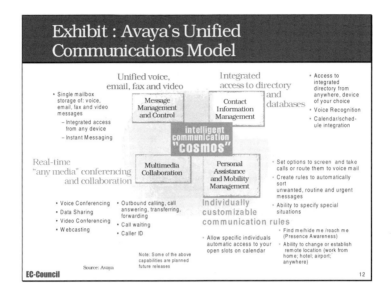

Avaya Unified Communication model -Illustrated

In today's growing mobile business environment, enterprises require cost effective ways to reach customers, coworkers and critical information whether their employees are at work or on the road. The exhibit shown here is Avaya's Unified Communication Center, which enables enterprises to provide mobile workers with productivity tools that help them work more efficiently, rapidly respond to customers by expanding the capabilities of current systems.

This is an integrated solution suite that delivers wireless, Web and speech-enabled access to applications including messaging, communications and collaboration tools. From phones, cellular phones, PCs or wireless handheld devices, workers can easily manage email, voice mail and fax messages, in addition to accessing business communications applications, such as calling, conferencing, company directories, desktop calendar and task functions.

The purpose of exhibiting this solution here is to highlight the trends in networking solutions that are available to enterprises in achieving increased collaboration across the enterprise and outside of it.

Call Center

⊙ Objectives

- Create many points of interaction between company and customer.
- Minimize the cost of those interactions.
- Identify those non-customers who might become customers.
- Give everyone outside the company the tools to gather information about the company.
- Gather as much information about those customers as possible.
- Provide that information to anyone in the company who can use it.

EC-Council   14

Call Center - Explained

The call center has emerged as the strategic weapon of choice for customer access in business today.

Incredible advances in the ability to integrate telephone and computer technologies with front and back office functions have made the call center the potent weapon in creating and maintaining long-term customer relations. What makes the call center so important is that it is affordable and available right now for use by both large and small businesses. Even as call centers are increasingly evolving into contact centers, the basic objective behind a call center still holds true.

Primarily, call centres were set up with the objective of creating many points of interaction between company and customer and also minimizing the cost of those interactions. The enterprise sought to increase revenues by identifying those prospects that might become customers and equip them with the tools to gather information about the company. Enterprises also sought to gather as much information about those prospects as possible and transform that into useful information to anyone in the company who could use it.

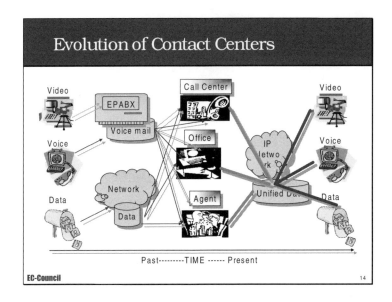

Evolution of Contact Centers

Enterprise infrastructures are growing increasingly complex. Networks are increasingly being required to support geographically distributed employees, customers, partners and suppliers, with usage requirements ranging from secure access for telecommuters and road warriors to support for remote agents in outsourced call centers.

CRM initiatives place high demands on enterprise communications. The top strategic imperatives driving new technology deployments can be categorized as:

➢ The need to enhance business performance, e.g., avoid missed opportunities, increase customer loyalty, increase employee productivity etc

➢ The need to improve business continuity, e.g., distribute enterprise functionality geographically, ensure continuous availability in case of emergencies, standardize on infrastructure components to simplify recovery procedures etc

➢ The need to reduce operational costs, e.g., facilitate access to outsourced resources, leverage common infrastructures and management, protect against system obsolescence.

On the functional side of the equation, as enterprises become increasingly distributed, their success depends on efficient and timely communications with the right people, at the right time, in the right place, using the right device.

Therefore, distributed enterprise solutions must address at least the following functional requirements through customer contact centers:

➢ A consistent user and customer experience when accessing communications services, regardless of the media or mode used.

➢ Mobility support for a user population that is increasingly on the go and working remotely.

➢ Rapid creation and delivery of new applications and services to support a new, dynamic business environment.

➢ Integration of applications into the heterogeneous environment of today's enterprise, ensuring continuity of features and processes.

➢ Secured, worldwide distribution of information and services.

Many companies have turned to customer contact center access as a means of delivering enhanced customer experience that result in increased satisfaction and the greater probability of long-term relationship.

Customer access must be used as a key component of a business strategy in order to deliver the strategic value possible from a contact center. Customer contact centers and Internet access are evolving as the central core of an overall strategy to allow customer access and deliver customer value anytime and anywhere.

e-commerce initiatives render assisted service an economic necessity for attracting and keeping customers. Understanding the need for a multi-channel contact center is becoming apparent to companies that realize the limitations of self-service options in meeting the needs of many online customers. The infrastructure to support delivery of cross-channel customer care is the contact center.

Contact centers span the entire organization, requiring that several business units become involved in their planning and implementation. Organizations often deploy multi-channel customer support for e-commerce and automating business processes.

The true strategic benefit of multi-channel strategy through contact centers can be derived only if the enterprise views the customer as a single account and manage the customer equally regardless of how they choose to contact a company.

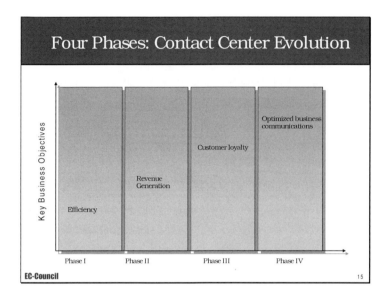

Contact Centers –Evolution Phases

During the early days which constitute the first phase, contact centers were seen as a necessary cost center. The objective behind setting up the call center was improving service efficiencies by focusing on cost reduction and productivity gains.

In next phase of evolution, contact center was seen as a potential profit center. Serving the objective of revenue generation, the focus was on turning the cost center to a potential profit center.

Driven by the quest for customer loyalty, the next phase saw contact centers gaining strategic importance as they were becoming central to building lasting customer relationships.

The fourth phase aims at optimizing business communications and by focusing on moving transactions beyond the contact center through the enterprise, contact centers have become true representation/extension of the enterprise itself.

CRM products have traditionally been thought of as efficiency tools for employees who interact with clients, and to some extent, as sources of data to guide customer oriented programs. Customers and prospects are increasingly communicating via e-mail, Web, Web chat, etc., in addition to the traditional communication channels like phone, fax, and personal sales call methods. They demand that each contact point, traditional or new, automated or human, be aware of their entire situation or profile. This demands enterprises to embrace new technologies as part of its CRM strategy.

The new generation of implementations is targeted less at faster and more efficient transaction processing, and more at performing the appropriate action for the particular customer.

Additionally, those organizations that pre-empt customer concerns and are able to reach out to customers proactively will give themselves the best opportunities to retain important clients.

Successful enterprises will focus on utilizing current insights on customers and getting those insights to the point of interaction between the employee and the customer. The ability to demonstrate to the customer that he or she is individually 'known' will make the difference between winning and losing that customer.

Three ingredients are crucial to make Collaborative ebusiness work:

➤ Integrating business processes between enterprises.

➤ Managing structured content.

Examples are personalized web portals driven by partner profiles.

A collaborative approach means the content can be syndicated throughout the value chain, managed securely across multiple enterprises and out to customers without re-publishing.

➤ Enabling multi-company team collaboration.

That means working with the unstructured data that are used in day-to-day operations. Examples are emails, documents, project plans, etc. About 80% of enterprise information is unstructured, and therefore highly unlikely to be captured into a CRM/PRM/ERP/SCM database or into a web-based content portal.

The slide above depicts the four phases seen in the evolution of call centers into contact centers.

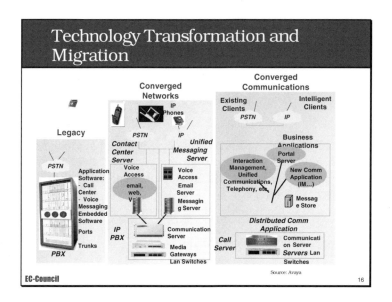

Technology Transformation and Migration

The illustration above depicts the transformation from legacy systems to converged communication networks. The prominent change has been the phasing out of exclusive dependency on PSTN or normal telephony to make way for VOIP (voice over internet protocol) or computer telephony.

To succeed, enterprises must learn new ways to use their network more intelligently and cost-effectively and to exceed their customers' needs and expectations. New applications that integrate voice, data and video can help provide better customer service, but they take a heavy toll on standard data networks.

The historical method of using a dedicated T1 circuit for the call center becomes very complex when it needs to deal not only with voice but also with customer databases, e-mail responses and Web interactions. The convergence of all these technologies onto one single IP LAN/WAN (Local Area Network/Wide Area Network) removes much of the complexity and makes the solution easier and cheaper to deploy and operate.

The inevitable shift to e-business means that there is a case for converged, Internet-based applications, to be deployed. Web-based customer contact centers therefore present the best business case for a convergence strategy.

To effectively facilitate the communication required for a collaborative environment among people a strong collaborative engine needs to be an integral part of the architecture. To further enhance collaboration between people, ebusiness streams also utilizes real-time communications technologies for managing telephony-based communication (using any Java Telephony Application Programming Interface [JTAPI] compliant Computer Telephony Integration [CTI] server) as well as Web-based/chat communication (using any Internet Messaging/Presence Protocol-based [IMPP] Web chat application).

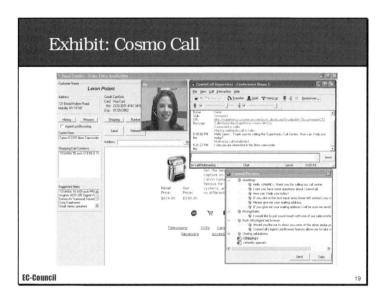

Exhibit: Cosmo Call

Customer interaction -illustrated

The nature of CRM activity and processes, including disparate teams and systems that need to interact, the presence of structured and unstructured customer data, planned and ad hoc activities, suggests a requirement for a strong workflow foundation.

The exhibit shown here is from Cosmo call, and illustrates how video interfaces; whiteboard sharing, agent prompt windows and ability to push portal pages to the customer are achieved.

Such applications allow interaction with the customer over multiple points thereby providing a rich customer experience. The key here is consistency over multiple channels. This can be achieved only if communication and business applications are well integrated. Readers may recall the discussion on the different layers in Avaya's communication's architecture here for an in-depth understanding.

Portals Address

- ⊙ "Single point of access to enterprise information assets"
- ⊙ First generation Portals - Next generation Intranets
- ⊙ Aggregate
  - People
  - Information
  - Applications
  - Business Processes

EC-Council

20

What do portals address?

The best way to view the community of users who can benefit from a people-centric collaboration strategy is to consider them as part of one of three categories: internal enterprise users, external customers or clients, and external suppliers or partners.

Each of these user communities can be described by the business processes accomplished in the course of their work, which in turn are best realized through the use of a Web-based portal. The link between user roles and portals is essential.

A portal doesn't just serve as the integration point for Web-based applications and services – it is also the environment that allows the expression of the workflow and business processes that define a particular role.

One of the key strengths of collaborative CRM offering is its focus on portals. For instance most vendors support three main categories of portals that define the scope of a collaborative enterprise – employee, customer, and partner.

These categories usually have more than a dozen individual roles, each with its own portal (as shown in illustrations in the subsequent pages). The portals offer the requisite single sign-on capability and security as well as serving as the platform for integrating applications, Web services, analytics and anything else that a user may want displayed in a portal window.

Portal offerings provide a highly functional set of role-based services that can form the cornerstone of a truly people-centric collaborative environment, providing operational and analytical information and processes to a broad set of users both inside and outside the enterprise.

 Some of the typical ROI benefits expected from portals are:

➢ Increased sales

➢ Print/mail cost savings

➢ Travel savings

➢ HR benefits enrollment

➢ Customer contract management

The Internet allows enterprises to extend business processes to customers and partners to create a collaborative network. This allows the enterprise to work together to meet common objectives - increased profitability through generating satisfied customers.

The use of a portal strategy with customers and partners facilitates information dissemination. Seamlessly connecting the front-office environments within the extended enterprise and enabling true enterprise-to-enterprise collaboration on any customer relationship of common interest can help corporates to realize the ultimate value of CRM.

 Portals focus on providing a single point of access to enterprise information assets and aggregates people, information, applications and business processes.

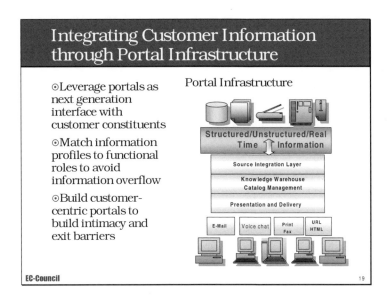

Integrating Customer Information through portals

Portal technology has been maturing quickly to provide complete, reliable, viable solutions to a common set of problems. Enterprises need to leverage portal technology to reduce costs and this requires integration and synchronization with existing systems.

While it is desirable to achieve a high level of transparency and knowledge sharing within the organization, enterprises must be careful to match information profiles to functional roles. Failure to do this might result in decreased productivity as employees handle information overload. Organizations should justify employee portal expenditures as enabling infrastructure.

The customer portals should be designed to ease interactivity while providing comprehensive yet personalized content relevant to nurture the customer relationship.

Partner portals need to incorporate necessary elements of the value chain to give a desirable value proposition to encourage further collaboration.

Enterprise portals need to be customer centric to build intimacy with the customer, grow the relationship and raise the exit barriers for the customer.

Key elements of a good portal design include:

➢ End-User Focus

    o   Process/task-based flow (Should have flows by life events)

- o Explicit personalization
- o Implicit personalization
- o Customization

➢ Transactional Capabilities

- o Scenarios (strings of related transactions tied together)
- o Blends with informational and collaborative patterns
- o Performance (Response times)
- o Confirmation of transactions

➢ Collaboration

- o User-to-user
- o User-to-site owner (ask the expert, e-mail in context, chat)

➢ Information Quality

- o Completeness
- o Current
- o Taxonomies (Good use of multiple taxonomies)
- o Search features (full-text, categorical, documents, images, etc.)
- o Dynamic FAQ based on searches

➢ Usability

- o Reasonable performance
- o Backward technology integration (ability to work with old technology versions)
- o Minimal scrolling on highest level pages
- o Navigation (consistent, understandable, complete)
- o Accessibility (color blind, deaf, poor eyesight)

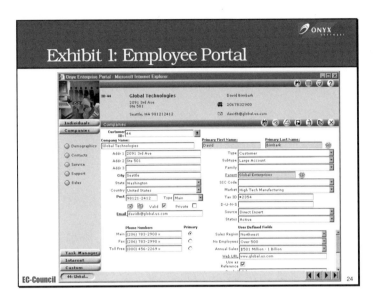

Employee Portal

Employee portals are collaborative CRM components that consolidate customer information gathered by sales, marketing and service departments to deliver a complete view of the customer to the employee.

The objective of employee portals is to turn every customer interaction into a potential revenue opportunity.

They facilitate employees to conduct targeted marketing campaigns, create account plan strategies, forecast new sales opportunities and rapidly respond to customer service inquiries. Featured here is the Onyx employee portal.

The standard features of most employee portals include a workspace that enables the employee to access all the information needed to maximize productivity with instant access to centralized customer data and relevant information from other business applications.

This is achieved through integration of Internet content such as corporate profiles, market research or other relevant data. Advanced products also integrate other productivity tools, such as web collaboration, product configuration, knowledge bases, expense reporting and more through a single portal interface.

As information access needs vary from department to department, employee Portals can be customized based on the differing needs of departments and individuals. Further, role based configuration can increase end-user productivity by sharing only information relevant to the job at hand.

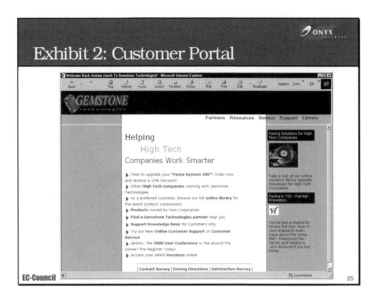

Customer Portal

The objective of customer portals is to transform the corporate web site into sophisticated, intelligent customer interfaces. They seek to optimize the effectiveness of customer online interactions and expand customer relationships through a convenient web front-end that captures customer information.

Customer Portals enable customers and prospects to access information and obtain service quickly and independently.

The benefit of customer portals to the enterprise include streamlining operational costs and strengthening customer relationships by extending the CRM application to the web to more effectively market to prospects and enable customer self service.

The features seen in most customer portals include the ability to automatically capture detailed prospect and customer information, thereby enabling the organization to better conduct targeted marketing in order to increase sales opportunities.

The customer can research products online in a faster and detailed manner. This encourages repeat visits and interactions. Customer portals also give customers the flexibility to research and resolve problems online, twenty-four hours a day, seven days a week. The bottom line is that customer portals have a heightened role to play in building better customer experiences.

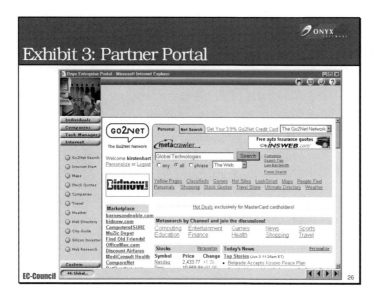

Partner Portal

Partner Relationship Management (PRM) is a business strategy for improving relationships between companies and their channel partners. Partner Portal is a PRM solution for organizations that depend in whole or in part on indirect channels to deliver their products and services to the market.

The collaborative features of a partner portal include lending the capability of extending the sales team to include partners and suppliers. This can be achieved through sharing leads by gathering detailed information from partners about new sales opportunities, assigning leads generated to partners using rules-based routing and escalation.

As discussed in earlier modules sharing sales pipeline information aids in managing and monitoring of channel sales processes for improved planning and forecasting.

Portal features such as online catalogs handles partner requests for self-service training, literature fulfillment enables partners to order sales and marketing collateral from the web, online product configuration empowers partners to configure custom products for customers online and online order processing allows partners to easily place orders with the enterprise over the web.

Summary

⊙ Collaborative CRM applications link the enterprise to achieve strategic CRM goals.

⊙ Enterprises are increasingly adopting multi-channel strategy and deploying contact centres to fulfill communication needs.

⊙ Portals frameworks have heightened visibility in supporting collaborative needs across and outside the enterprise.

EC-Council   27

Module Summary

Recap

➢ Collaborative CRM applications link the enterprise to achieve strategic CRM goals.

➢ Enterprises are increasingly adopting multi-channel strategy and deploying contact centres to fulfill communication needs.

➢ Portals frameworks have heightened visibility in supporting collaborative needs across and outside the enterprise.

Customer
Relationship
Management

Module VIII
CRM Project Management

CUSTOMER RELATIONSHIP MANAGEMENT (CRM)
Module VIII - CRM Project Management

Exam 212-16 - Certified e-Business Associate (CEA)

Module Objectives

- Understand the Phases of CRM Project
- Discuss the Pre-Implementation phase
- Comprehend the activities taken up in this phase
- Discuss Implementation phase
- Understand the stages of in implementation project methodology
- Discuss the post Implementation phase
- Discuss Change management and training issues

Objectives

👉 Module Objectives

In the previous modules we have discussed various aspects of CRM. We have seen that the intent of CRM is to create a dynamic environment of continuously improving customer relationships. In order to reap the benefits of this initiative, the enterprises need to internalize the CRM project. The CRM technology solution is to be implemented within the enterprise; the processes need to be tailored around the CRM solution and people need to adopt the new style of functioning. In this module we will discuss the CRM project – the issues and challenges.

On completion of this module you will be able to:

➢ Understand the Phases of CRM Project

➢ Discuss the Pre-Implementation phase

➢ Comprehend the activities taken up in this phase

➢ Discuss Implementation phase

➢ Understand the stages of in implementation project methodology

➢ Discuss the post Implementation phase

➢ Discuss Change management and training issues

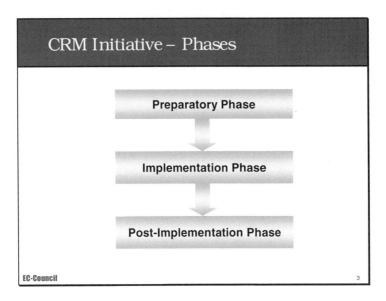

CRM Initiative- Phases

Any CRM initiative essentially goes through three distinct phases namely Preparation, Implementation and Post Implementation. It is necessary to tread diligently through all three of these phases in order to ensure a successful sail to gain strategic advantages from the initiative.

The preparatory phase is where the organization gets onto an introspective mode and crystallizes a vision for the new customer centric initiatives. In this phase issues with regard to the People, Processes and Technology are given utmost consideration in order to ready the organization to take on the challenges associated with the new initiative. We are dealing with the activities associated with this phase in great detail in this section.

The next section is devoted to the implementation phase and deals with the implementation of the CRM initiative. Here we look at the details regarding the project implementation methodology.

The CRM initiative is an ongoing process and therefore it is imperative to discuss the issues that we come across in the post implementation stage. Post implementation phase is detailed in this section.

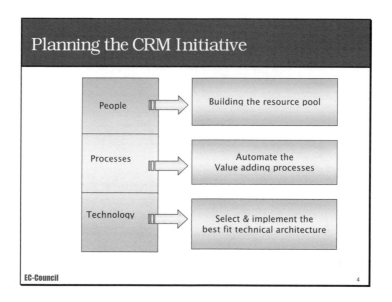

Planning the CRM initiative

Meticulous planning is essential to ensure successful completion of the CRM project and later on optimal adoption by the user community. The planning process takes into consideration, People, Processes and Technology issues relevant to the CRM initiative. The planning process sets forth the course of action starting from initial analysis to internalizing the newly implemented CRM processes.

The starting point is to set a Vision for the CRM initiative. Then we arrive at CRM project objectives based on the vision within the organizational constraints.

The key people issue under consideration is about building the resource pool to take on the new way of working that follows the CRM initiative. Similarly on the process front, intimate attention is needed on the candidate processes that need redesign or automation. Technology being an integral part of the initiative, the challenge lies in arriving the best technology architecture that suits the organization.

We are dealing with these issues in greater details in this section where in all the necessary activities that constitute the preparatory phase is explained.

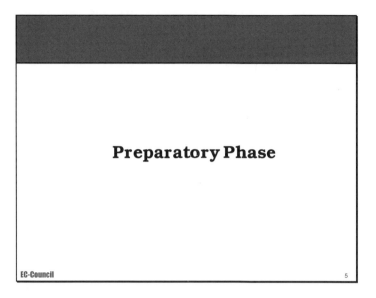

Preparatory Phase

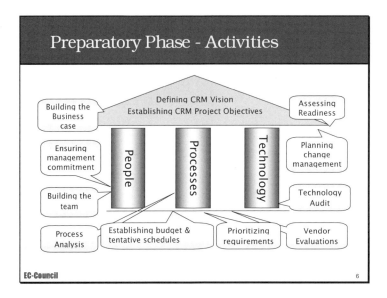

Preparatory Phase - Activities

Presented below is a list of essential activities that needs to be taken up on the run up to implementing the CRM initiative.

- ➢ *Defining A CRM Vision*

- ➢ *Assessing CRM Readiness (Organizational Perspective)*

- ➢ *Analyzing Business Processes*

- ➢ *Auditing The IS/IT Infrastructure*

- ➢ *Establishing CRM Project Objectives and key metrics*

- ➢ *Building A Compelling Business Case*

- ➢ *Ensuring Involvement Of Key People*

- ➢ *Building the best team*

- ➢ *Prioritizing The Requirements*

- ➢ *Establishing The Budget*

- ➢ *Establishing Tentative Timelines*

- ➢ *Short listing Prospective CRM Solution Vendors*

- ➢ *Selecting The CRM Solution*

➢ *Selecting The Solution Partner*

Each of these activities is dealt in detail in the subsequent pages.

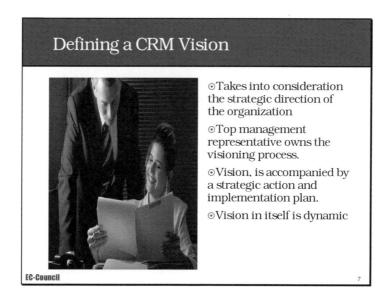

Defining the CRM vision

This is the starting point of an ambitious journey towards becoming a customer centric organization.

CRM vision is the reference point to both the internal as well as external customers of the organization. Organization's strategy is tightly interwoven into the CRM vision. Normally a top management representative owns the visioning process. The CRM vision is typically accompanied by a strategic action plan and an implementation plan.

Here is a sample vision statement for better comprehension of the concept:

➢ Vision

" To service the customers better".

➢ Strategy to achieve this Vision

Reorganize the internal Sales force and rationalize channel strategy.

➢ Implementation plan

Activity 1: Set up a dedicated customer support cell.

Activity 2: ....

Organizations should ensure that the CRM vision is kept relevant and alive feeding back performance information on a periodic basis for validations or effecting changes to reflect new market realities, customer preferences as well as competitive scenario. This means that the CRM vision should not remain static and may be revised in the event of changes in market places, customer requirements as well as competitive scenario.

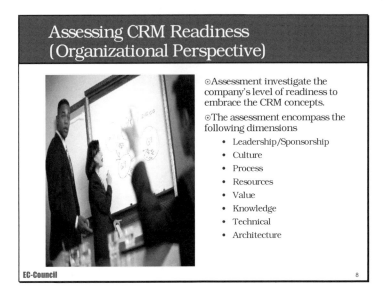

Assessing CRM Readiness (Organizational Perspective)

⊙Assessment investigate the company's level of readiness to embrace the CRM concepts.

⊙The assessment encompass the following dimensions
- Leadership/Sponsorship
- Culture
- Process
- Resources
- Value
- Knowledge
- Technical
- Architecture

Assessing CRM readiness (Organizational perspective)

The objective the assessment is to investigate the company's level of readiness to embrace the CRM initiative.

The Assessment process relies heavily on key staff interviews spanning different departments like:

➢ Marketing

➢ Customer support

➢ Sales

➢ IS/IT

➢ Operations

➢ Product management

is intended to throw light on the need (if any) for realigning organizational structure to deliver goods on the new customer-focused strategy.

The readiness assessment provides a detailed evaluation on the professional and technical skill levels of the CRM user community. This is useful in identifying and planning professional development opportunities for key personnel. Apart from this various change management issues that might arise with the new CRM initiative, concerning organizational culture, communication and compensation are also brought to light for review.

As per Meta group research, organizational readiness is to be assessed along the following dimensions:

➤ Leadership/Sponsorship

➤ Culture

➤ Process

➤ Resources

➤ Value

➤ Knowledge

➤ Technical

➤ Architecture

One key benefit of this assessment is that, it helps identifying the people and knowledge requirements for successful implementation of the new CRM initiative.

Now that the Organizational readiness is gauged, we need to analyze the Business process and technology needs that are crucial to ensure success of the initiative.

Analyzing Business Processes

⊙Business Process Analysis essentially consists of:

- Analysis of current business processes
- Envisioning desired business processes

⊙The analysis results forms the basis for arriving at the CRM project objectives

EC-Council   9

Analyzing business processes

Usually business process analysis looks into the current processes followed by the organization in the context of the changing customer-market-business scenario and attempts to set right the processes to suit the new realities.

Analysis of current business processes: The introspective analysis usually starts with an assessment of the current business processes. These analyses most usually lists down the pain points that hinder the team's productivity. They also include certain strengths within the current system.

Typically the analysis covers:

➤ The strengths and weaknesses of current sales, marketing, service and support business processes

➤ Identifying non-value adding processes

➤ Ways and means to improve concerned business processes

➤ Benchmarking the current processes with processes followed by market leaders /competitors

Envisioning the desired business processes: This process defines the basis for arriving at the CRM project goals. Having reviewed the current processes and taken cue from industry best practices, gap between the current and desired states are arrived at.

This analysis helps arriving at avenues for revenue enhancement as well as cost reduction that should follow the CRM initiative within the company. Essentially this is a listing of the benefit expectations out of the CRM initiative.

An indicative list of the benefits that the company could expect from the CRM implementation is given below. Some of them are tangible but many are intangible benefits.

Tangible benefits:

➢ Increase in profitability per customer

➢ Increase in revenue per customer

➢ Decrease in internal administration costs

➢ Increase in hit rates on forecasted sales

➢ Increase in profit margin on deals

➢ Improvement in cost per response marketing

➢ Increase in deal closure rates compared to competitors

➢ Reduction in deal close time through improved efficiencies

➢ Better customer issue resolution times

Intangible benefits:

➢ Increase in visibility of company with customers

➢ Increase in quality as perceived by customers

➢ Increase in number and timeliness of prospects followed up

➢ Increase in coaching of sales personnel

➢ Increase in customer service levels

➢ Improved internal communications and job satisfaction

➢ Standardization of business rules and processes

Thus the analysis lays down a clear direction for the CRM project and will also remain as a basis for arriving at project objectives as well as measuring the project success.

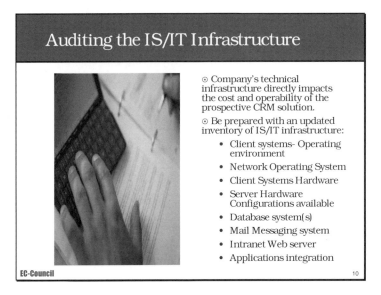

Auditing the IS/IT Infrastructure

⊙ Company's technical infrastructure directly impacts the cost and operability of the prospective CRM solution.

⊙ Be prepared with an updated inventory of IS/IT infrastructure:

- Client systems- Operating environment
- Network Operating System
- Client Systems Hardware
- Server Hardware Configurations available
- Database system(s)
- Mail Messaging system
- Intranet Web server
- Applications integration

EC-Council   10

Auditing the IS/IT infrastructure

It is critical to know the current components company's technical infrastructure, before embarking on any initiatives that affects the organization's information systems architecture. Getting ready with this information will have a direct impact on both the cost and operability of the prospective CRM solution.

Enterprise wide CRM solutions are designed for the client/server environment, Web-based environment or combination of the two. While some products will function in a variety of technical infrastructure configurations, others are designed for a limited number of platforms/configurations. The current technical infrastructure should support the prospective CRM application. If the new system demands costly changes to the existing infrastructure, those issues need to be probed further. Usually organizations prefer acquiring new systems that cost-effectively integrate with the existing technology architecture.

Typically, with the IS/IT infrastructure audit, details as presented below are collected and kept handy to be used while deciding on the technology architecture of the CRM solution to be selected.

➤ Client systems: operating environment:

Example: Windows NT Workstation™, Windows 98™

> ➤ Network Operating System:

Example: NT Server 4.0™, Novell NetWare 5.0™

> ➤ Client Systems Hardware:

Example: Pentium 166 Mhz with 64mb of RAM and a 10 GB hard drive

> ➤ Server Hardware Configurations available:

Example: Xeon Dual processor 512 MB of RAM and a 80 GB hard drive

> ➤ Database system(s):

Example: Microsoft SQL 7.0™, Oracle 9i™

> ➤ Mail Messaging system:

Example: Microsoft Exchange 5.5™

> ➤ Intranet Web server:

Example: Microsoft Internet Information Server 4.0™

> ➤ Applications integrate needs:

Example: ERP, Legacy Systems

By way of this process companies can be aware of what needs to be done in terms of addition of hardware/ OS/ Special software with regard to the technical infrastructure as plans for acquisition of the new CRM application is planned. Apart from this, requirements with regard to new technical skills within the IS/IT department needed to develop/maintain the prospective system can also be planned.

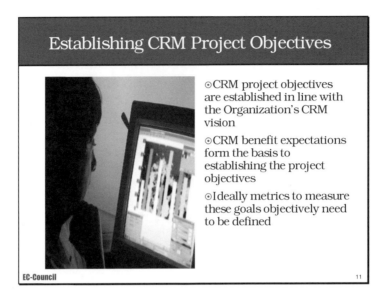

Establishing CRM Project Objectives

⊙CRM project objectives are established in line with the Organization's CRM vision

⊙CRM benefit expectations form the basis to establishing the project objectives

⊙Ideally metrics to measure these goals objectively need to be defined

EC-Council   11

Establishing CRM project objectives

After the initial analyses, we are clearer as to what could be realistically be expected from the CRM implementation.

With the CRM vision of the company as the guiding principle, more brainstorming, and thorough drilling down into the intangible and tangible goals, expected from of the project, the CRM project's objectives can be established. The CRM project's objectives typically aim at achieving a list of benefits, as expected by the organization.

Having a well-articulated set of project objectives are critical to the success of the project. These project objectives address the unique needs and requirements specific to the company.

A sample list of objectives for project could be:

➢ Decrease the turnaround time to generate sales proposals

➢ Provide self service capability to all the 'Service' customers

➢ Increase customer retention rate

➢ Achieve x% of profitability rise from top x% of customers

Here are a few examples of the project requirements translated from the objectives:

➢ Automate quote and proposal generation

> ➤ Create and distribute reports electronically

> ➤ Cut the time required to generate forecasting reports

> ➤ Eliminate duplicate data entry that happens presently

> ➤ Distribute pricing information, collateral materials

> ➤ Classify contacts by type, such as prospect, customer, reseller, supplier, business partner

> ➤ Automatically notify other team members of important plans, events or customer interactions

> ➤ Track customer referrals and lead sources

> ➤ Manage multiple marketing campaigns, projects and activities

> ➤ Create mailing lists and generate targeted direct mailings using fax, e-mail or mail

> ➤ Maintain an online encyclopedia of all marketing and sales collaterals

> ➤ Synchronize data changes, additions, deletions and modifications to records with mobile users

It is essential to have a comprehensive list of requirements. This can later form the part of RFP inviting proposals for CRM implementation.

Project objectives should be measurable and ideally metrics to measure the achievement of the project goals are also to be taken up simultaneously.

Building a business case for CRM

CRM implementations demand substantial amounts of funds as well as systematic involvement of senior management to reap envisioned benefits. It is therefore imperative to build a persuasive business case in order to secure the budgets required for the project as well as top management commitment necessary to effect organizational changes as in culture, processes and business practices.

 A compelling business case:

➢ Spells out the strategic fit of the CRM system in the organization's strategic game plan

➢ Lists out the tangible as well as intangible benefits brought about by the proposed CRM system

➢ Specifically charts out how these benefits could be achieved.

Here the cost of the project as well as the time and effort invested by top management is justified by way of appropriate ROI calculations so that the project has all the support from the senior executives concerned.

We are dealing with this topic in detail in a later module.

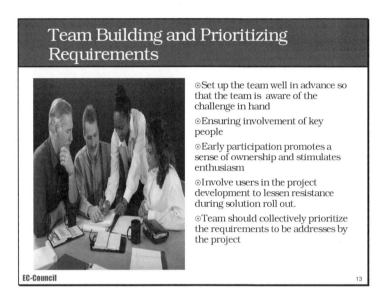

Building the team

The activity of setting up a team is taken up in advance so that the team is well aware of the challenge in hand even before the implementers are in.

Early participation by everyone affected by the CRM solution promotes a sense of ownership and stimulates enthusiasm before the solution is implemented. Failure to involve the users during the project development leads to user resistance when you roll out the solution.

It is this team, which owns the responsibility of successfully implementing the CRM solution within the company. Therefore ensuring involvement of key people is critical to the success of the initiative.

Ensuring involvement of key people

Success and failure of a CRM project as in any other project is dependent on the people who drive it and the people who adopt the new way of working once the implementation is through.

As a rule all successful CRM projects have an executive as the project champion/sponsor. It is this executive support and endorsements ensure that the CRM solution is well received by the users and becomes a part of the corporate culture as change management is involved.

The project team is to be drawn out from the best of the resources and should include all the relevant parties all the way to the user community representatives. If need be a steering committee can be drawn up to oversee the upcoming implementation.

Typically, the sponsor for a CRM initiative is a top management representative who has the clout within the organization to advocate adoption of new culture / process / way of functioning.

In order to ensure success of the initiative, it is necessary that the sponsor is

➢ readily available to team

➢ provides quick, decisive resolution to issues

➢ active, vocal and visible supporter of the initiative, and

➢ has realistic expectations

 Ideally the team will have representation from the key managers of all the user functions like:

➢ Sales,

➢ Marketing

➢ Service,

➢ Support and

➢ IS/IT department

More often the team constitution is skewed towards members from the functional teams. IS/IT is relevant because, these are the people who are responsible for the maintenance of the day to day functioning of the technical infrastructure. It is the coordinated effort of this multi-disciplinary team that is going to separate success from failure.

Prioritizing the requirements

It is essential to set up meetings where the team can discuss the opportunities to improve the current system and have them establish the priority of some must-do processes.

Since the CRM project will also impact management and information services (IS/IT department), it is vital to create representative teams to compile their critical success factors as well.

During the previous activities, the team had been generating a list of requirements to be incorporated in the new scheme of things enabled by the CRM solution. This list of requirements needs to be rationalized before going ahead to the next stages.

Once all the inputs are collected, priorities need to be set in order of importance to the business. The requirements list can be classified as 'must have', 'great to have', 'not necessary' etc. as per criteria devised by the team. This kind of requirements prioritization help to keep the project focused on the objectives set forth.

It is always appropriate to break down the project into definitive phases so that the each phase has a measurable ROI to deliver. Prioritization of the requirements should be taken up keeping in mind the fact that fast payback from the project strengthens the case for subsequent phases as well as keeps the management enthusiasm alive.

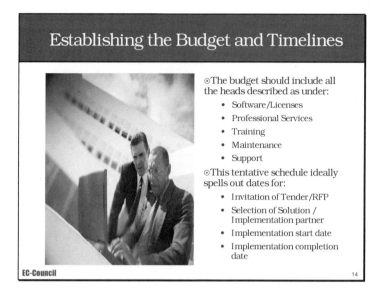

Establishing the budget

Here, we are not estimating the internal resource costs that are to be allocated for the CRM initiative. The focus is to arrive at a ballpark figure on the procurement of products/services involved.

CRM solutions vary from low-end, "off-the-shelf" products to high end, customizable solutions. The cost of these products varies significantly based on functionality, scalability and architectural elegance.

It is indeed true that the CRM marketplace is crowded and fragmented. In a subsequent slide, we are talking about how to compile a short list of systems to review based on the specific CRM objectives, business requirements and technical infrastructure. Once this shortlist is done, probably, list prices of these solutions can be compiled and used. Bear in mind the fact that, greater the functional requirements, greater will be the cost for the system. In fact, the CRM product cost is only a part of the cost. There are a host of other expenses that contribute to the total project cost. It is important that all the hidden costs are also estimated in order to arrive at the budgetary figure.

    The budget should include all the heads described as under:

➤ Software/Licenses

➢ Professional Services

➢ Training

➢ Maintenance

➢ Support

The figures arrived at here are no more than ballpark figures. An exercise like this makes sure that there are no surprises after the project is flagged off.

Establishing tentative timelines

Timelines are crucial to the success of any project. Now that various supporting information leading to the understanding of activities involved in the CRM project are available, tentative schedules can be arrived at.

 This tentative schedule ideally spells out dates for:

➢ Invitation of Tender/RFP

➢ Selection of Solution and Implementation partner

➢ Implementation start date

➢ Implementation completion date

Tagging dates to different activities involved brings about seriousness within the team. This helps planning the project in a detailed fashion so that all the intermediate activities are planned properly to fit within the schedule.

Short Listing Prospective CRM Vendors

⊙CRM marketplace is crowded, therefore shortlist prospects for thorough screening before selection.

⊙Shortlist solutions based on:

- Broad Functionality offered
- Technology Platform/Architecture
- Specific User needs

EC-Council 15

Short listing prospective CRM solution vendors

CRM marketplace is crowded and fragmented with over 500 vendors providing a variety of functionality. It is imperative to create a short list of 'Off-the-shelf' CRM systems to review based on the specific CRM objectives, business requirements and preferred technical architecture. The team can take it up on their own or engage external consultants for the same depending on the resource availability to handle the perceived complexity.

The short list of Off-the-shelf CRM solutions can be prepared on the basis of broad functionality offered by the packages under consideration, technical features on the offer as well as specific user needs. It is assumed that budgetary constraints are not considered at this stage. (Please note that if affordability is a key criterion, then that itself will shorten the list of CRM vendors.)

Broad Functionality: Remember, during the initial phase where in project goals and objectives were finalized, broad functionality to be covered by the CRM implementation is already decided.

For instance, the broad functionality to look for could be

➢ Sales Force Automation

➢ Marketing Automation

➢ Customer interaction management for the customer service department

Short listed prospective CRM software solutions should essentially be offering all the broad functionalities considered. Detailed investigations into individual functionalities are taken up in the package evaluation and selection stage.

Technology Architecture: What is required as technical architectural needs? These can be broken into things that IT platform needs and things that users need. Remember, that we had already done an IS/IT infrastructure audit, the results of which can be used for decision making at this stage.

Technology Platform / Architecture:

➢ Client/Server /Web based/ Mini-computer environment

➢ Operating system (Windows, Unix, Linux or Novell)

➢ Synchronization - (Direct Dial, Internet, VPN or wireless access)

➢ Database

➢ Ease of integration with back-office systems

Since there is a possibility of version incompatibility of Software / Hardware / Netware with the ones on the offer by the CRM software vendor, it is wise to be ready with a chart with the respective versions to check with the vendor.

User Needs: Specific needs as expressed by users representing different areas could fall under the following heads:

➢ Flexibility / Ease of Customization

➢ Calendar/Contact – integration through Outlook

➢ Computer Telephony Integration

➢ Data Communications

➢ Mail handling capabilities

➢ Intuitive Reporting

➢ Mobile/PDA/handheld-enabled solution

➢ User Friendliness

It is important that this driven largely by the user community. They will also have needs around the features they are looking for from the new CRM solution:

➢ Screen design (familiar look and feel for GUI) facilitating easy navigation

➢ Provide customer self-service via the Web

➢ Context sensitive help function

> ➢ Online chat

> ➢ Online training

> ➢ User documentation

> ➢ System support

> ➢ Painless release of new versions

Users might be low-usage, partners, customers and even prospects. Users know their jobs and they know when tools are not up to the mark. It is important that their views are taken into consideration.

Now with reasonable confidence a list of CRM software solutions that fit the bill can be drawn up. Also preliminary details with regard to pricing and effort requirements for implementation can be gathered by visiting websites of the prospects or from published information.

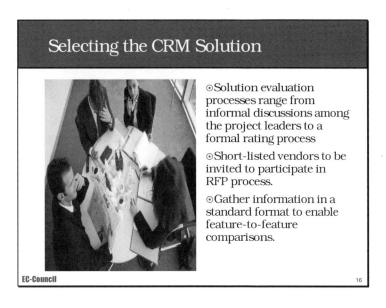

Selecting the CRM Solution

⊙ Solution evaluation processes range from informal discussions among the project leaders to a formal rating process

⊙ Short-listed vendors to be invited to participate in RFP process.

⊙ Gather information in a standard format to enable feature-to-feature comparisons.

EC-Council   16

Selecting the CRM solution

Theoretically there are two approaches for the CRM Application selection. Develop a custom built solution or procure a packaged solution and customize the solution to suit the company's business processes

The fact that long development cycle times, as well as technical resource constraints associated with the first approach, indeed hamper successful implementation. It is more practical to go in for customizing a packaged solution and therefore most companies prefer this route to CRM technology implementation.

Therefore, we shall talk more about the package selection in this section.

Success of the CRM initiative hinges on the company's ability to select the best fitting CRM solution available in the market as well as selecting a competent business partner to successfully integrate the newly selected tool into the existing technology architecture.

The more intensive the planning process that is done, the more rigorous the selection process will be. The must-do business processes are the benchmarks used to evaluate each solution's ability to effectively support the business processes and address the company's automation requirements.

The following is a representative list of generally used criteria for vendor evaluation:

➢ Ease of Use

➢ Functionality Fit

➢ Customizability

➢ Ease of Implementation

➢ Price

➢ Data synchronization

➢ Future Direction

➢ System Architecture

➢ References

➢ Support

Different organizations attach different weightings for each of these criteria in their vendor evaluation processes.

Solution evaluation processes

Solution evaluation processes range from informal discussions among the project leaders to a formal rating process involving the entire project team. Remember we have covered many aspects that lead to the selection at the short-listing stage itself. The complexity of business processes, the amount and detail of project requirements, and the number of solutions short-listed for evaluation will determine the format of the evaluation process.

The short-listed vendors can be invited to participate in the Request For Proposal /tendering process. This would help gather information about all the vendors to be collected in a standard format to enable feature-to-feature comparisons. It is ideal to have all the concerned vendors to present a demonstration of the software. If the demo can be based on a 'day in the life' of your sales, marketing & customer services users, it can directly foretell the suitability.

The evaluation team should actively participate in the demonstration. Each of the representatives from the concerned business area can take up probing the vendor on features and functionality concerning respective areas. The IS/IT representatives can concentrate on evaluating the technical fit of the prospective solution vis-a vis the current technology architecture.

Note: More often, Value added resellers/Systems integrator representing a specific CRM vendor presents the case for the CRM software vendor. These system integrators become the implementation partners in the event of the award of the project. This means that the systems integrator involved also needs to be evaluated for their ability to successfully handle the project.

Selecting the solution partner

Selecting a reliable, knowledgeable, reputable solution provider or systems integrator is more important than even selecting the best solution for the project. Partner should have the resources to provide full implementation support, including system design, customization, data conversion, installation and training.

It is vital to look for the following in a CRM implementation partner apart from other general qualifying criteria:

➢ **Quality of specialized resources**: Organizations that have consultants who specialize in the CRM area understand how to implement successful solutions. Organizations with resources dedicated to supporting CRM solutions in the industry domain are able to provide comprehensive services and ensure the long-term, ongoing success of the system. Accredited certifications and training can be considered as indicators of quality of these resources. Maintaining a staff of trained and certified professionals requires a significant allocation of a company's resources and is a strong indicator of their commitment to servicing the CRM solutions they represent. It is important that the implementation team assigned by the CRM partner includes experienced professionals certified to customize, integrate and provide training for the selected solution.

➢ **Experience of the firm in the CRM implementation area**– The CRM industry is growing, and so are the numbers of solutions and solution providers. It is important that the partner has the experience, both with implementations and with the product offered to understand both the technical and strategic aspects of CRM. Apart from this it is wise to see if the prospective partner has experience in the technology platform on which the implementation is planned.

➢ **Project methodology** – The solution provider should have a proven and documented project management methodology. Development of a successful, repeatable methodology is a strong indicator of the ability to deliver a reliable solution and their commitment to the CRM market.

➢ **Client testimonials** – Past customers are the best sources of information to judge performance for any solution provider. The best way to assure that the implementation experience will be positive and professional is to check client testimonials.

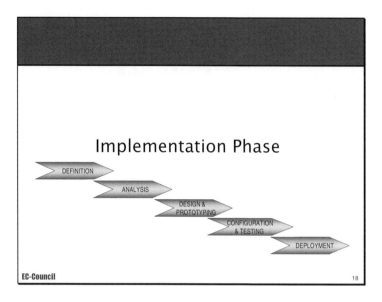

Implementation Phase

We have seen the activities that constitute the preparatory phase of a CRM initiative. Next phase deals with the implementation of technological solution. It is here that the software solution is configured and customized to suit the organization's CRM project objectives. This phase involves managing the project to successfully deliver the planned results as well as managing the change accompanying the implementation of the new initiative where in the users trained to use the new technology enabled customer centric way of working.

In this section, where in we are discussing Implementation phase, the CRM implementation methodology is dealt in detail.

In practice, depending on the CRM solution chosen to be implemented, implementation methodologies vary. In fact, most of the CRM vendors advocate organizations to follow proprietary implementation methodologies devised by them. For instance, mySAP CRM implementation follows an ASAP methodology for CRM; Siebel advocates a Siebel e-Roadmap for respective implementations. Apart from this, the solution implementation partner or the systems integration partner also may bring with them, their version of project implementation methodology. Most implementation methodologies use a Rapid Application Design (RAD) approach in the stated methodologies.

The details presented in this section are intended to provide a general understanding of what constitute a well drawn out CRM implementation methodology. The focus here is to present details with regard to different stages involved in the implementation phase and the milestones to look for.

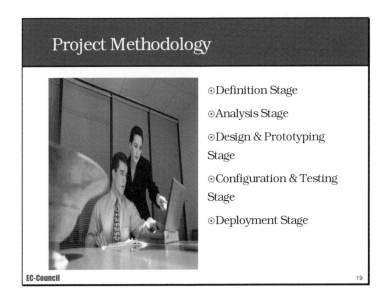

CRM implementation project methodology

The CRM implementation methodology ideally should focus on both the strategic and the tactical areas that maximize the customer's ROI. This implies that the implementation methodology needs to group major implementation process into different stages with clearly defined deliverables. Managing the implementation in stages enhances manageability of the project by applying checks and controls throughout the project implementation and ensures quality delivery at each stage of the project.

No implementation project methodology, as presented by vendors/ implementation partners is applicable 'as-is' for all CRM projects/types of customers. Therefore the methodology recommended by the vendor / implementation partner should be tailored to suit the specific project requirements. Here lies the advantage of a staged approach. Staged approach is flexible, and allows the project team to address all requirements and select specific techniques as required.

As mentioned previously, depending on the CRM solution chosen for implementation, implementation methodologies vary. However typically an implementation project methodology would consist of the following stages:

➢ Definition Stage

➢ Analysis Stage

➢ Design & Prototyping Stage

➢ Configuration & Testing Stage

➢ Deployment Stage

We shall deal with these stages in more detail in the subsequent slides.

Note: Various proprietary methodologies as recommended by vendors /implementation partners essentially consist of more or less similar activities.

The project management process, though embedded in the implementation methodology is vital to the successful completion of the implementation. The project management process must take into consideration:

➢ Project task breakdown, time management and resource allocation

➢ Issue log and resolution

➢ Project status monitoring and reporting

➢ Project scope and change management.

➢ Project quality assurance

➢ Project risk mitigation

Here the discussion pertains to the project team fielded by the implementation partner. The Project Manager works with the project team and the executive sponsor in assessing and resolving risks and issues throughout the project life cycle.

Project team typically consists of business analysts, certified CRM consultants, database administrator, programmer-developers and integration experts apart from the project manager. The number of project resources varies depending on the scope and complexity of the project.

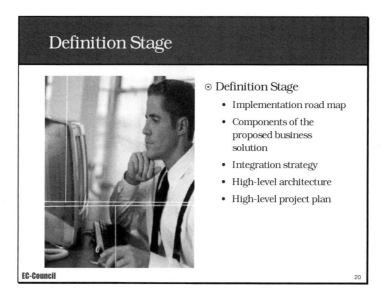

Definition Stage

This stage marks the start of the implementation project and is crucial in the sense that this stage sets the direction for the project.

The definition stage is where the implementation strategy is drafted. Depending on the broad scope of the project, the implementation can happen in single phase or multiple phases. Apart from this, project team organization structure and control structure for project management is defined. Here project stakeholders their roles and responsibilities, expected participation levels in the project are ascertained. The Implementation partner's team is also finalized with allocation of specific roles and responsibilities.

The deliverable at this stage consists of:

➢ an implementation road map document, which details components of the proposed business solution, integration strategy, and

➢ High-level project plan detailing the first phase (and subsequent phases) of implementation also form part of the deliverables for the project definition stage.

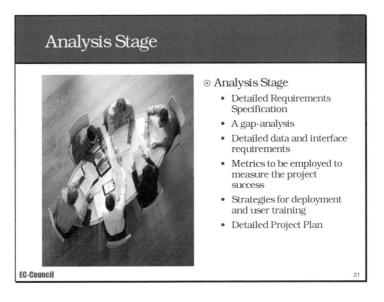

Analysis Stage

This stage takes cue from the pre-implementation preparatory phase. Analysis stage is where the detailed specifications that the project has to adhere to while designing the solution are prepared.

During this stage, consultants of the implementation partner look into customer's business processes, with a view to document functional, technical and training related requirements. They would undertake a gap analysis, which report the differences between the customer's requirements and the standard features of the relevant CRM application to be implemented.

Depending on the specific requirements, the implementation partners' project team analyzes the functionality that need to be custom created for the client.

There would be other application in the technology landscape, which might require interfaces and such interface requirements to external systems like ERPs or other legacy applications are determined. The extent of data migration that is required in order to have the CRM solution operational is also estimated.

Having analyzed the requirements and interacted with the client team all through this stage, the implementation partner develop strategies for deployment and user training. The training needs corresponding to different groups (as business users from different departments, technical users) of user community are ascertained before training materials and schedules are prepared.

All the documents that are produced forms the reference documents for the oncoming stages of the project. Though the deliverables are joint-developed by the implementation partner and the client teams, it is vital that the client team signs off and flags of the next stage of the project implementation.

Deliverables at the end of the stage include:

➢ Detailed Requirements Specification, which includes functional, technical, data, capacity, architecture, performance, and training requirements.

➢ Gap-analysis, report detailing gaps between the customer's requirements and standard features offered by the CRM application.

➢ Detailed data and interface requirements analysis document (data import requirements need to be carefully estimated.)

➢ Metrics to be employed to measure the project success

➢ Strategies for deployment and user training (estimation of training requirements is to be undertaken diligently)

➢ Detailed Project Plan covering the subsequent activities of the project

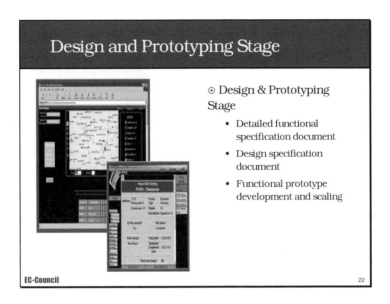

Design & prototyping Stage

The system design is undertaken based on the analysis findings and the signed of software requirements specification and related documents.

The deliverables typically include:

➢ Detailed functional specification document and

➢ Design specification document.

During this stage, the development environment is set up. Server and client installations, network hardware and software installations, etc is undertaken. Building of requisite databases interfaces with other application systems are also carried out.

During the design stage a solution that best meets the customer's business requirements is designed. Most of the solution vendors advocate an iterative design approach where in a consumable prototype is designed. This limited functionality prototype is demonstrated to the client's project team, clarifications sought and the prototype is extended to accommodate all the requisite functionality in an iterative fashion as per the detailed design specification.

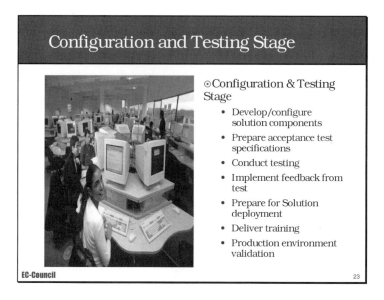

Configuration & Testing

Remember, most of the CRM functionality that the client requires comes built-in with selected CRM application.

During this stage, implementation partner's consultants take up the configuration of the application. Majority of the work is technical in nature. They also do the required customizations and extensions.

This involves accessing the source code of the software and making appropriate changes as per the customization specifications prepared. Interfacing with different application systems is also carried out. The number of applications in the systems landscape that needs to be integrated to the CRM system characterizes the complexity of the task. Disparate technologies on which these applications run add to the complexity of integration tasks.

The activities taken up during this stage can be summarized as follows:

➢ Develop/configure solution components as per the delivery plan of solution

➢ Prepare acceptance test specifications. This involves writing test scripts /test cases to be used for testing.

➢ Conduct testing: Unit testing, integration testing and acceptance testing

➢ Implement Feedback from test. Here bug fixing as well as functionality corrections are incorporated.

➢ Prepare for solution deployment. This involves preparing for migration from development to the production environment.

➢ Deliver training—as per plans developed during the analysis stage, prepare the users, and run pilot testing business / technical users (IS / IT maintenance staff).

➢ Production environment validation: to ensure that production hardware and software are ready, databases and interfaces are built, and data preparation is done.

Typically the interaction between the project team (members of client organization as well as implementation partner) is very high during this stage.

During this stage, the implementation partner's team also prepares the customer's organization for the deployment and support of the CRM solution. Training is a crucial element, which makes the change from the old way of functioning to the new way possible. This topic is separately addressed to take on specific issues with regards to training.

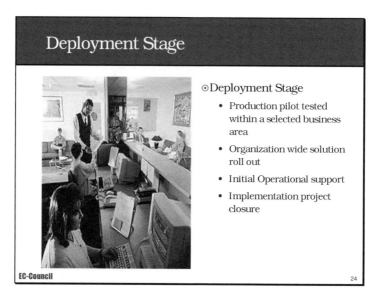

Deployment Stage

In the deployment stage, fully developed and tested application is deployed in the production environment. Normally, a production pilot of the application is used to test the solution's readiness for a full production deployment. This would avoid the possibility of an unwanted glitch stalling the business activities. Such a glitch can be costly and will work against the smooth roll out as the users might put in unwarranted resistance.

The pilot test is normally undertaken in one part of the business environment such as a business unit /territory as deemed appropriate by the joint project team. This pilot deployment tests the full impact of the deployment.

The production pilot experience leads the way to successfully completing full-scale enterprise wide deployment. The solution is rolled out to other business areas /a territory in a phased manner till the deployment is completed enterprise wide.

By now the user community have begun using the new system and the Implementation phase comes to an end. During this stage the implementation partner's project team hand holds the client's users to effectively use the solution.

Once the implementation project is formally closed, it is time to prepare for post-project review to appraise the outcome of the solution implementation. The implementation team hands over the responsibility of maintaining and growing the system to the IS/IT Support staff once they are coached to handle the situation. In the event that the client organization decides to retain the implementation partner with the job of supporting the system, a separate support contract is signed with the implementation partner to that effect.

Following the implementation, the client's CRM project team should engage in a review process where in they should assess the adoption of the new system, estimate the benefits achieved against the metrics defined in the analysis stage. If need be they can now plan for the next phase of development.

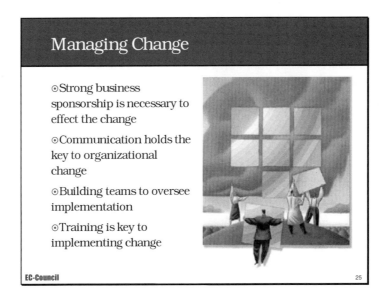

Managing Change

CRM implementation brings about a visible change in the way organizations function, at least this is true with the way the customer facing departments function. The implementation has more to do with a culture change within the organization than just a technology rollout. To be successful, it is necessary that we need to think about the project in terms of people, processes, and technology.

➢ **Strong business sponsorship is necessary to effect the change**

Organizations have a natural reluctance to change, as do individuals. Without strong business leadership and direction, organizational changes do not happen.

➢ **Communication holds the key to organizational change**

The compelling need to change should be communicated strongly through the ranks and files of the organization.

The key decisions regarding internalisation of the new way of working should be communicated strongly. For instance, the business sponsor deciding that sales forecasting needs to be communicated through the CRM tool only will force the concerned managers to begin using the software to enter related information.

It is essential that the project progress and accomplishments be posted to the user community effectively. This would clearly set the mood that the organization's seriousness with the initiative and the organization's expectations about participation and adoption of all concerned.

➢ Building teams to oversee implementation

As mentioned earlier, setting up a team is in advance is important. This will make sure that the team is well aware of the challenge in hand even before the implementers are in. Early participation by everyone affected by the CRM solution promotes a sense of ownership and stimulates enthusiasm before the solution is implemented. Failure to involve the users during the project development leads to user resistance when you roll out the solution.

It is this team, which owns the responsibility of successfully implementing the CRM solution within the company. Therefore ensuring involvement of key people is critical to the success of the initiative.

➢ Training is key to implementing change

Everyone concerned needs to be trained to use the new tools to enable them embrace the new way of working.

Training & Documentation

⊙ Everyone concerned needs training

⊙ The structured, hands-on training is essential.

⊙ Overview Training to cover all concerned

⊙ Training the trainers to impart in-depth knowledge transfer

⊙ Training content is to be carefully drafted

EC-Council

26

Training is key to implementing change

Everyone concerned needs to be trained to use the new tools to enable them embrace the new way of working.

The training needs as identified during the initial stage of implementation provides a clue as to how to deliver the training and who all need to learn what from these programs.

The training needs to be structured, hands-on sessions. It is ideal to have training materials prepared as reference books.

➢ **Overview Training:** It is ideal that overview training be conducted to everyone in the entire organization. This program should provide an overview of the CRM tool and present how it would help him or her on the job.

➢ **Training the trainers:** All the user groups need to be trained in-depth before they can successfully use the system. An ideal strategy for this is to follow the "training the trainer" approach. Here, the core project team is trained to be the trainers who would propagate the knowledge down the user hierarchies. It is essential to identify skills-set for each role and map against various candidates before training is scheduled.

➢ **Training content:** It is essential that the content to be delivered to the user groups should be relevant. For instance, user groups from the marketing department need to trained on how to use functions specific to them as well as an over view of any integrated business process involving other departments. The system administrators also need to be trained on the business side of things apart from technical aspects, as he should be equipped to answer queries from business users. It is ideal that the systems person should have a good mix of technical and business skills.

➢ The implementers will leave once the implementation is completed. It is necessary that all the training material and help documentation reflects the as-built system and incorporates all the customizations undertaken.

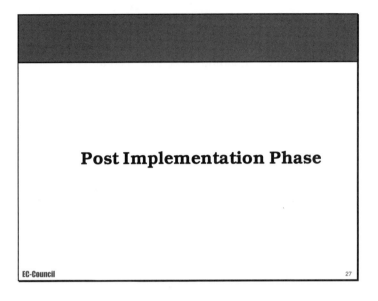

Post Implementation Phase

27

Post Implementation Phase

Post-implementation, it is time for review. The client's CRM project team should engage in a review process where in they should assess the adoption of the new system, estimate the benefits achieved against the metrics defined in the analysis stage. Depending on the assessment, if need be, they can now plan for the next phase of development.

Post Implementation Support

Common Problems:

- The help desk staff haven't been trained on the system.
- They know the system but they have no empathy with users.
- Problem logging is slow.
- Problem resolution is slow.
- The log does not work - no log number is issued.
- The response is not pro-active. "Wait for the User to call back."
- Users can't explain the problem.
- The help desk cannot replicate the problem.

EC-Council

28

Post Implementation Support

Once the implementation team moves out, it is time for the internal IS/IT organization to take up the day-to-day issues with the CRM system. Invariably, users will ask for help as often as they can, as they are finding it difficult to adjust to the new way of functioning.

An indicative list of common problems encountered is as follows:

➢ The help desk staffs haven't been trained on the system.

➢ They know the system but they have no empathy with users.

➢ Problem logging is slow.

➢ Problem resolution is slow.

➢ The log does not work - no log number is issued.

➢ The response is not pro-active. "Wait for the User to call back."

➢ Users can't explain the problem.

➢ The help desk cannot replicate the problem.

Well it takes time to resolve these problems. The only way out to eliminate these kind of issue is to foresee these problems beforehand and train the support staff adequately.

Devising a system for issue logging and resolution, preparing the support staff to work within service level agreements etc. could be thought of as remedies.

Another way of dealing with this problem, which is being increasingly adopted now, is signing up a support service contract with the implementation partner's organization, if they provide such services.

Here the client organization expects the supporting organization to provide an internal help desk to field calls from users. There are different models of support service provision. Post implementation support is crucial and needs to be planned in advance.

Problem Areas

⊙ Here are a few that could be prevented with thought and planning:

- The project budget runs out before the system is rolled out
- The estimates for data import are hugely low
- Holidays are planned for the end of the project
- A committee runs the project
- The framework for change is not strong enough
- The atmosphere at the start is unstructured as well as the budget
- The project manager is managing other projects

29

Problem areas to look out for

Here are a few that could be prevented by way of thoughtful planning:

➢ The estimates for data import are hugely low: This is a common mistake, if discovered earlier saves much time and effort later on.

➢ The project budget runs out before the system is rolled out: Under estimated the costs? Or begun the project without necessary management commitment? Either way the project is bound to fail. Therefore this is a pit fall that needs to be avoided.

➢ A committee runs the project: Delayed decision making could delay the project.

➢ The framework for change management is inadequate: handling the change requests and effecting changes are likely go out of control. It is essential to establish change management procedures beforehand.

➢ The project starts without proper planning: it will be disastrous to the project if planning for the project is not done proper.

➢ The project manager is a shared resource managing other projects: CRM projects need full time project management.

Summary

⊙ CRM project Management demands ample attention all through the Pre, Post and Implementation phases

⊙ Hard home work is essential to plan a successful CRM initiative

⊙ Project Implementation involves change with respect to People, Processes and Technology

⊙ Change management strategy is essential for enterprise wide adoption of the initiative

EC-Council   30

Module Summary

 Recap

➢ Managing a CRM project to successful completion demands ample attention through out the different stages viz. Pre, Post and Implementation phases.

➢ Meticulous preparation is essential to plan and execute a successful CRM initiative.

➢ Project implementation involves change with respect to People, Processes and Technology.

➢ Change management strategy is essential for enterprise wide adoption of the initiative.

CUSTOMER RELATIONSHIP MANAGEMENT (CRM)

Module IX – Building a Business Case for CRM

Exam 212-16 - Certified e-Business Associate (CEA)

Module Objective

⊙ Discuss the importance of building a business case

⊙ Comprehend the constituents of a good business case for CRM

⊙ Understand various aspects involved in CRM benefits and ROI estimation

EC-Council

2

Objectives

☞ **Module Objectives**

We have discussed the various aspects of customer relationship management in the previous modules. We have seen core concepts, technical functionality and various applications that assist in relationship management. However, one of the most challenging tasks that key personnel face in undertaking a CRM initiative is to convince the senior management and build a business case to establish the need and garner resources for a CRM program.

After completing this module you will be able to:

➢ Appreciate the importance of having a compelling business case

➢ Comprehend the constituents of a good business case for CRM

➢ Understand various aspects involved in CRM benefits estimation and CRM ROI estimation

Readers are encouraged to treat this module as an exploratory one, as the specifics will differ from organization to organization and is highly dependent on specific business scenarios.

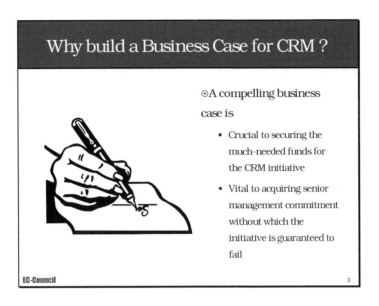

Need for a Business Case

Most CRM vendors tout the need to justify investment in their product using return on investment (ROI) calculated on different parameters. There is no dearth of literature or supporting documents that record a high return on investment on use of these products. What is being exhibited is one form of a business case on part of the vendors to initiate organization interest in their product.

We had earlier discussed the case of internal customers. Within an organization, the key personnel involved with a CRM initiative must sell their idea / concept / intent regarding CRM initiative to the senior management. To this end, they need to build a business case that exposes the key challenges, explores the opportunities and threats, discusses appropriate solutions, quantifies the benefits and justifies the need for investment.

This is especially true as any CRM implementation demands substantial resource commitments as well as systematic involvement of senior management to reap envisioned benefits.

We had discussed the need for evolving into a customer centric organization as well as the need for change management in earlier modules. Any CRM initiative calls for sweeping organizational changes across the enterprise. Evolving into a customer centric organization is an expensive proposition that not only calls for substantial financial investments, but also demands intellectual resource commitments.

Any capital-intensive technology implementation needs to have its merits documented and benefits quantified in a manner that has business value implications to the organizations. This is critical given the fact that most organizations would have already invested in other applications like ERP.

 Projects whose merits cannot be measured and projected to estimate the returns on the capital invested seldom find management sponsorship. It is here that a convincing business case can make all the difference.

The business case is particularly important to a CRM initiative because:

➢ It is crucial for securing the essential funds for the project.

➢ It is important to gain senior management appreciation and support, without which, internalization of the CRM program (which will effect changes in the organization's culture, processes and business practices) is a daunting task.

Probably, the most implicit benefit of having a good business case is that a comprehensive business case can drive the organization's CRM team to focus on where the main benefits and costs lie, and guide the team make better decisions around the scope and schedule of the project.

Moreover, business cases provide a framework for allocating accountability for delivering the benefits from an investment. They also serve as a benchmark against which the success of the project can be assessed.

This module is intended to make functional managers familiar with the key elements of a properly prepared CRM business case. This will enable managers to better assess how a CRM program can contribute to departmental or organizational business goals.

Elements of a good Business Case

⊙A definition and analysis of a business need, threat, opportunity, or problem

⊙The proposed solution expressed in terms that decision-makers can understand

⊙A discussion of alternative solutions considered and why they were rejected

⊙Life cycle cost estimates and estimated budget requirements

⊙A cost-benefit analysis

⊙Return on investment (ROI) analysis

⊙An investment risk analysis (including, technical, organizational, and financial risks), and

⊙Proposed project time frames and delivery schedules.

EC-Council   4

Elements of a good Business Case

A good business case is the foundation for establishing goals, buying-in management and staff, being funded, staying on track and measuring to achieve results and project success. The purpose of writing business cases is to provide management with a comprehensive evaluation of a significant issue for their decision, including:

➢ What needs to be done and why

➢ When it needs to be done and how

➢ Who is going to do the work

➢ How much will it cost, and

➢ The alternatives and risks.

Matters for consideration include full identification of implementation and life cycle costs, project sponsorship and ownership, human and organizational costs, intangible and tangible benefits, risk management and the time scale of likely benefits. It is critical that the business case shows that a project is aligned with identified business and organizational needs.

There is no one format to cover all these matters. Business cases will vary according to the maturity of the technology under consideration, the available finances and choice of systems, industry sector pressures, organizational business strategy and direction and the management and decision making culture.

Appropriate criteria for comparative assessment of CRM business cases are difficult. The area is relatively new and not yet fully understood. The cost/benefit relationship spans both intangible and tangible matters. Business cases based on financial criteria can be biased towards the short-term quick pay off and may overlook other areas where CRM can contribute to business value. In this broader perspective, value is regarded as the sum of the return for the resources deployed, the business impact (including organizational readiness and risk management) and the technology impact.

Adding value needs to be considered not just as a dollar return, but also as a performance return. Increasing value may result from improved performance towards the organization's mission, innovation, reduced cost, increased quality or speed, improved flexibility, or increased staff and customer satisfaction. Benefits come not from the technology, but from the new products and services or the enhanced business processes made available from innovative application of the CRM technology.

An indicative outline of a CRM related business case typically includes the following elements:

➢ A definition and analysis of a business need, threat, opportunity, or problem

➢ The proposed solution expressed in terms that decision-makers can understand

➢ A discussion of alternative solutions considered and why they were rejected

➢ Life cycle cost estimates and estimated budget requirements. This is the total estimated cost for the CRM program over the time period involved, including direct and indirect initial costs plus any periodic or continuing costs for operation and maintenance.

➢ A cost-benefit analysis

➢ Return on investment (ROI) analysis. A business case is more than a projection of ROI calculations for the project. In fact Return on Investment calculation is only one part of the business case.

➢ An investment risk analysis (including, technical, organizational, and financial risks). Risk analysis is used to identify and assess factors that may jeopardize the success of the project or achievement of desirable goals. This helps define preventive measures to reduce the probability of these factors from occurring and identify countermeasures to successfully deal with these constraints when they develop.

➢ Proposed project time frames and delivery schedules.

Business cases may also include additional information such as key assumptions made, and any constraints that may have limited the data gathering and analysis. Certain aspects that are of importance to the organization may be detailed such as critical success factors, strategic partner information, legal and regulatory impact, staffing and organization, competitive analysis and market research.

Some organizations may even have specialized requirements governing the form and content of a business case.

  In essence, persuasive business cases:

➢ Quantify the benefits CRM can bring about and talks about the ROI

➢ Demonstrates how the system will achieve those benefits (both qualitative and quantitative).

➢ Reveals how the CRM initiative is of strategic relevance to the company

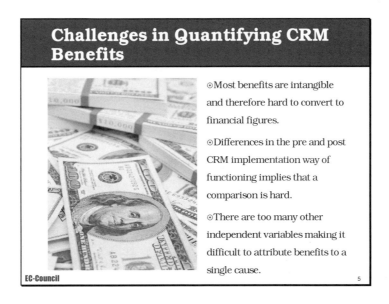

Challenges in Quantifying CRM Benefits

⊙Most benefits are intangible and therefore hard to convert to financial figures.

⊙Differences in the pre and post CRM implementation way of functioning implies that a comparison is hard.

⊙There are too many other independent variables making it difficult to attribute benefits to a single cause.

EC-Council 5

Challenges in quantifying CRM Benefits

Identifying and quantifying benefits from a CRM project can be a challenging task. This is especially true as organizations may assign varying priorities to the business value that can be derived from these benefits.

Enterprises may use a mixture of quantitative as well as qualitative benefits to evaluate a CRM initiative. Tangible benefits from CRM can be quite compelling to project in the business case, and are often done so at the cost of overlooking the intangible benefits. Demonstrable bottom-line and top-line benefits make up a strong business case, but addressing the additional benefits here can turn the CRM proposition into a persuasive one.

Therefore, it is crucial to address both the tangible (quantifiable) as well as intangible (qualitative) benefits when we talk of business benefits in the business case.

One of the most popular methods of quantifying benefits is the estimation of Return on Investment (ROI)

Estimation of ROI for CRM systems is particularly difficult for three reasons:

➢ A sizable proportion of CRM benefits are intangible and therefore hard to convert to financial figures.

For instance, being able to have intimate insight into the customer behavior is an intangible benefit that a CRM solution can bring about. The challenge here is to assign a financial value to this intangible benefit.

Examples of such benefits are:

- o Understanding up/cross-selling opportunities
- o Identification of drivers of customer retention and profitability
- o Discovery of new markets that was not known to exist
- o Discovery of new customer segment that was not targeted previously
- o In-depth knowledge of customer buying preferences, frequency, and seasonal variations
- o Identification of their top customers and what they are market basket
- o Ability to target content and marketing to the right audience
- o Better understanding of product mix

➢ There is a difference in the way of functioning once the CRM system is operational. This means that before and after comparison metrics is difficult.

For instance, increased efficiency resulting from an SFA tool implementation can result in both cost and timesavings. This can lead to increased productivity as the sales team has more customer facing time. The organization's approach to assessing productivity evolves as business processes evolve and as a result, new metrics emerge within the organization to measure a metric (such as increased productivity) previously non-existent.

Therefore, the metric used to assess a particular benefit (such as increase in productivity from SFA) may itself be out of context once the project goes live. It is therefore difficult to establish a baseline to compare both pre and post implementation results.

➢ There are too many other independent variables

For instance, increased revenue that was observed during the measured time period from a product line could have been caused by fleeing customers from a competitor, due to flaws in the competitor's market strategy and not attributable to any proactive customer acquisition strategy followed by the company.

The estimation of ROI is given special mention here, as most often; this aspect is widely projected by software vendors. The calculations involved in arriving at their respective ROI differ. The organization needs to arrive at its own estimation methods, projecting the benefits to be realized. The scope of discussion here is to emphasize the importance of backing each benefit or measurement with reliable and contextual facts pertaining to the organization in order to convince the stakeholders.

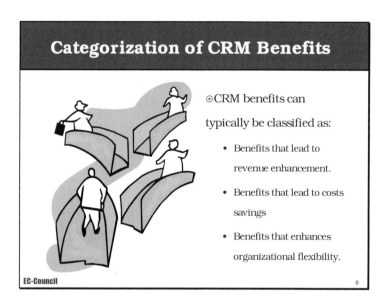

Categorization of CRM Benefits

⊙ CRM benefits can typically be classified as:

- Benefits that lead to revenue enhancement.
- Benefits that lead to costs savings
- Benefits that enhances organizational flexibility.

EC-Council

6

Categorization of CRM Benefits

It is easier to quantify benefits, if the organization can broadly categorize them, so that both tangible and intangible benefits are projected in terms of easily identifiable business value.

One broad set of categorization can be:

➢ **Benefits that lead to revenue enhancement**

In accordance to the business scenarios under consideration, one can arrive at other sales revenue enhancement opportunities.

- o **Acquisition of new customers:** New customers directly translate into increased sales.

- o **Increase in revenue per customer**: The CRM initiative makes the enterprise more responsive to customer needs. The initiative equips the enterprise capabilities to proactively attend to the customer needs. As a result of the new customer centric initiatives an increased share of the customer's wallet is reasonable to expect.

- o **Cross selling and up selling**: When the enterprise can analyze the loyal customer's genuine needs and come up with an offer to satisfy that need, chances that customer make a purchase is higher.

- o **Improved customer retention**: Retained customers are loyal customers. If a most probable retention rate could be reasonably estimated, by applying the average sales per customer figure, we can assign a number to the revenue contribution that can be expected of retained customers.

o **Efficiencies brought about by reduction in sales cycle times**: For instance, think of a scenario where in a sales cycle which previously took 8 weeks, is possible in 3 weeks, post CRM initiative. (Thanks to automation tools that generates proposals and other collaterals on the fly.) There are five extra weeks available for the sales reps to make more contacts. More contact time will reflect as more sales. Though the efficiency jump is a one-time affair, a sales improvement figure can be assigned to represent this efficiency enhancement.

➢ **Benefits that lead to costs savings**

There are various sources of cost efficiencies that are brought about by the CRM initiatives. Before starting out, it is appropriate to identify areas where savings can be made. It is necessary to consider the process improvement that can result from a CRM implementation.

A systematic analysis of current operations will serve as a detailed baseline from which to measure improvements.

An internal process improvement: More efficient and automated order fulfillment process, improves sales cycle time, cuts out rework, and improves the bottom line. Cost savings can come from lower inventory levels as well as reduced order to cash cycle.

Typically Sales force automation tools facilitate: (a) Automation of proposals, configuration, and quotations (b) Reviewing notes and files before calls (c) Preparing sales forecast and call reports (d) Providing better quality leads in a useable format (e) Finding and providing information (product, technical) to customers (f) Optimizing customer facing time (g) Leading to reduced deal closure times and savings contributed out of efficiency in sales process.

Service center efficiencies lend: (a) institutionalizing processes leading to quicker issue resolutions (b) reduced number of staff to deal with the problems (c) Ability to switch to lower cost operatives (d) reduced staff turnover due to increased motivation as the institutionalized processes improves the quality of work life (e) lower telecommunications line charges.

Marketing campaign expense reduction leads to: (a) Accurate targeting of customers leads to less advertising/promotion waste (b) lower campaign volumes (c) lower expense to revenue ratios. This means that at same cost or lesser better responses could be elucidated from mailing/ other types of campaigns.

➢ **Benefits that enhance organizational flexibility**

This is the capability to respond to competition or changes in the market place. Most CRM systems provide flexibility to rapidly respond to strategic changes to product, pricing and customer behavior. The ability to communicate customers of changes in prices or products or to adapt your sales pitch is invaluable in competitive and volatile markets. A value can be assigned to this flexibility tagging an opportunity cost for the absence of this future flexibility.

This categorization has greater appeal as most organizations list these as the most prominent sources of benefits from their investment in CRM projects. This makes it possible to highlight the intangible paybacks that work together to make the above-discussed benefits possible, and present them in a correlated and contextual manner.

CRM Benefits (Indirect revenue enhancement opportunities)

⊙ Benefits accrued to customer, leading to improved loyalty:
- Product/service meets customer needs
- Enhancement in the perceived value of the product/service
- Customer self service capability
- Immediate access to order status
- Greater breadth of solution options
- More responsive support service.

EC-Council

8

CRM Benefits –Customer's perspective

By way of the CRM initiative, the organization realigns itself as a Customer Centric Enterprise. This enhances customer experience across all channels of customer interaction. A customer derives the following benefits:

➢ Delivered product meets customer requirements

➢ Reduced costs of buying and using the product/service

➢ Customer self Service Capability

➢ Immediate access to order status

➢ Greater breadth of solution options

➢ More responsive support service

The purpose of highlighting the customer's perspective here is to emphasize the need to explore and include benefits of this nature, for which a financial figure can be arrived at and used in the ROI projections. The methodology to arrive at these figures varies according to the business scenarios. However, readers should bear in mind that, those which are difficult to quantify into financial figures should not be ignored as these benefits too has a role in justifying the CRM initiative.

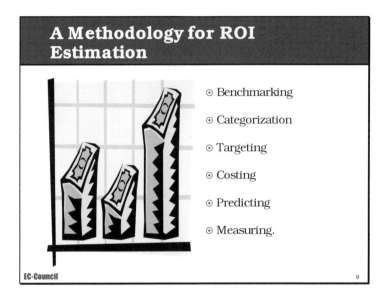

A methodology for ROI Estimation
- ⊙ Benchmarking
- ⊙ Categorization
- ⊙ Targeting
- ⊙ Costing
- ⊙ Predicting
- ⊙ Measuring.

EC-Council

9

A methodology for ROI Estimation

CRM implementations are significantly different for every company, and attempts to apply a 'one-size-fits-all' approach to measuring return on investment (ROI) would be a major blunder.

In any CRM implementation, several processes need to happen in order for projects to be proven a success. Listed below are processes that lead to a ROI estimation.

> **Benchmarking**

Before any solution provider is invited to pitch for business, and before design charts are drawn up, the enterprise should first take an objective view of its present operations. It is critical at this stage to work with all departments that will be affected by any proposed changes. These include, but are not limited to Sales, Marketing, Logistics/distribution, customer service, IS/IT, Human resources and Finance.

For a few projects, some of these departments may seem irrelevant. For example, if a proposed solution is to be put in place to improve the marketing campaign effectiveness, the obvious choice of departments to consult might be IT, sales and customer service. However, if no one consults the logistics department, they may find that the increased sales cannot be fulfilled because the department is already running at full capacity. For an enterprise-wide rollout of multiple processes and solutions, most of the departments or functions will be touched.

The next step is to take key data points, which will be measured throughout the project. These may include:

- o Customer service: (a) Customer service staff remunerations (b) Customer satisfaction scores (c) Cost of follow-up calls (d) Activity-based costs

- o Sales: (a) Promotion costs (b) Average deal size (c) Resale rates

- o IT: (a) Infrastructure costs (b) Ongoing maintenance charges (c) Training

Once the benchmark of where the enterprise is currently disposed has been established, a process of segmentation can begin.

➢ Categorization

When the metrics have been established, they can be categorized into types such as revenue enhancement, cost savings etc. (refer: Categorization of benefits). This makes it easier for the enterprise to focus more clearly on its strategic goals. The categorization stage is a useful tool to prevent the lack of focus that can cause ill-thought-out implementations to stagnate or miss achievable goals.

➢ Targeting

Once the metrics have been collected and segmented, the enterprise should have a better idea of which improvements should come first. Enterprises should look for financially measurable objectives to put into their ROI model. Intangibles are useful, but by their nature, they are impossible to add to the bottom line.

A market leader in a mature area may decide the following to be their key metrics for the first wave of CRM implementation:

- o Customer retention rate to improve by 15%

- o Sales cycle time to decrease by 2 week

- o Customer satisfaction rating to improve by 25%

Whereas a small player in a growing market may opt for these as the key metrics for improvement:

- o Increase average order sizes by 7%

- o Increase per salesperson revenues by 12%

- o Move into new geographical markets, increasing revenues by 20%.

From the benchmarking and targeting stages, the enterprise should have a good idea of where a small increase in efficiency or decrease in cost can make a major difference to profit. In addition, without the targeting stage to set up key performance metrics, the business will not know whether it has succeeded or failed.

> ### Costing

Calculating the cost of even a simple IT project means more than just totaling the number of software licenses being bought.

For CRM, this is even more complex. Businesses should try to understand the total cost of ownership involved with whatever technology-based solutions they decide to purchase. Even just on the technology side, this will include costs from various stages: (a) Analysis (b) Design (c) Implementation (d) Hardware (e) Software (f) Maintenance (g) Project management (h) Training.

As CRM is more than just technology implementation, enterprises must quantify human and business costs as well, for example: (a) Business process re-engineering (b) Re-tooling (c) Change management (d) Process management (e) Temporary decreased efficiency before familiarization.

Breaking these down tactically by project - for example, marketing automation- can make costing more manageable. However, businesses should be wary of looking for ROI on individual projects, as there are a large number of interdependencies that will affect the final outcome.

> ### Predicting

At this juncture, the enterprise has a heightened sense of self-awareness, and can understand both where revenues are coming from and costs are being generated. Major problem areas would have been identified at the previous stages, and possible solutions suggested and appropriate costs arrived at.

Now, it is important for the enterprise to perform a quantified cost-benefit analysis. Through comparing realistic targets for improvement in specific areas with the relevant total cost of ownership, the enterprise should then be able to forecast a break-even point where the investment is paid for by the improvements it brings. It is rare, and possibly counter-productive for all aspects of a CRM implementation to happen concurrently. The results of the cost-benefit analyses will target the enterprise's attention on the areas that have most to gain first from implementation.

It is important that focusing on these initial areas does not diminish the project team's wider view of the CRM implementation. There will be benefits and costs associated with the initial phase, but these will change over time as more projects are rolled-out and interdependencies emerge.

> ### Measuring

CRM can be a very long process. It is important to have at least one person with financial knowledge on the team who is dedicated to keeping costing and benefit metrics created in the targeting and costing phases up-to date.

Recalculation of costs and benefits are likely to take place throughout project lifecycles, as external and internal variables change. Project scope and functionality are likely to change, and assumptions that affect the rest of the CRM implementation should be checked every time a notable alteration is made.

Exhibit: Quantifying the Benefits

	Year 1	Year 2	Year 3	Year 4	Year 5
Increased Operating Profits from Revenue Enhancements					
Increased Average Revenue per customer	$220,000	$440,000	$687,500	$859,375	$1,074,219
Increased Customer					
Retention Rate	$1,250	$2,500	$3,906	$4,883	$6,104
Improved Close Rate	$82,500	$165,000	$257,813	$322,266	$402,832
Increased Number of					
Sales Opportunities	$619,489	$1,238,978	$1,935,904	$2,419,880	$3,024,850
Improved New Representative					
Performance	$17,500	$35,000	$54,688	$68,359	$85,449
Increased Operating Profits from Cost Reductions					
Reduced Customer					
Acquisition Costs	$12,250	$24,500	$38,281	$47,852	$59,814
Reduced Training Cost	$22,500	$45,000	$70,313	$87,891	$109,863
Reduced Employee Turnover Rate	$3,750	$7,500	$11,719	$14,648	$18,311
Reduced Order Errors	$6,250	$12,500	$19,531	$24,414	$30,518
Totals					
Total Revenue Enhancement	$940,739	$1,881,478	$2,939,810	$3,674,763	$4,593,453
Total Cost Reduction	$44,750	$89,500	$139,844	$174,805	$218,506
TOTAL BENEFITS (operating profit)	963489	1970978	3079634	3849567	4811959

EC-Council

10

Presenting the benefits - Illustration

The above exhibit depicts a sample projection of benefits in financial terms. We had discussed a methodology for arriving at an ROI figure earlier. Discussed below are notes on some of the probabilistic calculations for arriving at the best scenario for ROI. It is important to remember that risk management forms an integral part of any business case. Managing risks so the project runs to plan is more important than estimating their likely impact. However, as mentioned earlier, many CRM projects do have significant intangible benefits that can only be quantified on a 'best guess' basis.

To get a better grip on the intangibles, the following techniques may be used for easier comprehension.

➢ Analyze the costs and benefits more than once – using the optimistic/ pessimistic estimates in turn. The aim here is to identify how sensitive the cost benefit analysis is to the assumptions used on the monetary value of, for example, improved customer loyalty. The system can be cost justified neither on a best and worst-case basis, a best-case basis only, nor on a best or a worst-case basis.

➢ Use probabilistic estimates of the expected value of costs and benefits. If there is an uncertainty regarding the extent of future costs and benefits, and a number of possible outcomes are likely, probability theory can be used to calculate their value on a weighted average basis. A weighted average is best used in cases where there are a number of possible outcomes covering a continuum of benefits.

➢ Identify the cost of achieving the intangible benefits: This method works back from the known costs and benefits to identify the residual level of cost that can not be justified by the quantified benefits. To illustrate using a simplistic example, if the total cost of the system (including cost of capital and inflation) is $800,000 but only $600,000 worth of other (hard) benefits can be identified, to break even, the system would have to generate an extra profit of $200,000 in sales.

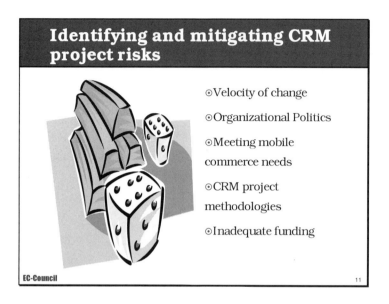

Identifying and mitigating CRM project risks

⊙Velocity of change

⊙Organizational Politics

⊙Meeting mobile commerce needs

⊙CRM project methodologies

⊙Inadequate funding

EC-Council   11

Identifying and mitigating risks

CRM projects differ from other systems projects in various aspects. Identifying impediments to a successful CRM program and taking proactive measures to mitigate them should be actively pursued and presented in the business case. Some of the areas where due consideration may be given are:

➢ Velocity of change

The rate at which marketing and sales requirements undergo change is exponential. There fore enterprise must factor them in a rapidly evolving requirements scenario. A project that for any reason takes longer than four - six months to implement in its first phase is in danger of stalling due to outdated processes, loss of interest and an ROI that is difficult to justify.

➢ Organizational Politics

Politics play a big part in the dynamics surrounding departments concerned with CRM, more so than in any other departments within the organization. CRM systems more often than not do change roles and responsibilities of many managers.

Successful implementations and use of systems requires the change management issues to be identified and managed. At the user level the question as to who owns the prospect or customer often needs to be addressed.

➢ Meeting mobile commerce needs

The aspect of mobile commerce needs is more specific to the implementation of sales / field service focused CRM systems. The logistical challenges that arise due to portability and accessibility requirements have to be met with complicated processes that need changing at an ever-increasing speed on part of the users. Mobility and its demands for data synchronization pose a dominant technical risk for CRM systems projects.

➢ CRM project methodologies

Whilst systems development methodologies can help standardize work and raise quality, their use is not without risk. First, many of these methodologies have been developed and work successfully for ERP, distribution or finance systems projects. But their use is unproven for CRM projects, which have different risks and challenges. It is also important to remember that what worked for one implementation need not necessarily work in an identical manner for another.

➢ Inadequate funding

Many CRM projects end up as under-funded due to poor estimates of the costs of process re-engineering and change management. Other projects run out of funds because of problems encountered on the way. Inadequate funding spells disaster for CRM projects.

Risk management has to be an ongoing practice and contingency plans should be put in place.

Summary

⊙ A good CRM business case will show how the CRM system support the enterprises strategies

⊙ The business case will have explored the 'real' costs and benefits

⊙ The business case will highlight the impact of risks and strategies to mitigate risks

EC-Council   12

Module Summary

 Recap

To summarize, a good CRM business case will show how the CRM system will support the enterprises sales and market strategies. It will have identified the best option and explored all alternatives. The business case will have explored the 'real' costs and benefits - the changes arising from the system and their likely associated cash flows. It will highlight the impact of risk (financial, market, operational and technical) on the estimated/most likely cash flows and portray how the system will maximize utilization of scarce resources or assets.

Presenting the ROI of CRM systems' initiatives is difficult and has to be done well, as the ROI demonstrates and build support for the changes needed for CRM initiatives to succeed. It is critical to get the necessary funds allocated and for the senior management to appreciate and support the necessary changes in organization, culture, processes and business practices.

Most ROI calculations are multi-purpose. They satisfy the need to convince, obtain resources and control. Senior management needs to be convinced that the system will add value, increase profits and shareholder value, and is a better investment than other alternatives under consideration.

CUSTOMER RELATIONSHIP MANAGEMENT (CRM)

Module X – CRM Product Comparisons

Exam 212-16 - Certified e-Business Associate (CEA)

Module Objectives

- ⊙ Provide input to initiate thought process towards zeroing-in on the appropriate solution that best fits the organizational needs.

- ⊙ Present a feature list that best serves as a platform to compare and contrast products to ascertain their suitability for value addition within the organization.

- ⊙ The purpose of this section is not to endorse any particular vendor or product, but to present salient features of the products in focus.

EC-Council

2

Objectives

- **Module Objectives**

This module is aimed at:

➢ Providing input to initiate thought process towards zeroing-in on the appropriate solution that best fits the organizational needs.

➢ Presenting a feature list that best serves as a platform to compare and contrast products to ascertain their suitability for value addition within the organization.

The purpose of this section is not to endorse any particular vendor or product, but to present salient features of the products in focus.

This module does not deal with an all inclusive vendor list but presents an indicative list of CRM products that fall under the large enterprise and SME categories. The information presented is collated from different sources including vendor web sites and CRM community opinions.

The list of products presented is not an exhaustive list of CRM solutions available in the market.

The prime determinant in the CRM product selection process being the organizational requirements and expectations from the CRM system, the feature list presented best serves as a platform to compare and contrast products to ascertain their suitability for value addition within the organization.

Therefore on completion of this module you will be:

➢ Familiar with a few prominent CRM solutions available in the marketplace

➢ Familiar with distinctive features offered by these solutions

➢ The focus areas as covered by these solutions and

PS. It should be noted that the vendors introduce new features and enhanced products hit the market very quick in the highly fragmented CRM market. It is therefore advised that the readers should visit the concerned vendor websites for the latest information with regard to the products under consideration.

Approach

- ⊙ Featured in this section is a list of CRM products that fall under the following categories.
    - -CRM solutions for Large enterprise and
    - -CRM solutions for SMEs
- ⊙ Salient features of these products are listed along with other pertinent product information.
- ⊙ The list of products presented is in no way complete and the appearance of products in the list does not convey that the products not represented are inferior to the ones presented.

EC-Council   3

Approach

The approach followed through this module in presenting the CRM solutions and their salient features is presented here in order to better comprehend the details presented in the right perspective.

A select list of CRM products are featured in this module. It can be observed from the product-market positioning, of the CRM projects, that the products can be classified as:

- ➢ CRM solutions for Large enterprise (100 + users)and

- ➢ CRM solutions for Small (<10 users) and /or Medium businesses (10-100 users)

Salient features of these products are listed along with other pertinent product information for the purpose of understanding the products per se.

We have been following a common thread through out the courseware with regard to the core areas that need to be addressed by a CRM solution within an organization. These core areas are Sales, Marketing and Customer service. Not all organizations expect CRM solutions to cover all these areas. Some implementations are enterprise wide, some are specific to a function say 'Sales'. In the feature comparison that is undertaken in the pages to come, we are addressing a head - 'coverage' which presents which all of the above mentioned core areas are addressed by the solution under consideration. Apart from this another dimension focused through out the feature comparison exercise is whether analytics is embedded in the product offering or not.

The list of products presented is in no way complete and the appearance of products in the list does not convey that the products not represented are inferior to the ones presented. It is advised that the readers may visit the vendor websites for latest information. More often than not the analyst reports on market positions and evaluations vary widely from analyst to analyst and therefore any basis of decision should be arrived at referring to different sources.

PS. Please note that providing an in-depth analysis of each of the products mentioned is beyond the scope of the discussion. Pricing details are not included. It is advised that for the pricing details, vendor may be approached directly as many pricing options and discount options exist with most of the products.

Large enterprise solutions

Product	Vendor	URL
AMDOCS Clarify CRM	AMDOCS	http://www.amdocs.com
E.piphany 6.0	E.piphany	http://www.epiphany.com
Kana iCare	Kana	http://www.kana.com
Oracle 11i CRM	Oracle	http://www.oracle.com/applications/index.html
Peoplesoft 8 CRM	PeopleSoft	http://www.peoplesoft.com/corp/en/products/line/crm/index.asp
mySAP CRM	SAP AG	http://www.mysap.com/solutions/crm
Siebel 2000	Siebel Systems	http://www.siebel.com

EC-Council 4

Large Enterprise solutions

➢ **AMDOCS Clarify CRM**

Ordering / billing system major AMDOCS acquired Clarify CRM and hence the name AMDOCS Clarify CRM. Clarify CRM had a good clientele prior to the acquisition. The new CRM system has integration to Order management and Billing and is capable of delivering value to AMDOCS traditional target industry segments like communications, and utilities industries.

Coverage: AMDOCS Clarify CRM solution covers all the basic CRM focus areas viz. Marketing, Sales and Service by way of its product offerings:
- o Service and Support
- o Sales and Ordering
- o Marketing and Analytics
- o ClarifyCRM Services

Probably the areas not covered by the solution map include: Partner Relationship Management, field sales or sales configuration.

Clarify is strong on field service, call center and e-service components, e-mail response management systems surveys, service requests and status checking, as well as service analytics.

Since the customers belonging to the large enterprise segments are interested in CRM integration to the backend systems as well, AMDOCS Clarify CRM is a solution to be considered for AMDOCS billing/order management customers.

➢ E.piphany E.6

E.piphany E.6 solutions are built web-based CRM architecture on the J2EE platform. The modular architecture and interface support enables flexible deployments.

Coverage: The E.piphany E.6 system covers all the basic CRM focus areas viz. Marketing, Sales and Service by way of its product lines:

- o E.piphany Marketing which includes: Campaign Management, E-mail Campaign, Real-Time marketing with real time analytics, E-Commerce analytics etc.
- o E.piphany Sales which includes: Sales, Direct Sales analytics, Real time sales etc.
- o E.piphany Service which include: Contact Center, Customer Support, E-mail Response, Web Self-Service, real time service capabilities as well as contact center analytics

Probably the areas not covered adequately by the solution map include: telesales, field sales and dispatch for complex work environments as also is the case with industry vertical support.(say for eg. consumer goods, pharmaceuticals etc.)

Excellent analytics and call scripting for customer service center etc are features to lookout for.

➢ The KANA iCARE Suite

The KANA iCARE solutions integrate marketing and customer service activities in a multi-channel interaction environment.

Coverage: The KANA iCARE eCRM solutions can be deployed as complete solution suites or as individual components. The product covers the basic CRM focus areas viz. Marketing and Service and not the Sales area. The solution components include:

- o **Contact Center** - a multi-channel customer service application for contact centers that provides complete request management, solution publishing, self-service capabilities, and extranet workflow for complete, high-quality service at lower cost.
- o **Marketing** - multi-channel marketing automation solution
- o **Analytics** - Facilitates measurement and analysis of customer service, marketing and commerce operations irrespective of the customer touch points.

Other components include: a customer self-service solution along with an assisted-service solution for contact center agents called Kana IQ; an intelligent e-mail management suite that manage e-mail responses called Kana Response IQ and another e-mail response system which provides agent assisted service, called Kana Response.

➤ **Oracle 11i CRM R5.x**

Oracle's suite key strength and selling point is its tight integration with the rest of its enterprise applications. It also has integration capabilities with legacy products.

Coverage: Oracle CRM application covers all the basic CRM focus areas viz. Marketing, Sales and Service by way of its E business suite product offerings that deal with:
- o Marketing
- o Sales
- o Service
- o Interaction Center
- o Contracts and
- o E-Commerce

For large enterprise customers running oracle back-office applications, looking for CRM integration to the backend systems, Oracle CRM is an option to be considered seriously due to the ease of integration.

➤ **PeopleSoft 8 CRM**

PeopleSoft 8 CRM product offering is most appropriate for large enterprises as the company comes from an ERP background and the fact that the CRM application was to serve the front office application requirements. PeopleSoft also has an offering - PeopleSoft accelerated CRM cut out for small and mid-sized enterprises. PeopleSoft CRM is strong on the Field sales and service areas. PRM is an area to be addressed by the product.

Coverage: PeopleSoft CRM product suite covers all the basic CRM focus areas viz. Marketing, Sales and Service processes by way of its CRM core products:
- o Configurator
- o CRM Portal Pack
- o CRM Warehouse. Enterprise Warehouse
- o Support, Help Desk, Help Desk for H R
- o Marketing, Online Marketing, Site Marketing, Telemarketing
- o Customer Behavior Modeling
- o Customer Scorecard
- o Field Service, Mobile Field Service
- o Sales, Mobile Sales

- o Multi-channel Interactions
- o CTI Integration
- o Order Capture, Order Capture Self-Service
- o Quality Management

With people soft CRM suite, Analytics (profitability customer behavior etc.) come embedded in the application. PeopleSoft provide enterprise integration points (EIP), for easy integration with third-party systems non-PeopleSoft applications.

Apart from this PeopleSoft have industry specific CRM solutions that cater to the following industry verticals:
- o Communications
- o Energy
- o Financial Services
- o Government
- o High Technology
- o Insurance

➤ mySAP CRM

mySAP CRM combines back-office and front-office functions across the enterprise.

Coverage: mySAP CRM product suite covers all the basic CRM focus areas viz. Marketing, Sales and Customer Service processes spanning the entire 'customer interaction cycle'. Presented below are the key areas addressed by mySAP CRM
- o Marketing: Enterprise marketing, Field marketing, E-marketing, Telemarketing, Channel marketing, Analytics
- o Sales: Enterprise sales; Field sales, E-selling, Telesales, Channel sales, Channel commerce, Analytics
- o Service: Enterprise service, Field service, E-service, Customer service, Channel service, Analytics
- o Analytics: Analytical scenarios; Analytical methods
- o Field applications: Field marketing, Field sales, Field service, Analytics
- o E-commerce: E-selling, E-service, Analytics
- o Interaction center: Telemarketing, Telesales, Customer service, Analytics
- o Supporting processes
- o Channel management: Partner management and analytics, Channel marketing, Channel sales, Channel service, Channel commerce

By way of its native integration to the core SAP ERP system, CRM offers seamless order fulfillment capabilities. The campaign management features both for the traditional and Internet sales are rich. As seen in the solution map, each of the functional areas comes equipped with analytics.

Apart from this mySAP CRM solution has industry specific offerings that cater to the following industry verticals:
- o Aerospace and defense -
- o Automotive
- o Banking
- o Chemicals
- o Consumer products
- o Engineering, construction, and operations
- o Financial service providers
- o Healthcare
- o High tech
- o Industrial machinery and components
- o Insurance
- o Media
- o Mill products
- o Oil and gas
- o Pharmaceuticals
- o Public sector
- o Retail
- o Service providers
- o Telecommunications
- o Utilities

For large enterprise customers running SAP R/3 ERP, looking for CRM integration to the backend systems, mySAP CRM offers excellent value. This is particularly true as many of the CRM functions have deep linkages to the SAP transactions. Having said that it has to be born in mind that mySAP CRM integration to other systems could be time and effort intensive.

➢ **Siebel**

Siebel remains the fore runner in the CRM market, leading the high-end of the market with a multiplicity of CRM product offerings catering to a wide audience. Apart from the large enterprise product, Siebel Mid-market is the product from the Siebel stable that addresses the mid-market customers.

Coverage: Siebel CRM product suite covers all the basic CRM focus areas viz. Marketing, Sales and Customer Service processes spanning the entire 'customer life cycle'. Presented below are the areas addressed by Siebel.
- o Sales,

- o Marketing,
- o Call Center and Service
- o Interactive Selling
- o Partner Relationship Management
- o Employee Relationship Management
- o Analytics etc are some of the product offerings (Siebel offers over 200 application modules)

Apart from this Siebel have industry specific offerings that cater to the following industry verticals:

- o Aerospace and defense -
- o Automotive
- o Communications
- o Consumer sector
- o Energy
- o Financial Institutions
- o Healthcare
- o Homeland Security
- o Industrial Manufacturing
- o Insurance
- o Life sciences
- o Oil, Gas, Chemical
- o Public Sector
- o Travel and transportation

Front office to back office integration is a major issue plaguing many CRM vendors. Siebel has developed connectors that link into popular back-office applications like Oracle SAP, JDE and PeopleSoft.

CRM solutions for SMEs

Product	Vendor	URL
Applix	Applix	http://www.applix.com
Clientele, e	Epicor	http://www.epicor.com
Onyx Enterprise CRM	Onyx Software	http://www.onyx.com
Pivotal CRM	Pivotal Software	http://www.pivotal.com

EC-Council   5

CRM Solutions for SMEs

> **Applix**

Applix's CRM product is positioned as a Low cost product aimed at Small and medium enterprises. Applix has two lines of product namely– iCRM and iPlanning, the former being the CRM offering and the latter an analytics product.

Coverage: The Applix's CRM offering- iCRM basically covers the Sales and Service areas and has limited marketing functionality. iCRM addresses these areas by way of the following components:
   o   iSales offers SFA and base marketing automation
   o   iService offers service and support as well as customer self service
   o   iHelpdesk and
   o   iCustomerInsight.

iCustomerInsight is a product from Applix offering customer analysis features.

The areas not addressed by the Applix suite include: e-commerce, field service, and Partner Relationship Management. Applix has recently sold off its CRM business to Platinum Equity LLC.

➤ **Epicor – Clientele CRM Suite**

The product Clientele CRM an integrated Windows NT based application,from Epicor is positioned at small and medium sized companies.

Coverage: Clientele CRM offering covers the Sales, Marketing and Service areas by way of the following components:
- o Sales and Marketing (Contact, Lead, Opportunity and Account Management)
- o Customer Support (Customer call handling, Customer FAQ for self help etc.)
- o Connector (bi-directional data synchronization)
- o Conductor (work flow tool)
- o Clientelenet (internet/intranet/portal application)

It is to be noted that the coverage could be limited to certain functionalities alone within the broad areas of sales, service and marketing.

Since Epicor offers a back-office suite (manufacturing, financials, e-commerce, etc.)as well, it can offer the front office products integrate seamlessly for clients of its back office aaplications. There is an analytics tool named Epicor eIntelligence for data access data and analysis.

➤ **Onyx**

The Onyx Enterprise CRM is a web based offering which comes as Onyx-Employee Portal, Customer Portal, and Partner Portal. Onyx operates in the mid market segment touching up to the large enterprise segments.

Coverage: The Onyx CRM offering covers the Sales, Service and Marketing automation areas by way of the:
- o Employee Portal which offers a single interface for accessing sales, marketing, service and support functions. The features provided by these functions in turn are as follows:

  Marketing : Campaign management and analysis, Permission marketing, Target list management, Product tracking, Surveys and customer profiling, Collateral and literature fulfillment, Marketing Encyclopedia

  Sales: Opportunity management, Pipeline management, Quotes and proposals, Order generation, Win/loss analysis, Sales team management, Forecasting analysis, Channel management, Reporting and analytics

  Service and Support: Service/support request management, Service/support escalation, Queue management, Knowledge base, Online service inquiries, Call center performance analysis, Quality management, Computer Telephony Integration (CTI)

- o Partner Portal consisting of:
  Partner Recruiting, Channel program management, Partner profiling, Lead distribution and management, Pipeline management, Indirect sales forecasting, Performance assessment, Online catalog, Online knowledge base, Online service inquiries features

- o Customer Portal Product consisting of:
  Online lead capture and profiling, Permission-based marketing, Online catalog, Online surveys, Literature fulfillment, Online service inquiries, Product registration features enables internet customer self service.

As we have seen Onyx lacks inbuilt analytics. Cognos' solutions Business Intelligence solution doubles up as the analytical engine for the Onyx CRM. Onyx is gearing up with industry solutions currently financial services and health services vertical solutions are available.

➢ Pivotal CRM

Pivotal positions itself as a mid market CRM solution provider offering marketing, sales, service and support automation solutions.

Coverage: The Pivotal CRM offering covers the Sales, Service and Marketing automation areas by way of the:

- o Pivotal sales Suite consisting of Sales, Contact Center, Wireless applications and Sales Analytics

- o Pivotal Marketing Suite consisting of: Campaign Portal, Lead Manager, Direct Marketing Manager, Prospecting Assistant, Event Manager, Contact Center, Marketing Analytics.

- o Pivotal Service suite consisting of: Contact Center, eService, Wireless and Service Analytics

As you might have noticed, Pivotal suites come with built in analytical capabilities.

Apart from this Pivotal offers interactive selling and Partner management solutions. The beauty of the solution is that these works across Web, wireless and traditional communication channels. Pivotal support the industry verticals, Insurance, Financial Services and Real estate & construction.

CRM solutions for SMEs (..Contd)

Product	Vendor	URL
Act	Interact Commerce	http://www.act.com
Maximzer7 Enterprise	Maximizer	http://maximizer.com
SalesLogix	Interact Commerce	http://www.saleslogix.com

EC-Council

6

CRM Solutions for SMEs (Contd..)

➤ **ACT! 6.0**

ACT! is a world leading contact management software with more than 3.5 million users. It does not fall under a full feature CRM category.

Coverage: ACT! 6.0 do not cover the core CRM areas like marketing or service management, but deals with contact management functions like company and contact data storage, registration of activities and contacts, calendars and schedules. Apart from this ACT!6 deals with a part of the SFA functions as sales (opportunity) management and pipeline analysis also .

ACT!6.0 is available at a License Fee per Copy: $200, the price that makes it sell to over a million companies.

➤ **Maximizer 7 Enterprise**

Maximizer 7 Enterprise is a new CRM solution targeting small and mid size firms. There is a product Maximizer 7 which is a sales and contact management solution offered by the same vendor targeted at small businesses and individuals.

Coverage: Maximizer 7 Enterprise is a CRM suite with Sales, Service and Marketing automation areas addressed.

- o Sales consist of processes that facilitate sales incidents management from opportunities to closure, as well as forecasting and analytical reporting capabilities.
- o Marketing consist of campaign tracking and management, marketing collateral distribution, customer profiling etc.
- o Customer Service and support consists of service incident management and resolution, online customer self service, Service level tracking and reporting.

Maximizer Enterprise talks about remote access to critical data from anywhere on any device through the web, Palm OS device, or a web-enabled PDA.

Maximizer7 Enterprise comes in three different flavors: SQL eCRM suite for SMBs with multiple sales channels, SQL CRM suite for SMBs and Pervasive CRM suite for small businesses.

➤ **SalesLogix**

SalesLogix is the market leading CRM product in the mid-size enterprise segment.

Coverage: SalesLogix is a full fledged CRM suite with Sales, Service and Marketing automation areas addressed.

- o SalesLogixSales consists of contact management, lead and opportunity management sales team management, revenue forecasting as well as sales activities and effectiveness reporting features.
- o SalesLogixMarketing consists of campaign tracking and management, campaign ROI measurements and metrics reporting features.
- o SalesLogixService consists of Support ticket management, Defect tracking, Contract management, Return material authorizations (RMAs), Standard problems and resolutions, Web self-service. Etc.

SalesLogix has connectors to prominent ERPs like Great Plains, Solomon, J.D. Edwards, and SAP. And therefore is an easy candidate for front to back office integration.

Module Summary

- There is a multiplicity of CRM products catering to different market needs.
- The products can generally be classified into Large enterprise products and products catering to Small and Medium Businesses.
- Enterprise products normally have Sales, Marketing and Service area coverage along with embedded Analytics.
- Small and Medium business products have niche area focus rather than having strength across all core CRM areas.

EC-Council   7

Module Summary

 Recap

➢ There is a multiplicity of CRM products catering to different market needs.

➢ The products can generally be classified into large enterprise products and products catering to Small and Medium Businesses.

➢ Enterprise products normally have Sales, Marketing and Service area coverage along with embedded Analytics.

➢ Small and Medium business products have niche area focus rather than having strength across all core CRM areas.

Having seen some of the distinguishing features of 14 popular CRM solutions available in the market, you are in a better position to evaluate the best fit solution for your organization. Bear in mind the point that it is imperative to do a thorough search of the market place before zeroing in on the products for short listing. Visit all respective vendor sites for up to date information.

Section 1a

Sample Exam - Multiple Choice Questions

Module I: Overview of CRM

1. **Which of the following statements most appropriately defines the concept of CRM?**
   a) CRM can be widely defined as a strategy
   b) CRM is about technology enabling processes and practices in sales, marketing and service areas
   c) CRM is a packaged software solution for managing customer relationships
   d) CRM is a comprehensive set of processes and technologies for managing with potential and current customer relationships.

2. **Broad categories of CRM are:**
   a) Marketing, Sales and Service automation
   b) Campaign Management, Customer Interaction management, Customer analysis
   c) Operational, Analytical and Collaborative CRM.
   d) Analytics, Marketing, sales and Service automations

3. **eCRM helps organizations to formulate enterprise wide business rules that ensure:**
   a) Buying and selling of goods and services on the web
   b) Consistent customer experience across multiple contact channel
   c) Sales force productivity enhancements
   d) Marketing campaign effectiveness

4. **eCRM is the CRM concept that tries to:**
   a) Provide a web point of sale to the customer
   b) Provide self service capability over web
   c) Integrate multiple channels through a web access point.
   d) Integrate sales department with marketing

5. **Collaborative CRM is the:**
   a) Application of collaborative services to facilitate interactions between the customer and the organization.
   b) Application of collaborative services to facilitate interactions between the customers.
   c) Application of collaborative services to facilitate interactions between the departments within the organization.
   d) Application of collaborative services to facilitate interactions between the customer service representatives and the customers.

6. **Analytical CRM involves:**
   a) Capturing, storing, extracting, processing, analyzing and interpreting of production data to the corporate user.

b) Capturing, storing, extracting, processing, analyzing and interpreting of Sales data to the corporate user.

c) Capturing, storing, extracting, processing, analyzing and interpreting of marketing data to the corporate user.

d) Capturing, storing, extracting, processing, analyzing and interpreting of customer data to the corporate user.

7. **Analytical CRM makes use of:**
   a) Data bases and build a data warehouse at the back end by using both transactional data and market research data.
   b) Data mining models and build a data warehouse at the back end by using both transactional data and market research data.
   c) Data available in production and marketing databases to make various analytics.
   d) Data available from data sources external to the enterprise only.

8. **By way of operational CRM it is possible:**
   a) To facilitate interaction between different customer facing departments within the enterprise
   b) To facilitate interaction between customers of the enterprise
   c) To achieve the automation of horizontally integrated business processes including customer touch points, and other back office systems.
   d) To facilitate interaction between different departments within the enterprise

9. **Which of the following comes as an example for Operational CRM tool?**
   a) A Customer data warehouse
   b) A Sales Force Automation tool
   c) A Customer Interaction center
   d) Customer communication channels

10. **An organization, before embarking on a CRM implementation strategy:**
    a) Must define its business focus, organizational structure, business metrics, marketing focus and technology
    b) Must re-engineer the marketing business processes
    c) Must select appropriate CRM solution
    d) Must engage management consultants to prepare a CRM road map

Module II: Developing a Customer Strategy

1. **The purpose of formulating a Customer strategy**
   a) Is to build brand equity
   b) Gain customer loyalty and achieve satisfaction
   c) Gain competitive edge through media focus
   d) Is to influence stock prices

2. **Transactional measurement of customer loyalty**
   a) Are based on customer attitudes, opinions, and customer satisfaction.
   b) Is directly proportional to switching costs – such as search costs, transaction costs and learning costs
   c) Is influenced by perceived and actual barriers to switching to another provider
   d) Is a composite mix of customer satisfaction and transactional history

3. **Customer satisfaction and customer loyalty are not identical concepts.**

   a) Satisfaction measures attitudes, while loyalty measures repurchase behavior.
   b) Satisfaction looks at current impressions, while loyalty focuses on customer history.
   c) Customer satisfaction results from a process of external customer evaluation, while loyalty depends on the success of loyalty programs.
   d) Customer satisfaction is influenced by functional value of a product or service, while loyalty is influenced by transactional value.

4. **Emotional value of customer satisfaction**
   a) Is a skewed measure of product market share
   b) Is considered to have greater prominence in enhancing business value
   c) Is not measured through customer surveys
   d) Serves as the sole indicator of customer's loyalty

5. **Characteristics of good customer profiling are:**
   a) It uses recency, frequency and monetary methods
   b) It reflects on the measurements of customer satisfaction and loyalty programs
   c) It employs customer models in order to elicit action
   d) It reflects the corporate business model, unique selling proposition and customer value statement

6. **Customer Models need to be challenged regularly**
   a) As market research indicates a change in market share
   b) To indicate possibility of technology upgradation

c) As rapidly changing customer dynamics can outdate a predictor model
d) As customer scoring is static in nature

7. **A customer centric organization attempts to**
   a) Facilitate customers to interact across multiple channels and organizes itself around its customers.
   b) Give the customer different experiences each time it interacts with the organization.
   c) Has a customer strategy that projects a popular brand promise, and does not require superiority of products and services.
   d) Has an open loop feedback reporting ensuring transparency and accessibility.

8. **Information collection pertaining to a profitable customer**
   a) Includes customer wants and needs, customer purchase cycle, customer interaction opportunities, customer profile and a customer lifetime value.
   b) Includes customer wants and needs, customer purchase cycle, customer interaction opportunities, customer model and a customer life cycle.
   c) Includes customer wants and needs, customer purchase cycle, customer interaction opportunities, customer profile and a customer life cycle.
   d) Includes customer wants and needs, customer purchase cycle, customer satisfaction levels, customer profile and a customer life cycle.

9. **Customer value focused enterprise differ from customer centric enterprise**
   a) By considering them as profitable cost centers
   b) By minimizing customer management costs by reducing wastage on servicing customers of lesser strategic value
   c) By seeking to leverage the inherent ability of the customers to shorten the learning curve and provide innovative leads
   d) By looking up to their customers as innovators

10. **The three precepts of any successful CRM initiative are**
    a) Know the customer, Reach the customer and Grow the customer
    b) Meet the customer, Learn the customer and Value the customer
    c) Acquire the customer, Profile the customer and Profit the customer
    d) Know the customer, Empower the customer, Refer the customer

Module III: Customer Lifecycle Management and Customer Value

1. **The purpose of the customer life cycle is:**
    a) To define and communicate the stages through which a customer progresses when considering, purchasing and using products
    b) To define and communicate the stages through which a product progresses when conceptualizing, manufacturing and selling products
    c) To define and estimate the value a customer /prospect can deliver while considering, purchasing and using products
    d) To define and communicate the life time value a customer /prospect can deliver while considering, purchasing and using products

2. **A prospect typically is somebody, who is:**
    a) Uninterested in the company's product/service offerings
    b) Considering the purchase of a product or service
    c) Already using the company's product or services
    d) Well passed the 'customer moment'

3. **The term 'customer moment' signifies the point**
    a) Where in the prospect considers to purchase the product or service
    b) Where in the prospect decides to purchase the product or service and becomes a customer.
    c) Where in the customer decides to ditch the company and ceases to be a customer.
    d) Where in the customer decides to be a loyal customer.

4. **The term "loss" signifies:**
    a) The capture of a prospect from a competitor at or before the customer moment.
    b) The loss of a customer to a competitor
    c) The capture of a prospect by a competitor at or before the customer moment.
    d) The capture of a customer from a competitor after the customer moment

5. **The term 'Attrition' denotes:**
    a) The erosion of customer loyalty before the customer moment leading to their capture by a competitor.
    b) The erosion of customer loyalty after the customer moment leading to their capture by a competitor.
    c) The capture of a prospect from a competitor at or before the customer moment.
    d) The loss of a prospect to a competitor

6. **The final goal of CRM is to:**

a) Raise the exit barriers so that prospects are not easily lost to competitors and attrition of hard earned customers is prevented.
b) Raise the entry barriers so that prospects are won from competitors
c) Lower the entry barriers so that prospects are won from competitors
d) Cut down the attrition of hard earned customers

7. **Intrude and Engage stage of the Customer life cycle is where the corporate:**
a) Attract the prospect's attention, increase awareness about the organization and engage the prospect in a dialogue to move him or her into the customer life cycle
b) Attract the prospect's attention, and fulfill his/her needs by transacting sale with the customer
c) Raise the exit barriers to the customer so that prospects are not lost to the competitors
d) Cut down the attrition of hard earned customers

8. **By calculating CLV,**
a) A business can measure the expected financial benefits from customer retention investment to build customer loyalty.
b) Customer acquisition programs can be planned accurately
c) A business can measure the expected financial benefits from customer acquisition.
d) Short and long-term profits can be predicted

9. **Maximizing the "lifetime value" equation requires:**
a) Maximizing the rate of new customer acquisition and conversion rate of prospects to buyers
b) Maximizing the rate of new customer acquisition and the repeat frequency of existing buyers
c) Maximizing the rate of new customer acquisition, the conversion rate of prospects to buyers and the repeat frequency of existing buyers.
d) Maximizing the rate of new customer acquisition, the conversion rate of prospects to buyers and minimizing the repeat frequency of existing buyers.

10. **The purpose of CLV is to:**
a) Maximize the rate of new customer acquisition and conversion rate of prospects to buyers
b) Allow the corporate to allocate a weighted version of its resources and focus on specific customers depending on the projected CLV of that customer.
c) Allow the corporate to plan resource allocation to acquire new customers
d) Allow the corporate to better target and convert prospects into customers

Module IV: CRM Technology

1. **Enterprise CRM strategies focus on**
   a) Integrating ERP, SCM and CRM applications across the extended enterprise
   b) Automation of horizontally integrated business processes to provide end-to-end coordination
   c) Automation of vertically integrated businesses to balance costs and customers
   d) Interchanging people with technology to transform into leaner enterprises

2. **Operational CRM enfolds:**
   a) Customer facing applications such as sales automation, enterprise marketing automation, customer service/support, and miscellaneous components
   b) Customer information backing applications such as data warehouses, business intelligence applications and statistical tools
   c) Customer interacting applications such as interactive voice response system, customer portals and web based operational tools
   d) Customer facing applications such as call centers, corporate website, customer service/support, and miscellaneous components

3. **Collaborative CRM forms the**
   a) Backbone of CRM technology solutions map by binding different applications
   b) Strategic customer information scrutinizing part of CRM technology map enabling strategic decision making
   c) Communication and coordination model across the ETFS life cycle between channels and customer touch points
   d) Exclusive closed networks for partners, customer interactions and channel alignment.

4. **While operational CRM constituents have enhance visibility, analytical CRM components address**
   a) The needs of the marketing function by rendering enhanced decision-making abilities.
   b) Binding all the three functions with the customer that is essential for the smooth functioning of the organization's internal departments
   c) A pivotal role in the evolution of corporate service delivery
   d) Customer facing applications that integrate the front, back, and mobile offices

5. **CRM initiatives must be measured**
   a) Against post implementation metrics determined during the analysis and planning phase
   b) On an iterative basis to refine initiatives and to justify initiatives, continuing the CRM analytic cycle
   c) To enable organizations to segment their customer bases across a variety of characteristics

    d) To establish the lifetime value of customers beyond the transaction to create a partnering relationship

6. **Evolving a people-centric collaborative environment can**
   a) Deviate the focus from enhancing capability of handling second sourcing, product or personnel substitution to increasing manual processing.
   b) Impede creation of a platform for changing partnerships and business processes
   c) Can be detrimental to achieving customer and partner satisfaction due to increased level of people dependency
   d) Streamline operations to offer lower transaction costs and lower error rates

7. **Service automation involves use of**
   a) Loyalty Management, Segmentation, Personalization, Content Management and Campaign Management
   b) Loyalty Management, Contact and Territory Management, Win/Loss Analysis and Distributors/agents
   c) Segmentation, Web Self-service, Automated voice Dispatch, E-mail Routing and Response systems
   d) Segmentation, Telesales, Field Sales, Call Center Automation and Field Service Dispatch

8. **The three pillars of CRM are considered to be**
   a) Finance, Sales and Marketing
   b) Sales, Service and Strategy
   c) Sales, Marketing and Service
   d) People, Technology and Marketing

9. **An enterprise CRM application architecture must combine**
   a) Transaction oriented business process management across multiple channels using various collaborative technologies
   b) Transaction oriented business process management technologies and data mart centered business performance management technologies across multiple channels using various collaborative technologies
   c) Data mart centered business performance management technologies across multiple channels using various collaborative technologies
   d) Transaction oriented business process management technologies and data mart centered business performance management technologies alone

10. **Which of the following can hold transactional level data on individual products, customers and transactions?**
    a) Customer Interaction Center

b) Customer Data warehouse
c) Sales force Automation Applications
d) Call Center

Module V: Operational CRM

1. **The strategic objective of implementing SFA application is to:**
   a) Provide the sales force with ways to leverage technology to achieve field reporting
   b) Provide the sales force with ways to leverage technology to achieve overall operational efficiency.
   c) Provide the sales force with ways to leverage technology to achieve sharing of data
   d) Provide the sales force with ways to leverage technology to access Customer information

2. **Lead Management deals with**
   a) The generation of leads based on multi-channel marketing campaigns to introduce new products or target specific customer segments.
   b) Collection of information about the customer/prospect and utilize this information to close the deal.
   c) Provision of a comprehensive view of the sales potential to the sales force.
   d) Provision of a bird's-eye view of sales opportunities

3. **The goal of opportunity management is to:**
   a) Collect details like financial details, decision dates, proposal and probability of deal closure.
   b) Generate opportunities for the organization
   c) Provision of a comprehensive view of the sales potential to the sales force.
   d) Collect any and all information about the customer/prospect and utilize this information to close the deal.

4. **Sales forecasting, another standard functionality of sales force automation software, provides:**
   a) The enterprise sales force with a comprehensive view of the sales potential.
   b) The enterprise sales force with capability to predict the sales potential
   c) The enterprise sales force with capability to interact with the potential customers
   d) The enterprise sales force with capability to predict success rates of campaigns

5. **A sales funnel offers:**
   a) Funneled set of opportunities for the organization to pursue
   b) A bird's-eye view of sales opportunities and provides managers with information for sales forecasting.
   c) Capability towards selection and segmentation of customers
   d) Capability to measure the results derived from customer contacts

6. **Suspect, prospect and sponsor are typical terms used to qualify the leads in:**

a) Campaign management
b) Opportunity management
c) Sales funnel management
d) Service management

7. **Which of the following application facilitates, selection and segmentation of customers, tracking contacts made with the customers, measurement of the results derived from these contacts and modeling the results to efficiently target customers.**
a) Marketing automation applications
b) Contact management applications
c) Sales automation applications
d) Service automation applications

8. **"Campaign management" is the term used to refer to:**
a) Executing marketing campaigns
b) Executing marketing campaigns and measuring effectiveness
c) Segmenting customers and executing marketing campaigns
d) Segmenting and analyzing customers

9. **Cost per response, qualified lead / opportunity / sale, etc are measures to:**
a) Ascertain efficiency of the sales force
b) Ascertain efficiency of opportunity management
c) Ascertain efficiency of the marketing campaign management
d) Ascertain efficiency of service management

10. **Outbound e-mail management capabilities:**
a) Provide views that are limited to contact history and channel, and exclusive of the transactional system.
b) Provide the ability to construct and execute permission-based marketing campaigns
c) Provide the ability to e-mail enable the organization
d) Provide the ability to respond to customer queries by e-mail

Module VI: Analytical CRM

1. **Personalization and data transformation represents:**
   a) The strategy for achieving a beneficial relationship with the customer
   b) The rules required for performing customer data analysis
   c) The rules required for achieving an integrated view of the customer
   d) The strategy for implementing a customer data warehouse

2. **Analytical CRM is the use of**:
   a) Sales data for analysis, modeling and evaluation to create a mutually beneficial relationship between the company and the customer
   b) Customer data for analysis, modeling and evaluation to create a mutually beneficial relationship between the company and the customer
   c) Customer data warehouse for analysis and reporting
   d) Product data for analysis, modeling and evaluation to create beneficial relationship between the company and the customer

3. **CRM analytics can be said to comprise of:**
   a) Special-purpose data warehouses and business intelligence applications designed to draw content from the CRM core systems, streamline the content as needed, and support reporting, analysis, and data mining.
   b) Customer data warehouse for analysis and reporting
   c) Customer data warehouse and business intelligence applications for analysis and reporting
   d) Special-purpose data warehouses and business intelligence applications designed to draw content from the Enterprise systems, streamline the content as needed, and support reporting, analysis, and data mining.

4. **CRM analytics differ from traditional data warehousing and business intelligence as follows:**
   a) Traditional data warehousing and business intelligence increasingly feed the results of the analytical processes into other transactional business processes, where as in CRM analytics the reporting and analytic activities tend to be ending points with regard to online activity.
   b) CRM analytics increasingly feed the results of the analytical processes into other transactional business processes, where as in traditional data warehousing and business intelligence the reporting and analytic activities tend to be ending points with regard to online activity.
   c) CRM Analytics draw content from the CRM core systems, and support reporting, analysis, and data mining unlike traditional data warehousing and business intelligence applications

d) Traditional data warehousing and business intelligence applications draw content from the CRM core systems, and support reporting, analysis, and data mining unlike CRM Analytics

5. **Which of the following is a critical factor for success in CRM strategy?**
   a) To up sell/cross sell to the customers
   b) To deliver consistent customer experience across multiple channels.
   c) To be able to take out relevant reports
   d) To deliver differential customer experience across channels.

6. **Which of the following forms a genuine value proposition of analytical CRM?**
   a) Ability to identify a customer at a point of need.
   b) Able to take out relevant customer details
   c) Ability to sell to a customer at any touch point.
   d) Ability to service customers through multiple touch points.

7. **A 'customer touch' is a term to describe:**
   a) Any interaction between the customer and the organization or someone representing the enterprise.
   b) Any interaction between the customers of an organization
   c) Any interaction between the customers through multiple interaction channels
   d) Any interaction between the customers of an organization through a single interaction channel

8. **All analytical CRM capabilities at its foundation have:**
   a) A robust customer centric operational data store
   b) A robust customer centric data warehouse
   c) A business intelligence application
   d) An integrated customer database

9. **Data acquisition, cleansing/integration, loading/ unloading, aggregation and distribution represents:**
   a) Processes managed by an analytical CRM environment
   b) Processes managed by an operational CRM environment
   c) Processes not managed by an analytical CRM environment
   d) Processes not managed by an enterprise CRM

10. **The two forms of customer data analysis typically handled by analytical CRM are:**
    a) Predictive and reporting analyses
    b) Predictive and retrospective analyses
    c) Feed forward and Feedback analyses

d) Predictive and behavioral analyses

11. **Predictive analysis of customer data:**
    a) Uses real-time customer data to uncover customer patterns, behavior and relationships.
    b) Uses historical customer data to uncover customer patterns, behavior and relationships.
    c) Uses online customer data to uncover customer patterns, behavior and relationships.
    d) Uses predicted customer data to uncover customer patterns, behavior and relationships.

12. **When companies need to understand existing customer data by transaction, location, product and time:**
    a) Predictive analysis is a good solution
    b) Reporting analysis is a good solution
    c) Retrospective analysis is a good solution.
    d) Behavioral analysis is a good solution

13. **Predictive modeling is a system:**
    a) That aids an entity in predicting what the users will do next
    b) That produces reports based on historical customer data
    c) That provides slice and dice analytics on customer data
    d) That predicts the value of the customer to the organization

14. **Event modeling enables organizations:**
    a) To understand which events are to be organized and at what costs to add value to the organization's products and services.
    b) To understand which events in a customer's life can lead to opportunities that add value with the organization's products and services.
    c) To understand which event managers can add value to the organization's products and services.
    d) To understand responses to the events organized to add value to the organization's products and services.

15. **The principle behind channel optimization is to:**
    a) Continuously evaluate ways to drive sales and service activities to the highest cost channel that can successfully execute the desired value proposition.
    b) Continuously highest cost channel that can successfully execute the desired value proposition.
    c) Continuously lowest cost channel that can successfully execute the desired value proposition.
    d) Continuously evaluate ways to drive sales and service activities to the lowest cost channel that can successfully execute the desired value proposition.

16. **The term Data enhancement denotes:**
    a) Deleting duplicate information from an existing customer database for more accurate analysis.
    b) Adding additional intelligence to an existing customer database for more in depth analysis.
    c) Deleting wrong information from an existing customer database for more accurate analysis.
    d) Deleting product information from an existing customer database for more accurate analysis.

17. **The process of identifying consistent patterns within customer or prospect data that provides information, which can be used to make business decisions and take appropriate actions.**
    a) Predictive modeling
    b) Retrospective modeling
    c) Customer profiling
    d) Behavioral profiling

18. **Which of the following techniques utilize predictive patterns to identify which prospects are most likely to make a particular type of purchase.**
    a) Customer acquisition profiling
    b) Customer product profiling
    c) Customer purchase profiling
    d) Customer retention profiling

19. **Which of the following techniques are used to identify additional selling opportunities for customers or prospects that are already in a buying mode.**
    a) Customer acquisition profiling
    b) Customer product profiling
    c) Customer purchase profiling
    d) Customer retention profiling

20. **Which of the following techniques are utilized to identify which customers are likely to remain loyal to the business and which ones are in jeopardy.**
    a) Customer acquisition profiling
    b) Customer attrition profiling
    c) Customer purchase profiling
    d) Customer retention profiling

Module VII: Collaborative CRM

1. **Collaborative CRM focuses on:**
   a) Providing operational infrastructure to support customers better.
   b) Providing visibility into enterprise sales, service, marketing, and product development to support customers better.
   c) Providing analytical ability to serve and support customers better.
   d) Providing customer segmenting and targeting to serve and support customers better.

2. **_____ greatly enhance customer and partner satisfaction and help leverage all partners' investments in technology and business processes.**
   a) Analytical CRM environments
   b) Collaborative CRM environments
   c) Operational CRM environments
   d) Analytical and Collaborative CRM environments

3. **An emerging KPI metric directly affecting Customer Interaction Center (CIC) operational performance goals is:**
   a) CIC infrastructure consistency
   b) CIC service level agreements
   c) CIC agent efficiency
   d) CIC Call closure times

4. **Establishing ---------------------------- will enhance customer experience and eliminate variables that affect staffing forecasts, that can result in shift(s) understaffing (i.e., risk not meeting service levels) or overstaffing (i.e., paying too much to meet service levels).**
   a) CIC service level agreements
   b) CIC agent efficiency
   c) CIC infrastructure consistency
   d) CIC Call closure times

5. **The need to deliver personalized access, and enable transactions at anytime and anywhere drives the investment in:**
   a) Service centers
   b) Contact centers.
   c) Logistics center
   d) Communications center

6. **_____ focus on providing a single point of access to enterprise information assets and aggregates people, information, applications and business processes.**
   a) Websites
   b) Portals

    c) eCRM
    d) Collaborative Planning

7. _____ are collaborative CRM components that consolidate customer information gathered by sales, marketing and service departments to deliver a complete view of the customer to the employee.
   a) eCRM
   b) Employee portals
   c) Customer Portals
   d) Partner Portals

8. The objective of _____ is to transform the corporate web site into sophisticated, intelligent customer interfaces that optimize the effectiveness of online customer interactions and expand customer relationships through a convenient web front-end, which captures customer information.
   a) Employee portals
   b) Customer portals
   c) Partner portals
   d) eCRM

9. The benefit of ---------------------------- to the enterprise include streamlining operational costs and strengthening customer relationships by extending the CRM application to the web to more effectively market to prospects and enable customer self service.
   a) Employee portals
   b) Customer portals
   c) Partner portals
   d) eCRM

10. Partner Relationship Management (PRM) is a business strategy:
    a) For improving relationships between companies and their internal customers
    b) For improving relationships between companies and their external customers
    c) For improving relationships between companies and their channel partners.
    d) For improving relationships between the managing partners of the company

Module VIII: CRM Project Management

1. **The CRM Vision is typically accompanied by:**
   a) Strategic plan to achieve the vision
   b) Implementation plan
   c) Strategic Plan and Implementation plan
   d) Implementation

2. **CRM readiness assessment helps in identifying**
   a) The budget requirements
   b) People and knowledge requirements
   c) The time commitments needed
   d) CRM functionality requirements

3. **Auditing the IS/IT infrastructure prior to a CRM initiative helps formulating:**
   a) CRM solution evaluation
   b) IS/IT strategy planning
   c) Technical infrastructure acquisition/development plans
   d) Technology project management

4. **One of the most important reasons for building a business case for CRM is:**
   a) To secure the much required sponsorship for the project
   b) To quantify the benefits from the initiative
   c) To be able to build the project team
   d) To define the project requirements

5. **Typically CRM project requirements are prioritized in the order of:**
   a) Complexity
   b) Ease of implementation
   c) Ability to deliver fast payback
   d) Ability to automate existing processes

6. **A key factor considered while short listing a CRM solution vendor is:**
   a) Budget constraints
   b) Brand image
   c) Broad functionality offered by the solution
   d) Project schedule

7. **Effective CRM implementation methodologies:**
   a) Have defined implementation processes

b) Consist of different stages with defined deliverables
c) Have implementation plans
d) Are suggested by the solution vendors

8. **Project team organization and project management control structure is defined in the:**
   a) Analysis stage
   b) Definition stage
   c) Design stage
   d) Deployment stage

9. **CRM solution customization is undertaken during:**
   a) Analysis stage
   b) Design Stage
   c) Configuration and Testing stage
   d) Deployment Stage

10. A **major impediment to organizational change management is:**
   a) Inadequate monetary incentives for the employees
   b) Lack of management commitment to effect change
   c) Lack of training and development to effect change
   d) No motivation for change

Module IX: Building a Business case For CRM

1. **A business case must essentially demonstrate:**
   a) The functionality of the CRM solutions available
   b) The CRM initiative's alignment with the organization's strategies
   c) The competency of the project team
   d) The effectiveness of the technology solution

2. **One of the reasons why ROI calculations for CRM are particularly difficult is:**
   a) A sizeable amount of benefits are intangible in nature
   b) Costs are not easy to estimate
   c) Cots are often fluctuating too much
   d) Lack of financial analysis skill sets

3. **Business Cases also provides with a framework to:**
   a) Schedule project tasks
   b) Allocate accountability for delivering benefits from the investment
   c) Allocate resources for project implementation
   d) Cost CRM projects

4. **Acquisition of new customers is an example of CRM benefit that can be categorized under**
   a) Benefits leading to revenue enhancement
   b) Benefits leading to cost savings
   c) Benefits enhancing organizational flexibility
   d) Benefits leading to enhanced customer experience

5. **Ability to quickly communicate pricing decisions is an example of CRM benefit that can be categorized under**
   a) Benefits leading to revenue enhancement
   b) Benefits leading to cost savings
   c) Benefits enhancing organizational flexibility
   d) Benefits leading to enhanced customer experience

6. **Success of CRM strategies are best measured at:**
   a) Departmental level
   b) Enterprise level
   c) Business Unit level
   d) Territory level

7. **More responsive after sales support is an example of**
   a) Benefits leading to revenue enhancement
   b) Benefits leading to cost savings
   c) Benefits enhancing organizational flexibility
   d) Benefit accrued to customer because of the CRM initiative

8. **One of the commonly used methods of de-risking the ROI estimates is:**
   a) Using only tangible benefits
   b) Using probabilistic estimates for arriving at expected CRM costs and benefits
   c) Discarding hidden costs
   d) Using best guess estimates of intangibles

9. **Correct measurement of CRM ROI pre-supposes:**
   a) Measurement of costs of current operations as a basis for comparison
   b) Measurement of performance of current operations as a baseline for comparison
   c) Accurate measurement of costs and performance of current operations as a basis for comparison
   d) Enterprise level benefits estimation

10. **One of the major sources of risk that spells disaster for CRM projects is:**
    a) Inadequate funding
    b) Hidden costs
    c) Inaccurate Benefits estimation
    d) Faulty customer strategy

Key to MCQs

Module I

| 1. d | 2. c | 3. b | 4. c | 5. a | 6. d | 7. b | 8. c | 9. b | 10. a |

Module II

| 1. b | 2. c | 3. a | 4. b | 5. d | 6. c | 7. a | 8. d | 9. b | 10. a |

Module III

| 1. a | 2. b | 3. b | 4. c | 5. b | 6. a | 7. a | 8. a | 9. c | 10. b |

Module IV

| 1. b | 2. a | 3. c | 4. a | 5. b | 6. d | 7. a | 8. c | 9. b | 10. c |

Module V

| 1. b | 2. a | 3. d | 4. a | 5. b | 6. c | 7. a | 8. c | 9. c | 10. b |

Module VI

| 1. c | 2. b | 3. a | 4. b | 5. b | 6. a | 7. a | 8. b | 9. a | 10. b |
| 11. b | 12. c | 13. a | 14. b | 15. d | 16. b | 17. c | 18. a | 19. c | 20. d |

Module VII

| 1. b | 2. b | 3. a | 4. c | 5. b | 6. b | 7. b | 8. b | 9. b | 10. c |

Module VIII

| 1. c | 2. b | 3. c | 4. a | 5. c | 6. c | 7. b | 8. b | 9. c | 10. b |

Module IX

| 1. b | 2. a | 3. b | 4. a | 5. c | 6. b | 7. d | 8. b | 9. c | 10. a |

Scenario Questions

This objective of this section is to highlight the need to apply the concepts learnt in the course to real life instances. The scenarios given here depict real world problem. The caselets appended in the case studies section are pointers to real world solutions that have addressed the issues highlighted. This section does not serve the purpose of vendor endorsement or customer testimonial. Students are encouraged to explore all aspects of the scenario before proceeding to read the caselet recommended.

Scenario 1

Richard, a very experienced service representative, is working for a third-party service provider of Quaero Telecom. Quaero Telecom selected Richard's company to cover peaks in its own daily service business.

Richard is a telecommunications equipment specialist and he likes to fix problems. Although he's never been particularly keen on using new technologies himself in the past (despite the fact that he repairs and services high-tech equipment all the time).

His nature of work requires him to prepare a daily service visit agenda, prepare service jobs, report on the parts used, and record the time and expense involved, to facilitate timely sharing of information with Quaero Telecom. They also find it desirable that he prepare information on material returns or repair requests, and enter reports on the reasons for service activities.

> ❓ *Envision a solution to cater to the needs of Richard and Quaero Telecom to collaborate in this partnership.*

> ❓ *List how can it help Richard improve his customer focus.*

> ❓ *Quaero would like Richard to assist them in case of emergency cases. How can the solution help Quaero improve customer service?*

> ❓ *How can the two companies involved share a common knowledge base to add mutual value and better their service offerings?*

 Refer case on Continental Telecom.

Scenario 2

A leading player in the hospitality industry wants to improve its customer loyalty and guest satisfaction ratings. The organization has always measured its success by hotel occupancy rates. In addition to measuring revenue per available room, now they want to measure revenue per available customer.

The organization takes pride in the fact that eight out of ten business travelers stay on its properties and avail its facilities in any given year.

The organization would like to achieve higher revenue per customer, and manage customer touch points across all channels. The organization seeks to be a truly customer centric by establishing unified set of customer data accessible by all its customer-facing employees, and offer every customer a highly personalized experience

> 2 *Discuss how the organization can attain its goal of being more customer -centric.*

> 2 *How can the organization increase its revenue per customer and also elicit additional revenue from its available customer?*

> 2 *How can the organization empower its customer-facing employees to create consistent customer experiences?*

 Refer case on Marriott.

Scenario 3

A leading international financial services companies and among the top 50 global asset managers wants to explore how to combine different interaction channels with other contact points, such as call centers and the Internet.

The increasingly competitive nature of the financial services sector and ever changing needs of its customer base, together with the enhanced market visibility meant that the company has to compete more aggressively in the marketplace to maintain the loyalty of its customers.

The company has an extremely broad range of financial products and services, and would like to improve its ability to up-sell and cross-sell to its customer base.

The company had relied on a network of company-branded and independent financial planners to sell products and services through traditional means such as face-to-face meetings. The company is now keen to exploit four primary channels—the phone, Web, mail and the financial planning community to provide customer service.

> *Discuss how the company can go about integrating its various interaction channels.*

> *How can the company achieve its objective of cross selling and up selling various products and services among its client base?*

> *What additional benefits can the company realize by investing in a CRM solution?*

 Refer case on AMP Financial Services.

Section 1b

Case Studies

This section presents a few case studies to highlight the importance of Customer Relation Management in an organization's business strategy. They are intended for the sole purpose of reference and to facilitate discussion of various practical aspects of CRM.

Collaboration Enhances Continental Telecom Customer Focus and Service Processes

Background

Bob, a very experienced service representative, is working for a third-party service provider of Continental Telecom. Continental Telecom selected Bob's company to cover peaks in its own daily service business.

Bob is a telecommunications equipment specialist and he likes to fix problems. Although he's never been particularly keen on using new technologies himself in the past (despite the fact that he repairs and services high-tech equipment all the time), he has had to get to grips with some new information technology tools in his current job.

Customer focus

Bob is proud to be a real service representative. He wants to help customers and fix problems, and despite the time pressure of the business he is in, socializing and maintaining close contact with his customers is very important to him and remains a key focus of his job. Bob has just been informed by Continental that he can avail information systems tools to support him in his daily work, allowing him to view his daily service visit agenda, prepare service jobs, report on the parts used, and record the time and expense involved. He can also prepare information on material returns or repair requests, and enter reports on the reasons for service activities.

List of orders

Bob has just received instructions from Continental Telecom on his beeper directing him to log on for an emergency service alert. He connects with Mobile Service and his schedule shows that all his afternoon preventive maintenance appointments have been rescheduled for a visit to the local departmental store where the telephone system has performance problems. The screen shows a list of the service orders dispatched to Bob. *A service order is a basic document that contains a request for a service activity.* The activity to be carried out today is a maintenance object at a customer site.

View of service order details

Bob clicks on the first item in his order list so that he can view the order overview information. On the initial screen, he sees a display of the key information: details of the customer to be visited and the contact person who reported the malfunction.

Bob checks the desired start and finish date and the schedule for the service job, and then selects the hyperlink to the installed base information. (He could also have viewed to further information on the customer, the contact person or the equipment involved in the service order).

View of the installed base

Bob examines the installation diagram and checks his van's inventory to make sure that he has all the parts he may need. By looking at the diagram, Bob can see exactly where the equipment to be serviced is located, and how the installed base hierarchy is set up. He then selects a hyperlink to take him to the equipment detail.

View of equipment detail

Here, Bob can see the technical equipment specifications and important business information, such as the customer contract and the business partner for the equipment concerned. By referring to the warranty contract overview, Bob can see that the equipment was purchased the previous year and is still covered by a service contract. This means that he will probably not charge the customer for the service he provides on this occasion.

View of service order operations

Planning his approach to the job, Bob reads the recommended solution in the CRM Solution Database. His first action will be to check the telephone closet to determine whether the main circuit is malfunctioning. If nothing is amiss there, he will inspect the desk sets at the two receptionists' stations, from which most calls are routed.

The system has already allocated and reserved components for Bob's service job. These are visible at the bottom of the screen.

Create time confirmation

To complete the commercial side of the job, Bob needs to enter the time spent carrying out the service activity. This usually involves entering two different times: travel time and working time. Each time type has a different charge assigned to it and is stored in a separate activity type. Bob enters two working hours and then confirms which materials will be invoiced. He used the materials that had been automatically allocated and reserved and uses drag and drop functions to confirm consumption. Bob is now ready to complete back reporting and create the technical confirmation.

Create technical confirmation

As part of technical back reporting, Bob can assign items, error codes, and actions for use in quality assurance. Once the job is completed, and time, materials, and technical back reporting have been confirmed, Bob sets the status of the order to closed. The next time he connects his laptop to the server, all the information will be transmitted to the CRM system for online processing.

Source: *Jörg Rosbach, SAP AG, Sap Info.*

Marriott International Enhances Customer Loyalty and Boosts Profitability

Business Profile

Marriott International, Inc.

Offering international hotel rooms, vacation clubs, and senior living services as a leader in the hospitality industry

Industry

Travel

Geographies

Worldwide

Deployment Summary

3,000 users dispersed across different sales and service functions spanning the globe

Deployed to more than 2,000 locations

The Application deployed include Siebel *e*Business Applications, Siebel Sales and Siebel Service

Background

Marriott International, Inc. is a leading hospitality company with over 370,000 rooms, spanning more than 2,000 properties, 58 countries, and 13 lodging brands, including Marriott Hotels, Resorts and Suites; Renaissance Hotels; Courtyard by Marriott; and Residence Inn. So extensive is Marriott's presence that an estimated eight out of ten business travelers stay at a Marriott property in any given year. Marriott attributes its success to one simple factor: guest satisfaction. Their sales and marketing philosophy is centered on creating a superior experience for their customers.

Challenges

While customer service has always been associated with Marriott's brand name, the company has always measured its success by hotel occupancy rates. In addition to measuring revenue per available room (REVPAR), Marriott wanted to measure revenue per available customer (REVPAC).

Goals

To achieve higher revenue per customer, Marriott sought to implement an eBusiness solution that managed customer touch points across all channels, establish a unified set of customer data accessible by all customer-facing employees, and offer customers a highly personalized experience based on a rich profile of information. Marriott wanted an eBusiness solution that could be implemented quickly, without spending a lot of time and resources on custom development. Marriott chose Siebel *e*Business Applications for their support of marketing, sales, and service across all channels.

Benefits

- ➢ Improved customer satisfaction
- ➢ Increased profitability
- ➢ Strengthened brand loyalty
- ➢ Increased corporate account sales
- ➢ Increased cross-chain sales

Highlights

Embracing the Customer

By using Siebel *e*Business Applications, Marriott was able to embrace its group customers in new ways.

For instance, in the past the company had waited for its large corporate accounts to call to reserve rooms and did little to proactively drive sales. However, Marriott is now able to collect and consolidate information on all corporate accounts, manage contacts, and record leads and opportunities.

Marriott's sales teams now call corporate customers well in advance of trade shows and conferences to book arrangements. Furthermore, as Marriott account managers have all system wide information at their fingertips, they're able to close a sale while the customer is still on the phone. There's very little price negotiation, and this is helping the organization achieve a higher closure rate.

Selling the Way Customers Want to Buy

Marriott is able to sell the way customers want to buy, regardless of which channel they use. Business travelers, in particular, have several ways to approach Marriott, and they expect Marriott to have the same information and provide a consistent level of service across the entire chain.

Building Brand Loyalty Across Hotel Properties

Marriott's solution also helped the company build loyalty and awareness across its 13 lodging brands. Before implementing its CRM application, Marriott's sales force logged information in disparate databases based on the hotels or hotel groups to which they were assigned.

If a guest wanted to book a room at a hotel that was full, Marriott's salespeople had no way of knowing whether another Marriott hotel in the same city was available. Now, Marriott's salespeople have visibility of rooms inventory at multiple Marriott properties and can easily book a customer in a different Marriott property—a capability that allowed Marriott to record cross-chain sales of U.S.$55 million last year.

Cross-selling Additional Products and Service

Marriott has improved its ability to cross sell additional products and services in other ways as well. For example, seven Marriott leisure hotels now provide the "Personal Planning Service," creating personalized vacation itineraries for guests well in advance of their arrival. The guest experience starts when Marriott starts planning the itinerary, and not when the guest arrives on the property. This helps Marriott deliver a more lasting memory of the stay. When a customer calls and makes a reservation, Marriott builds an itinerary based on the customer's requests and stored preferences.

When the customer arrives at the hotel, tee times have already been scheduled, dinner reservations arranged, and shopping itineraries created. Marriott has found that guests who participate in the program show noticeably higher guest satisfaction scores and spend an average of U.S.$100 more per day at hotel golf courses and restaurants.

Industry-leading Results

Since implementing its Siebel CRM solution, Marriott has experienced substantial benefits. The company's hotels are achieving occupancy levels that are typically 10 percentage points or more above the industry average. In addition, the company's revenue per employee is practically double that of its two closest competitors, Hyatt and Starwood Hotels & Resorts.

Marriott is now able to deliver superior customer service, and that has been the key to building customer loyalty across Marriott's hotels.

Source: Siebel Systems

AMP Financial Services Unites Multiple–Channels to Enhance Customer Satisfaction

Business Profile

AMP Financial Services

Providing wealth management products and services for corporate and private clients

Industry

Financial services

Geographies

Australia and New Zealand

Deployment Summary

- 3,700 total users

- Phase one implemented on budget within four months

This was a Siebel implementation involving Siebel eBusiness Applications, Siebel Analytics, Siebel Call Center, Siebel eChannel, Siebel eFinance, Siebel eInsurance, Siebel Marketing

Background

AMP Ltd. is one of Australia's leading international financial services companies and among the top 50 global asset managers, with almost U.S.$144 billion in assets under management. With more than 17,000 employees and financial planners and 8 million customers, AMP is acknowledged as a worldwide leader in wealth creation and management.

AMP Financial Services, a key business unit for the company, provides a wide range of products and services in the areas of insurance, banking, asset management, retirement savings and income, and financial planning. It is the leader in the Australian and New Zealand retail pension sectors and one of Australia's top retail fund managers.

In June 1998, AMP demutualized—that is, the company converted from a policyholder company to a publicly traded company. The increasingly competitive nature of the financial services sector and ever changing needs of its customer base, together with the enhanced market visibility brought about by the demutualization, meant AMP Financial Services had to compete more aggressively in the marketplace to maintain the loyalty of its customers.

Goals

AMP set itself an ambitious goal of building its business around a renewed focus on customer relationship management. AMP's vision was to become not just a leading financial services provider, but also a leading customer-centric organization.

Road Map - From Traditional to Multi-channel Customer Contact

To achieve its goals, AMP Financial Services began to rapidly expand the number of channels it used to communicate with its customers. In the past, the company had relied on a network of company-branded and independent financial planners to sell products and services through traditional means such as face-to-face meetings.

AMP Financial Services recognized the need to explore how to combine this form of interaction with other contact points, such as call centers and the Internet. Additionally, given AMP Financial Services' extremely broad range of financial products and services, the company was eager to improve its ability to up-sell and cross-sell to its customer base. AMP Financial Services was in need of an integrated eBusiness solution that would enable it to market to, sell to, and provide service to customers seamlessly across its four primary channels—the phone, Web, mail, and through the financial planning community.

Challenges

Broad Deployment Demands Change Management Support

Embarking on one of the broadest ebusiness applications deployments in its sector, AMP Financial Services sought a vendor that could not only provide industry-leading technology, but could also help AMP reengineer its business processes and instill a customer-focused approach throughout the business. The availability of industry-tailored solutions, together with the change management support, was critical factors in the vendor selection process.

Siebel Systems' strength in banking and insurance and change management support provided through its professional services arm enabled it to win the project.

In line with its strategy to implement a series of "quick win" projects, AMP Financial Services also decided to deploy Siebel *e*Finance and Siebel *e*Insurance to its call center representatives and deploy Siebel *e*Channel to its financial planner network.

Phase I - Rapid Rollout to 3,700 Users in Four Months

AMP Financial Services worked closely with Siebel Professional Services to define its eBusiness requirements and took the important step of involving the financial planner network in configuring the Siebel *ebusiness* solution. With financial planners responsible for around 75 percent of AMP Financial Services' business, the implementation focused on providing these critical stakeholders with functionality that would help them increase revenue and customer satisfaction.

In the first phase of the implementation, AMP Financial Services set out to rapidly replace many of its existing systems and processes with Siebel *e*Channel, the industry's leading partner relationship management application.

Siebel *e*Channel helped AMP deliver an enterprise-wide partner management platform that works collaboratively with partners over the Web. Within four months, Siebel *e*Channel was deployed to approximately 1,500 financial planner organizations (3,500 individual users) and 200 internal AMP users, providing lead generation, routing, and monitoring capabilities as well as access to a unified repository of customer information.

At the same time, Siebel *e*Finance and Siebel *e*Insurance were deployed to AMP's call center representatives.

The Siebel eBusiness solution rapidly improved the effectiveness of AMP's business development process. Where a lead was once routed to a planner in hard copy via a spreadsheet or fax, it is now sent electronically via the Internet. This has fundamentally changed a hitherto time consuming manual task into a fully automated process. Each planner is notified automatically via email when a lead has been sent. Planner managers distribute the leads to the financial planners by region and monitor the leads throughout the sales cycle. Planners have 48 hours to accept or reject a lead before it is passed to another planner—a process that managers can now track. A select number of planners are now also using Siebel eChannel to generate quotes online for the first time.

Insight into the Future

The second phase of implementation, which includes the deployment of Siebel Marketing and Siebel Analytics, is now under way. In the third phase of its eBusiness initiative, AMP plans to implement Siebel eMarketing, which will provide the company with email and Web-based marketing capabilities.

Benefits Accrued
  ➢ Provided consistent view of customers across multiple channels
  ➢ Improved cross-selling and up-selling opportunities
  ➢ Increased sales productivity and effectiveness
  ➢ Helped diversify product and service offerings to relevant customers
  ➢ Improved customer satisfaction

Highlights

Productivity Increases Five-fold

Since the deployment of Siebel ebusiness Applications, AMP Financial Services has seen measurable improvements in the efficiency of lead routing and lead management. With manual processes now automated, the capacity of the planner network to manage leads has increased 500 percent. In the past, a lead often took up to two weeks to get into the hands of a planner; it can now be distributed in just 30 minutes via the Siebel eBusiness system.

In addition to accelerating lead distribution, the Siebel eBusiness system has improved lead quality. Siebel eBusiness Applications provided AMP with a complete feedback loop: Call center agents could capture important details about a prospect at the first point of contact; planners then knew how to approach the prospect and could ensure that the products or services offered were in line with specific needs.

Source: Siebel Systems

Bibliography

A. Sarner, W. Janowski, T. Berg, "Personalization: Customer Value Beyond the Web", (September 10, 2001), Gartner Group

Baldwin, C. Y. & Clarke, K. B. (September-October 1997). Managing in an Age of Modularity.

Markets of One, Harvard Business School Press

Berger, P.D. / Nasr, N.L. (1998), "Customer Lifetime Value: Marketing Models and Applications", Journal of Interactive Marketing, 12, 17-30.

Bixner, R., Hemerling J. & Lachenaur R. (1999). "Managing Brands for Value", Boston Consulting Group, Inc.

Bowden, Cheryl "Creating an Effective Customer Relationship Strategy in a Digital World" CRM Project, Montgomery Research, Inc. Sponsored by Accenture

Britton Manasco, William S Hopkins, Carter J Lusher, "CRM Redefined: Beyond the Front Office and Out to the Customer", KCG Market Review

Brown, S.A. (2000), "Customer Relationship Management - A Strategic Imperative in the World of e-Business", Toronto.

Chaudhry, Rajiv, CRM white paper, November 2002, Zen & Art, zenart.com

Claudio Marcus, Wendy Close AV-16-2572 - Gartner Research

Dickie, Jim "CRM Solutions-How Do I Evaluate This Stuff? Fundamentals of picking the CRM solution that's right for you." May 2001, CRM Magazine

Dan, Remenyi Dr., (1999) "IT Investment -making a business case". Butterworth Heinemann

Davenport, T. (1998, June). "Managing Customer Knowledge." CIO Magazine. (June 1, 1998.)

Erin Kinikin "How Valuable Are Your Customers?"(September 2001), E Business Advisor Magazine

Firat, A. F., Dholakia, N. & Venkatesh A. (1995); Marketing in a Postmodern World. European Journal of Marketing. Vol 29, No. 1.

Fung, Mei Lin "Customer Lifetime Value" www.isoe.com

Gale, B T (2002). "Trends in Customer Satisfaction, Loyalty and Value." www.cval.com/into.html

Gallagher, R. W & Kordupleski, R. E. (2000). Customer Value Management, The CVA 2000 Collection

Greenberg, Paul (2001) "CRM at the speed of Light". Tata McGraw-Hill

Hampshire, Stephen "Customer satisfaction, loyalty and profit - understanding the links" (October 2002) http://www.ecustomerserviceworld.com

Hanson, W (2000), "Principles of Internet Marketing", Cincinnati (Ohio).

Imhoff, Claudia et al. "Building the Customer-Centric Enterprise, November 2000, DM Review

Ireland, Linda "Channel Integration Strategies" September 2001, Target Marketing

Jim Barnes "Build Value for Customers to Create Lasting Relationships" (October 2002)

Johnson, M. D. & Gustafsson A. (2000), "Improving Customer Satisfaction, Loyalty and Profit", Jossey-Bass.

Johnson, Rod "The Promise and Peril of CRM: Building a Business Case, Choosing a Vendor, and Planning for Risks" CRM Project-Montgomery Research, Inc. Sponsored by Accenture

Kalakota, R. / Robinson, M. (2001), "e-Business 2.0: Roadmap for Success", New York.

Kellen, Vince "Adaptive CRM and Knowledge Turnover" 6/30/2001

Kellen, Vince "CRM Measurement Frameworks" March, 2002

Levy, Doran J. "Segmentation: Key to Efficient CRM", September 2001, DM Review

Murtha, Kevin "Launching a CRM Initiative: Base it on a Customer Centric Business Model" September 4, 2002, DM Direct

Nelson, S. & Kirkby, J. (2001). "Seven reasons Why CRM Fails". Gartner Research Note

Newell, F. (2000), "Loyality.com: "Customer Relationship Management in the New Era of Internet Marketing", New York.

Peppers, D. & Rogers, M. (1997). "Enterprise One to One, Currency Doubleday"

Pine, J.B. II, Peppers D. & Rogers M. (1995) "Do you Want to Keep your Customers Forever?" Markets of One. HBS Press.

Reichheld, F. F. (1996). "The Loyalty Effect". Bain & Co.

Rust, R. T., Zeithaml, V. A. & Lemon, K. N. (2001); "Driving Customer Equity". The Free Press.

Scott Nelson, Rahul Singhal, Walter Janowski, Ned Frey, Customer Data Quality and Integration: The Foundation of Successful CRM, November 26, 2001, Gartner Group

Schultz, D. E. Ph.D. (2001, March). "Measuring and Managing Brand Value." ACNielsen

Shahnam, E. (2000), "The Customer Relationship Management Ecosystem", Stand: 25.09.2002.

Shahnam, Elizabeth "Industry Overview- CRM Infusion Program" (2002), MetaGroup Customer Insight.

Shostak, Barry "Bridging the Gap -- A Maturity Model for CRM" (May 2002)

Souza, R. (2001, September). How to Measure What Mattters. The Forrester Report.

Swift, Ron "Analytical CRM Powers Profitable Relationships: Creating Success by Letting Customers Guide You" (February 2002) DM Review

Tanoury, Doug & Ireland, Kit "Why CRM Projects Fail - Common Strategic & Tactical Mistakes" (July 2002)

Walsh, Scott J "Building a Winning Business Case" (May 2002). The Customer Group, LLC

Winer, R.S. (2001), "A Framework for Customer Relationship Management", California Management Review, 43(4), 89-105.

"Calculating Actual Value (or Lifetime Value)", August 2, 2002, 1to1.com

"Critical steps to successful CRM" CRM Forum Resources (October 2002) crm-forum.com

"Customers as innovators, a new way to create value." (April 2002) Harvard Business Review

"Customer value management and the measurement system". APQC. (2001, March). http://www.apqc.org/

"CRM. Talk" (on different CRM topics) (from Jun 2002), Expert opinions from crmguru.com

"Independent Reviews of CRM Products" (June 2002), CRMguru.com

"Integration: Critical Issues for Implementation of CRM Solutions" study commissioned by Oracle corporation, February 15, 2001 MetaGroup

"Making a compelling business case for CRM" (February 2000) Hewson Group

"Realizing Return on Investment from CRM" (June 2002) Cap Gemini Ernst & Young Whitepaper
"Secrets of CRM Success", February 8, 2001, CRM Guru.com

"The CRM Bible from Pyinna" (June 2001) Pyinna Limited"

"The Evolution to Converged Communications" -Avaya's Vision for Migrating Beyond Converged Networks – Avaya, www.avaya.com

Why Climb the CRM Mountain?", December 2001, CRM Guru.com

Online resources

The following online CRM community resources were referred to during November–December 2002, for information and expert advice.

http://www.crmcommunity.com,
http://www.1to1.com/Building/CustomerRelationships,

http://www.crmassist.com,
http://www.destinationcrm.com,
http://www.crm-forum.com,
http://www.crmdaily.com,
http://www.crmguru.com,
http://www.crmproject.com,
http://www.intelligentcrm.com,
http://www.crm2day.com,
http://www.ecrmguide.com,
http://www.crmxchange.com,
http://searchcrm.techtarget.com,
http://www.dmreview.com

Online Vendor resources

The following online CRM community resources were referred to during November–December 2002, for information gathering.

http://www.amdocs.com,
http://www.epiphany.com,
http://www.kana.com,
http://www.oracle.com/applications,
Zttp://www.peoplesoft.com/corp/en/products/line/crm/index.asp
http://www.mysap.com/solutions/crm
http://www.siebel.com
http://www.applix.com
http://www.epicor.com
http://www.onyx.com
http://www.pivotal.com
http://www.act.com
http://www.maximizer.com
http://www.saleslogix.com
http://www.teradata.com
http://www.sas.com
http://www.spss.com

Trademarks/Registered Trademarks

Computer hardware and software brand names mentioned in this book are protected by their respective trademarks and are acknowledged.

Copyright Disclaimer

EC-Council syndicates information from several hundred sources. We give all due acknowledgement to the source of information and where possible, try to seek the owner of the information to obtain permission for inclusion of content. Any copyright material unacknowledged is totally unintentional and if brought to our notice, we will be glad to incorporate the same and take necessary measures.